Psychology
in
Progress

General editor: Peter Herriot

Small Groups
and
Personal Change

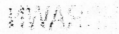

Psychology in Progress

Already available

Philosophical Problems in Psychology
edited by Neil Bolton

Thinking in Perspective
Critical essays in the study of thought processes
edited by Andrew Burton and John Radford

The School Years
Current issues in the socialization of young people
edited by John C. Coleman

Aspects of Memory
edited by Michael M. Gruneberg and Peter Morris

Issues in Childhood Social Development
edited by Harry McGurk

Brain, Behaviour and Evolution
edited by David A. Oakley and H. C. Plotkin

Forthcoming

Applications of Conditioning Theory
edited by Graham Davey

Personality
edited by Fay Fransella

Small Groups and Personal Change

edited by
PETER B. SMITH

METHUEN

First published in 1980 by
Methuen & Co. Ltd
11 New Fetter Lane, London EC4P 4EE

Published in the USA by
Methuen & Co.
in association with Methuen, Inc.
733 Third Avenue, NY 10017

This collection © 1980 Methuen & Co. Ltd
Individual chapters © 1980 the respective authors

Printed in Great Britain by
Richard Clay (The Chaucer Press) Ltd.,
Bungay, Suffolk

British Library Cataloguing in Publication Data
Small groups and personal change. — (Psychology in progress).
1. Group relations training
I. Smith, Peter Berington
158'2   HM134   80-40557
ISBN 0-416-72790-5
ISBN 0-416-72800-6 Pbk

Contents

Notes on the contributors

Michael Fullan holds a chair in the Department of Sociology of the Ontario Institute for Studies in Education. His main work is research, training and consultancy in the planning, implementation and assessment of educational change. He works with the Ontario Ministry and School Boards, the US National Institute of Education, the OECD and IMTEC.

Robert T. Golembiewski is Research Professor of Political Science and Management at the University of Georgia. His books include *Sensitivity Training and the Laboratory Approach* (Peacock, 1970), *Renewing Organizations* (Peacock, 1972) and *Learning and Change in Groups* (Penguin, 1976).

Kathy M. Lippert is a consultant for business, educational and social organizations. Her interests include laboratory training and affirmative action strategies, and she is completing a dissertation on the impact of consultant gender in organizations.

Nano McCaughan is a consultant with the Grubb Institute, London, working on a project concerning the transition to working life. She has practised social work in both the UK and the USA and has edited *Group Work: Learning and Practice* (Allen and Unwin, 1978) as well as publishing a number of articles and papers.

Matthew B. Miles is Senior Research Associate at the Center for Policy Research in New York. His interests include the study of small groups, organizational change processes and educational innovation. His books include *Organization Development in Schools* (National Press Books, 1971), *Encounter Groups: First Facts* (Basic Books, 1973) and *Measuring Human Behavior* (Teachers College Press, 1973).

Keith Oatley lectures in psychology at the University of Sussex and was also visiting Associate Professor of Psychology at the University of Toronto. His research interests include the phenomenology of human perception and the nature of mental schemata. He is the author of *Brain Mechanisms and Mind* (Thames and Hudson, 1972) and *Perceptions and Representations* (Methuen, 1978).

W. Brendan Reddy is Director of the Community Psychology Institute and Associate Professor of Psychology at the University of Cincinnati. His interests include the dynamics of small groups and organizational behaviour and he has served as consultant to government, business, educational and religious organizations.

David Robinson is Senior Lecturer in Sociology at the Institute of Psychiatry in London. His books include *Patients, Practitioners and Medical Care* (Heinemann Medical, 1972), *From Drinking to Alcoholism* (John Wiley, 1976) and *Self-help and Health* (Martin Robertson, 1977)

Gerald G. Smale is a Lecturer in Social Work at the National Institute for Social Work, and visiting research fellow at the University of Sussex. He is the author of *Prophecy, Behaviour and Change* (Routledge and Keegan Paul, 1977).

Peter B. Smith is Reader in Social Psychology at the University of Sussex. His principal interest is in the analysis of sensitivity training and allied group training methods, and he has undertaken numerous empirical studies in this field. He is the author of *Improving Skills in Working with People: The T-group* (HMSO, 1969), *Group Processes* (Penguin, 1970) and *Groups within Organizations* (Harper and Row, 1973).

Heather Wood is temporary Lecturer in Social Psychology at the University of Sussex. She has recently completed a doctorate on the processes and outcomes of therapeutic communities.

1 Introduction

Peter B. Smith

Small groups have provided the setting for the creation of personal change for many thousands of years. Whether one considers the role of families in childhood socialization, the effects of the differing types of developing organizational structures in society or the role of conspiracies, crowds and social movements in history, small groups are ever present. The developments of recent decades constitute not so much the invention of the small group as an agent of change, but rather a belief that through more systematic theorizing and practical testing of theories we might make better use of a mechanism which is already closely woven into the structure of society. This theorizing and testing has occurred largely within the present century and provides us with an ever-growing diversity of identified types of group-work, each apparently tailored to the creation of slightly different types of personal change. Many of these forms of group-work seem to contrast strikingly with those likely to have occurred in previous centuries. Back (1972) has made a compelling analysis of the manner in which the growth of group-work in contemporary society must be seen as but one element in a wider pattern of social change. The present century has seen much wider diffusion of education, raised standards of living, increased life expectation, enormous changes in geographical mobility and communication technology. All of these changes contribute to a decline in monolithic authority systems and the growth of demands to participate in and take control of significant decisions concerning oneself. The precision with which the contemporary small group movement can be seen to fit into these major social trends should not lead us to overlook the parallels to be found at other points in history. For instance Back himself points out the substantial parallels between some types of contemporary small group procedures and earlier religious movements.

Socio-historical analysis provides only a blunt instrument with which to examine the small group movement. Just a few years subsequent to Back's (1972) analysis, Back (1978) has collected a series of essays examining the decline of sensitivity training. No systematic data are presented to establish that sensitivity training or the small group movement more generally are in decline, but it is argued that since contemporary sensitivity training seeks to recreate that sense of cohesive community which large industrial societies can no longer sustain, it is inevitable that it has been no more than a passing fad. At one level this argument has a good deal of plausibility – if sensitivity training or other group methods are or have been conducted in a manner where more is claimed for them than can be achieved, they are indeed likely to be cast aside. But at another level the arguments advanced by Back in his earlier analysis are still true, and likely to remain so for some time. For this reason one or other types of group-work can be confidently expected to have a continuing prominence. This book is addressed to the question of what type(s) of group-work we have so far developed and how choices shall be made as to their relative usefulness in particular settings.

In the early stages of development of a field of expertise it is inevitable that innovation shall be haphazard and unplanned. Since no one knows how best to advance the field, what seems like progress to one may seem irrelevant or even harmful to another. Dispute is likely as to how to evaluate what is achieved by a particular method, and even as to whether the method ought perhaps to be achieving something different. All of these difficulties have characterized the first few decades of the small group movement. No speedy remedy is likely for this circumstance. The best that we can hope for is a gradually evolving agreement as to what small group methods are and are not good for, and how it shall be judged whether they have achieved their goals. Such an agreement needs to take account both of the subjective reactions of those who conduct and participate in small group experiences and of more sustained attempts at 'objective' research evaluation. Since discussions of the small group movement rather frequently ignore or pass cursorily over the available data, this volume seeks to redress that balance. Wherever research data are available which are relevant to a point of discussion, these data will provide a framework for that discussion. This emphasis expresses a viewpoint about the future development of this field: while impulse and spontaneity have provided much of the energy which developed the range of group-work methods we have available today, a knowledge of what has already been tried and why it does or does not work is essential to the coherent future development of the field. There is no need for practitioners of group-work to stop attending to their feelings, but there is a need for us to start thinking more about what we are doing.

Defining the field

This chapter has so far been written as if the term 'group-work' had a commonly accepted meaning. It is by no means certain that a defensible definition can be advanced which encompasses the range of current activity. Much of the fabric of society comprises small groups of people, who come together for a huge variety of purposes. To designate all such meetings as 'group-work' would be absurd. We can begin to narrow the field a little by stating that group-work is an activity set up with the publicly stated intention of creating some change in members' own behaviour or feelings. This takes out the numerous groups in which social influence may occur without any shared intention or awareness of change, but it leaves in any group which periodically sits down together to review its performance.

Two further defining attributes of group-work are frequently employed. The first of these is that the group has an external consultant or facilitator, i.e. someone who is not normally present and who has skills relevant to the facilitation of change. The second is that the group's procedure is based on an examination of its own behaviour, past or present. Both of these attributes are problematic, in the sense that they imply that some of the material in the present volume should not have been included. A variety of otherwise similar group activities are found in which no special facilitator is present. These range from human relations training groups working through written exercises, and groups following the tape-recorded 'Encountertapes', to project groups within organization development programmes and the great majority of self-help groups. The requirement that the group attend to its own behaviour is no more successful in differentiating group-work from other activities. While attention to the here-and-now has been central to some types of group-work there are others where it is peripheral or absent. Some types of encounter make extensive use of fantasy, dream-work or bodily awareness exercises, while some forms of social group-work and self-help groups may have attention focused outside the group for much of the time. One could of course argue that the presence of a leader and attention to the here-and-now are such important aspects of the concept of group-work that they must be preserved within the definition. The case for not treating them as central rests primarily on the finding that neither presence of a leader nor attention to the here-and-now by themselves differentiate groups which are successful in creating change from unsuccessful ones (Lieberman et al., 1973).

One attribute that does provide assistance in defining the nature of group-work is its temporary nature. Group-work is most usually seen as a finite intervention, whether it be through the provision of a learning experience for an individual, or as an attempt to introduce change within an organization. In some types of group-work such as therapeutic communities, social group-work and self-help groups, it may be the member rather than the group which is temporary. Such groups typically continue on a semi-permanent basis with members joining and leaving in accordance with their own particular needs. In other types of group-work the group itself is temporary, being set up for a finite training purpose. A third variant occurs where the group is semi-permanent and the occurrence of group-work is signalled by the temporary addition of a group facilitator or therapist. Instances of this are provided by some forms of organizational development and by family therapy. In each of these types of group-work there is some kind of modification of the time boundaries of the group. Group-work may thus be crudely differentiated from other types of group experience by the existence of a contract, implicit or explicit, to create change within some finite time boundary. Longer-term group experiences, such as living in a family or working in a group which is part of an organization may also have change goals, but these will be intermingled with other priorities such as maintaining a stable system and ensuring long-term survival, so that the time boundaries of any change effort are likely to be more diffuse.

Any definition of group-work must also consider the size of group encompassed. Although we can now make some statements about the processes underlying change (see Chapters 3 and 4), we still know little about the impact of the size of group on these processes. At the one extreme one might argue that marital work with couples could properly be termed group-work. At the other, one finds that Carl Rogers and his colleagues have recently been experimenting with groups of several hundred, while the Synanon community in California makes use of video to share their encounter 'game' with up to a thousand residents (Simon, 1978). Most group-work continues to be done with small face-to-face groups of seven to fifteen, and it does appear likely that the processes found most salient in such groups, for instance trust, self-disclosure and the taking of personal responsibility for one's actions, would be more difficult to achieve in larger groups.

This discussion of some of the defining attributes of group-work leaves us with a crude but serviceable characterization: *Group-work is a finite activity whereby a small group seek to create change within their own behaviour and feelings*. Because it omits any reference to leadership or to procedures, this definition errs on the side of over-inclusiveness. Until such time as we have greater certainty about the distinctive mechanisms of group-work, such an error is preferable to a definition of group-work which would exclude whole areas of current practice.

The origins of group-work

The difficulties encountered in constructing a definition of group-work are not unexpected. They derive from the heterogeneity of current developments. Back's analysis of the reasons why group-work 'fits' within the social change of the current century was touched on earlier. If such analysis is correct it should be no surprise to find that group-work methods have been repeatedly 'invented' throughout the century. Since many of the professional groups in society who have developed and sustained group-work are isolated from one another, the present heterogeneity is in part due to the multiple origins of group-work and the relatively slight degree to which different traditions have intermingled. It is only relatively recently that these traditions have developed much awareness of one another. One of the principal goals of this book is to enhance that awareness, by considering how group-work has faced up to various issues in each of the fields in which it has arisen.

One of the earliest origins of group-work is found in the work of Jacob Moreno in Vienna from 1908 onwards. While Moreno was himself a student he developed a variety of activities with children, meeting in the parks of Vienna after school hours. Over subsequent years he sometimes drew in also the parents of the children, and his methods evolved into the range of techniques now known as psychodrama. By the early twenties (Moreno, 1970) he was already using such terms as encounter, sensitivity training, role-playing, psychodrama and group therapy. As we shall see, many of these terms have achieved wide usage among contemporary practitioners. The essence of Moreno's approach was that change arises through the portrayal of problems or issues in a here-and-now manner. To aid the development of such expression he devised an enormous variety of structured 'warm-up' exercises, many of which were also subsequently reinvented by the encounter leaders of the sixties. After his move to the United States, Moreno conducted regular psychodrama workshops and by the mid-thirties these included marathon groups.

Another pioneer in the development of group-work was Joseph Pratt who organized out-patient groups for tuberculosis patients in Boston, Massachusetts, from 1906. His clients were those who could not afford hospitalization and his goal was to provide support plus a certain amount of instruction in how to make the slum environment more similar to the type of treatment and life-style available in sanatoria (Shaffer and Galinsky, 1974). The subsequent development of group therapy in the United States was strongly influenced by psychoanalytic thinking. Although Freud and Moreno were both in Vienna for many years, they had little impact on one another. Moreno was actually present in the USA from 1925 onwards but it was Freud who had the greater effect on the development of American group therapy. By the 1930s Samuel Slavson had developed activity group therapy for children, which emphasized the free expression of repressed feeling. Psychoanalytic groups for adults were developed by Wolf and Schwartz, who maintained that concepts deriving from individual psychoanalysis, such as transference and resistance, provided an adequate guide for the conduct of psychoanalysis in groups. Thus within the clinical context a transition was made from seeing group-work as primarily supportive to seeing it as having a more directly therapeutic intent.

The development of group methods within the field of social work shows some parallels with those in the clinical field. Informal types of group-work were found in the settlements of the late nineteenth century, as developed by people such as Jane Addams in the USA and Octavia Hill in Britain. Supportive work with groups of children or those in deprived circumstances has continued through youth clubs, adult education and community centres. More recent developments in this field have involved an extension of the goals of social group-work to accommodate more overtly therapeutic methods, in line with the increasing professionalization of social work. While the professionalization of social work and psychotherapy met the needs of some clients, many others remained unprovided for. The thirties saw the beginnings of the first of the contemporary flood of self-help groups: Alcoholics Anonymous.

The advent of the Second World War marked a quickening of the pace of innovation in group-work methods. While some American psychoanalysts had by this time developed group methods, British ones had not. There was at that time a substantial divergence between American analysts' interest in ego-psychology and the much wider popularity in British psychoanalysis of Melanie Klein's object relations theory. Thus when a number of Kleinian analysts worked together on the rehabilitation of stressed soldiers at Northfield Hospital, Birmingham, a series of new developments occurred, which contrasted with all previous approaches. The Kleinians argued that the essence of group-work is that the group as a whole is a unified system. To interpret or relate to individual members of the group as though the others were not present is in their view a failure to utilize the opportunities afforded by the use of groups rather than individual treatment. Perhaps the most influential member of the Northfield team was Wilfred Bion. In the years after the war Bion developed an approach usually referred to as the Tavistock study group, in which the group leader remains aloof, declines to respond to questions, and when he does speak, speaks only about the behaviour of the group as a whole, never about individuals. As Bion (1961) reports, his group members were found to respond in a variety of ways intended to cope with his 'odd' behaviour. Study groups have had a wide impact in human relations training and in social work in Britain. At some times it has seemed to Americans that study groups were *the* British way of doing group-work, but in fact there have always been arguments and a variety of approaches in Britain as in the United States.

A colleague of Bion's at Northfield was S. H. Foulkes. Foulkes subsequently developed an approach to group therapy closely allied to Bion's method (Foulkes and Anthony, 1957) which he termed group-analysis. Here the group leader treats the conversation as a process of collective free-association. Interpretations are based on the themes which are apparent in this process. This approach has also had a substantial impact.

A further innovation which arose in Britain at this time was the concept of the therapeutic community. Here the suggestion was that the therapeutic efficacy of in-patient therapy was often destroyed by the elaborate and contradictory hierarchies of authority found in mental hospitals. By isolating a relatively small treatment unit and sharing authority within that unit between patients and staff, it was argued that there was a much better prospect of the system enhancing the mental health of participating patients. One of the earliest to use these methods was Maxwell Jones (1953), whose first experiments were also concerned with the rehabilitation of soldiers after the war. Jones's background was psychiatric rather than psychoanalytic, but others quickly developed communities with a more psychoanalytic emphasis.

While these developments were under way in Britain, the most frequently identified 'origin' of group-work took place in the USA. This was the invention of the T-group by Kurt Lewin and others. Lewin was a distinguished theorist and researcher into group behaviour who had also a firm commitment to training and application. T-groups arose at a training programme in 1946. Course members expressed an interest in sitting in on discussions between Lewin and his team of research observers about their observations of the course members' meetings earlier in the day. Thus was created a form of group-work which lays great stress on discussion of the here-and-now behaviour of the group, mutual sharing of perceptions and a participating role for the group leader. Many of the elements of the T-group had earlier been devised by Moreno. Lewin's collaborators, Bradford, Lippitt and Benne, were all familiar with psychodrama and had earlier made substantial use of role-playing in their training programmes. The origin of the T-group is sometimes presented as an isolated event, but it appears more accurate to see it as an extension and popularization of of Moreno's ideas. The establishment of National Training Laboratories under the leadership of Leland Bradford enabled the development of the T-group on a scale which Moreno's individualistic manner and extravagant claims had never made likely.

Lewin's role as a key figure in the development of social psychology assured the continuing involvement of social psychologists in the development of T-group methods. Unlike almost all the earlier approaches, sensitivity training, as it became known, had at this time little linkage with therapeutic concerns and was construed instead as a part of a growing range of methods available for training in human relations skills. Human relations training developed rapidly during the fifties, largely in response to the needs of industrial management. By the end of the fifties, different schools of thought were visible within the now greatly expanded National Training Laboratories. One school of thought saw that human relations training for individual managers was achieving much less change in organizational behaviour than had been hoped for. They experimented with ways of taking the training within particular organizations in order to enhance its lasting effects. This approach was adopted by Robert Blake and many others in the Esso company and it became known as organization development. Application was initially within industrial organizations in the USA, but attempts were soon made to extend the approach to many other types of organization and to most countries. As organization development gained strength it became clear that group-work need only be one among the range of methods available to induce organizational change.

The second school of thought within National Training Laboratories saw the T-group not as an agent of potential organizational change but as new and potentially valuable mode of personal learning. This school was centred principally in California. Will Schutz (1967) for instance developed a whole range of non-verbal activities designed to encourage the more direct interchange of feelings between group members. Through these innovations a more actively structured form of group-work evolved, which became known as encounter and drew on a variety of techniques which had developed earlier for use in some types of individual therapy, such as gestalt therapy, bioenergetics, massage and so forth. The term encounter is also frequently used to describe the approach of Carl Rogers (1970). The approach of Rogers and his associates is much more similar to the procedures of sensitivity training, since structured learning exercises are rarely used. There is a continuing consequent confusion between the various types of encounter and sensitivity training. Encounter methods have diffused widely, although they are still perhaps most firmly rooted in 'personal growth' centres. While some protagonists of encounter see its function as being to provide a new form of personal therapy, others stress its potentiality as an avenue of personal growth among those whose functioning is already adequate.

This brief survey of the development of group-work methods has presented only the broadest outline. In virtually all areas of group-work further differentiations of approach are to be found and the search for newer and hopefully better approaches continues unabated. Depending upon one's stance it is possible to construe this search as a process of creative ferment, a gradual refinement of a developing technology, or as a random sequence of variations which is tailored by the whim of passing social fashion. Most probably we shall with hindsight be able to see all three aspects of this search. For the present, perhaps the most pressing question is to consider what reasons there are for seeing group-work as an appropriate intervention to employ in some circumstances.

Why group-work?

The process of interpersonal acquaintance and attraction has received much attention from researchers in recent years (Duck, 1977). While a good deal of uncertainty remains as to just how stages in the acquaintance process succeed one another, some overall conclusions are clear. If we bring together a group of people for any substantial period of time, they will come to like one another. While some groups may like one another more than do other groups, the circumstances under which liking does not increase at all are markedly unusual. Press reports of some of the more spectacular hijackings and kidnappings of recent years have underlined the way in which even hostages frequently finish up feeling rather warmly toward their abductors. Duck argues that increasing intimacy in a relationship is not facilitated by any specific triggers. As he sees it, any relationship will develop toward increasing levels of intimacy unless one or other of the parties acts to prevent this occurring. In everyday living, we rather frequently emit such 'preventative' signals, thereby maintaining most relationships at non-intimate levels. Group-work establishes a circumstance in which members see a good deal of one another and have less reason than usual to use such preventative signals, since they know that their relationship with others in the group is a temporary one. If the group is an intensive short-term one, there is a finite end in view. In other types of group, members will know either that they are free to leave when they wish, or that an end to the group is envisaged even if it is not yet in view. As with other types of temporary systems (Miles, 1964) this finiteness provides a spur to the growth of intimacy in the group. If there is only so much time remaining, it makes more sense to go ahead with expressing those feelings and concerns one has, rather than awaiting some more ideal occasion, as might happen in everyday living.

It is sometimes argued that the intensity and temporary nature of groups provides just as much of a spur to the expression of hostility and dislike as they do to liking and affection. Critics of group-work would argue that the way groups are often set up offers a free rein to some of the less admirable aspects of human nature and are therefore dangerous. Later sections will give some consideration of how to cope with whatever dangers there may be in group-work. Here it will simply be asserted that in most circumstances the warmth and affection which groups generate outweigh their hostility and destructiveness. The manner in which this occurs is illustrated by an anecdote recounted by Farson (1978). Early in his career as a group leader, Farson found himself faced with a group member who spoke to him between sessions, explaining that he intended to leave the group forthwith. Farson asked him first to come to the next group session in order to explain to the others why he was leaving. Predictably, once the member had expressed his frustrations with the group he changed his mind and decided to stay. Farson, and most likely many other group leaders, have seen the same effect on other occasions. Once the member chooses to share hostility with the group, his ultimate acceptance is assured. This anecdote illustrates the general proposition advanced by Duck: the growth of intimacy through continuing contact is assured, unless one acts to prevent it. In everyday living such preventative actions are all too easily accomplished. In a group they are not.

If groups can be said to create a climate of warmth and affection, the choice as to when they should be employed becomes a question of specifying the circumstances under which this climate will give rise to some kind of intended, lasting change. The next two chapters explore some of the principal ways in which learning in groups has been conceptualized, and evidence as to how far the hypothesized processes of learning have indeed been found to occur. In these chapters the focus is on what happens in group-work, once a decision is taken to employ some form of group-work. A prior question is a consideration of why one might prefer group-work to some form of work with individuals or to no intervention at all. As will emerge in some of the later chapters, there does exist a substantial literature of evaluation studies, although it has been far from equally distributed across the various forms of group-work. In some fields such as sensitivity training and encounter, numerous studies are available, contrasting the effects of group experience with measures obtained for untrained controls. In many of the other fields, control data are rarely reported and more informal reports provide the only basis currently available for examination.

Although the choice between group-work and no intervention is the one most frequently examined by researchers, it is not necessarily the choice of greatest practical interest. Considerations as to whether or not to engage in group-work most frequently arise when some type of diagnosis has been made that a problem exists. The option of deciding to do nothing and seeing whether the problem resolves itself is always present, but other options are likely to include a variety of individually oriented intervention strategies. Research comparing any type of group-work with intervention focused on the individual is rare indeed. In the varying professional fields, different types of interventions lend themselves to research evaluation. For instance a programme of organization development may include individual consultancy or training to specific managers, but most of the available studies focus on the impact of group-based interventions. By contrast, in the clinical field, studies of individual therapy far outweigh those of group therapy, and studies which compare the impact of group therapy and behaviour therapy are usually concerned with extremely brief forms of group-work. Whether this divergence between fields means that very few practitioners do in fact debate the choice between individual and group-based intervention, or whether it merely reflects the ease or difficulty of differing research designs in the varying fields is hard to say. Table 1.1 details some attributes of individual and group-work which may have importance in making a choice between them. The table suggests that the potentialities of individual work are strongest for quickly focusing the leader's expertise on a specific client problem. Individual work would most likely be the method of choice where the client problems encountered were diverse and where the leader has one or more specific areas of expertise relevant to these problems. Group-work appears from the table as a procedure which is substantially more difficult to initiate and which may require a substantial time commitment. It would therefore only be the method of choice where clients' problems had a good deal in common, where they were as likely to learn from one another as from the leader and where the establishment of a continuing support network was desirable. Later chapters may shed some light on the degree to which the circumstances under which group-work currently occurs do approximate this hypothetical model.

Table 1.1   Some attributes of group-work compared to work with individuals

	Group-work	Individual work
Utilization of leader resources	Economical	Intensive
Potential responsiveness to needs of individual client	Moderate	High
Client's choice of models from whom to learn	High	Low
Problems in scheduling sessions, finding appropriate setting	High	Low
Potential for continuing support from other clients	High	Low
Minimum time required for effective work	High	Low

Problems and choices in the conduct of group-work

Once the decision is reached that there is a good match between one's diagnosis of a particular circumstance and the potentialities of group-work, a sequence of decisions and actions ensue, which will now be considered. It is suggested that these decisions and actions are unavoidable in any field in which group-work is practised, and contributors to later chapters have therefore been asked to comment on how these issues have been most effectively handled within their particular field. The decisions and actions to be considered comprise the design of training, the recruitment of group members, the activities of the leader during training, the assessment of programme outcome, the management of hazards and provision for continuity.

Training design

Many of the origins of the small group movement are closely associated with beliefs in the importance of participative decision-making rather than an emphasis on the technical expertise of the leader. Both in the T-groups and the Tavistock groups of the fifties the early stages in the development of a group often consisted of group members demanding that the group leader use his expertise more directly to structure events, while the leader either did not respond or asserted that he was no more of an expert than anyone else as to the behaviour occurring within the group. This confrontation between dependent members' wishes and the leader's unwillingness to provide traditional leadership was seen as a key element in the growth of a group. Some of the confusion which this approach can generate may occur because the leader is seeking to convey a highly complex message to group members. This is that although he is willing to exercise a traditional leadership role in setting up the programme, delineating various different types of session within the programme, composing groups and organizing procedures to be followed in some of the sessions, he is not willing to do this within that sequence of sessions which comprises the major part of the programme and is often presented as the most 'real' and important.

There are still large divergences in the degree to which group-work practitioners see it as appropriate to structure some or all of a programme. One current example of the 'no-design' design is the series of Facilitator Development Institutes conducted by Carl Rogers and his associates. These are residential ten-day workshops, largely for professionals, typically with a membership of fifty to a hundred. On arrival members are informed that the staff have undertaken a bare minimum of planning, but that the staff are willing to contribute their resources in whatever manner is agreed. The bare minimum of planning comprises the recruitment of an appropriately sized staff group and the provision of food and accommodation for the duration of the Institute. The resolve of the staff to undertake no prior planning beyond this minimum has sometimes meant that a workshop finds on arrival that not all of them can speak the same language (Clark, 1978).

Another instance of a minimal design is the minisociety (Higgin, 1972). In this approach a ten-day residential workshop is again employed, but the staff actively attempt to recruit to the workshop groups representing different facets of contemporary society. Each participant is free to determine how much money he or she will contribute to the costs of the workshop and the provision of food during the workshop is dependent upon agreement being reached as to procedures for collecting and spending the money necessary for obtaining it. Beyond this the staff group proposes an initial allocation of workshop members to the varying types of accommodation available and requires that members of the minisociety all meet with the staff group for one session each day. This session is devoted to reviewing what other events have been occurring in the preceding twenty-four hours.

These two designs illustrate attempts by particular practitioners to minimize the degree to which the leaders impose a training design. There are varying arguments for and against such approaches, but the point most relevant to this discussion is that such 'no-design' designs may well turn out to have predictable consequences. Facilitator Development Institutes spend a lot of time as a large group, struggling to agree a design (McLeod, 1977), while minisocieties frequently address disputes about money and resources (Higgin, 1972). Paradoxically, the minimal training design may have just as much effect on what happens as occurs where the leaders design workshops in a more active manner.

While some early protagonists of group-work (e.g. Moreno) have always favoured a leader style in which the leader actively structures events, it is certainly true that this approach has become more popular in recent years. Advocates of structured training designs would most likely concede that the unstructured groups favoured at earlier times have an important historical role in the development of group-work. In the fifties, they might argue, we had become aware of the potentialities for the creation of change which are inherent in group experience, but we were naive in our attempts to facilitate that change. Unstructured group-work proved, in their view, to be unnecessarily time-consuming and diffuse. By leaving the group unstructured the leader makes possible many types of change, but gives no impetus to any particular kind of change. The chances that all members of a group want to work on similar issues is not great, so that for substantial minorities in any group the experience will be fruitless. The growth of structured training designs is illustrated by the current popularity of techniques which focus on one particular goal or issue. One instance is transactional analysis, in which the group leader concentrates on the provision of a specific diagnostic framework which group members may use to describe their past and present behaviour. Another is gestalt therapy, in which the leader provides very specific instruction to members in accepting personal responsibility for all aspects of their own personal behaviour, including not only actions but also non-verbal behaviours and dreams. A third instance is provided by work in the field of organization development, in which group members are all drawn from the same place of work, and in which the enhancement of working relationships therefore becomes the primary agenda.

The continuing debate between advocates of structured designs and more open ones is illustrated by Farson (1978), who is a colleague of Rogers. Farson suggests that group-work, and humanistic psychology more generally, has been transformed from a movement with a good deal of vision and humanism to a set of techniques which are applied in ways which are increasingly difficult to distinguish from those employed by, for instance, behaviour therapists. From establishing group-work as a procedure where people met as equals and confronted the dilemmas they faced, we have moved gradually until it appears as a setting in which members utilize techniques introduced by a leader acting as a skilled technician. Farson illustrates how inexorable this process may be by considering the member wishing to leave his group, who was referred to earlier. When this first occurred, Farson could, in all innocence, ask the dissatisfied member to explain to the group why he intended to leave; he did not know what would be the outcome. Being pleased that the member chose not to leave, Farson naturally repeated it next time a similar event occurred. However, each time he repeats the procedure he is less innocent about its probable effects. He knows, even if the group member does not, that the effect of his request will most likely be to prevent the member from leaving his group. Faced with a dissatisfied group member now he must either accept that he is employing a somewhat manipulative technique, or abandon the technique, or else engage in a rather elaborate explanation to the dissatisfied member.

Farson's dilemma crystallizes the problem of trainer design. Shall the prime criterion of effective group-work be the provision of a circumstance where group members can experience autonomy, feel responsible for their own choices and have available to them a real choice of models as to how to cope with this or that problem? Or shall group-work increasingly be judged for the effectiveness with which it provides training techniques which are tailored to previously diagnosed training needs? One might anticipate that Rogerians, those influenced by the various psychoanalytic models and the self-help group movement, would opt for the first criterion, while the newer encounter therapists, organization development and family therapists would go for the second.

Recruitment of group members

The circumstances under which participants are recruited to groups vary somewhat. Almost always the groups will be sponsored by some type of agency or other, whether that agency be comprised of volunteers or professionals. The simplest circumstance is perhaps that where an agency publicizes some form of group-work, to which a prospective group member responds by enquiry and subsequent enrolment. Such an idealized sequence may in fact be relatively rare. An alternative sequence occurs where the individual contacts the agency concerning a current problem, to which the agency responds by proposing some form of group experience, either by itself or in combination with other more individually-focused activities. This sequence is frequently found in the fields of organizational consultancy, social work, clinical practice and the self-help group movement. A third alternative arises where the agency is contacted by the representative of an organization who arranges for one or many other members of that organization to participate in groups. The other members are typically also consulted about whether or not they wish to participate, but their decision is taken in the light of the fact that the organization is in favour of their participating. This sequence is found in most types of organization, particularly in regard to residential forms of group-work such as sensitivity training and Tavistock groups and in residential institutions such as prisons and hospitals. Still another basis for participation arises within organization development programmes. Such programmes may arise at the initiative of either the agency or the organization, but at the time individuals are required to decide whether or not to participate, they need to weigh up not only the attitude of the organization but also of their various specific work associates who are faced with similar decisions. A similar need to weigh up others' views is present also in family therapy. A final basis for enrolment is that which occurs when a student enrols in some programme of study which is taught in a predominantly traditional manner, but finds that a required element of the course is some form of group-work, which may even be formally assessed.

The originators of sensitivity training laid some stress on the creation of a 'cultural island' as an optimal setting for group experience. By this they had in mind not only that the group should be protected from the pressures and distractions of everyday living, but that members should be wholly committed to being present in the group. The ideal trainee was seen as one who had made a freely given commitment to participate. Staff members of National Training Laboratories sometimes jokingly comment that one of the reasons why Bethel, Maine, was so suitable for their developing T-group programmes is that it is such a long way from anywhere. Once arrived, the member whose commitment might wane is faced with a formidable discouragement from embarking on the long journey home again. Thus even in the heartland of the T-group, group leaders are not averse to a little pressure on members to stay committed. The variety of bases of participation which have been outlined indicate that the participants' decision to attend can range from a free choice to an acceptance of coercion. This broad range of bases for participation in groups has no doubt ensured that over the past few decades many more people have attended groups than would have been the case if group leaders ran groups only where a free choice was practicable. Group leaders differ rather widely as to how important it might be to attend closely to bases on which members attend groups. One line of argument would be to assert that the basis for attendance sets the contract, implicit or explicit, for much of what happens subsequently in a group. On this view it would be vital to have a clearly agreed basis for members' attendance, since it would define both the goals and the limits of subsequent learning. The alternative view is that much of the impact of groups arises from the spontaneity and creativity of the assembled group. Thus even if members arrive feeling coerced or hesitant, they are likely to enter into the spirit of the group as they become acquainted with others in the group and the procedures to be followed by the group. If this view is correct, there is much less reason to be concerned with the basis upon which people attend groups.

These differing conceptions of the basis of group participation have some parallels with the preferences for different types of design discussed earlier. The group leader who sees participant autonomy as crucial to learning will most likely favour unstructured designs and a free choice to attend. The leader who sees group-work as a technique will pay less attention to how members are recruited and more attention to improving training design.

Activities of the leader during training

Almost all students of group-work see the behaviour of the leaders as a key element in the procedure. Group leaders do however undertake an astonishing variety of actions. These range from prolonged inactivity to the very high rate of activity inherent in, for instance, gestalt therapy. In some types of group, such as therapeutic communities and self-help groups, the leadership function may be quite widely shared among participants. This diversity engenders a certain amount of caution in making generalizations about leadership skills in group-work. Consider three possibilities:

(1) Group-work provides a setting in which individuals are able to create changes in their feelings or behaviour in relation to their own specific needs. The skill of the leader lies in enabling participants to draw from the group what they specifically require.

(2) Group-work provides a setting in which individuals are able to focus on their behaviour and learn ways of controlling it to achieve their goals better. The circumstances under which participants achieve such learning are the same for everyone and certain leader's behaviours will facilitate this learning more than will other behaviours.

(3) Group-work provides a setting in which individuals can compare their feelings and behaviour with that of others and thereby achieve desired changes. The leader's behaviour will be no more important in achieving this effect than will that of anyone else.

As will be seen in later chapters we cannot yet reject any of these possibilities with any confidence. Indeed, although at first reading each may seem to exclude the possibility of the other two being true, even this may not be so. In order to make each possibility exclusive of the others, it would in addition be necessary to assume that group-work was a unified, homogeneous entity. Since this clearly is not currently the case, the possibilities above could be considered as statements about how group-work can on occasion be set up. Supposing in each of the statements the initial word 'Group-work' were to be extended to read 'Group-work can be conducted in such a way as to . . .', the statements appear more clearly as non-exclusive of one another.

This way of thinking about the diversity of current leader behaviours implies that it is unlikely to be fruitful to ask, for group-work as a whole, which style of leader behaviours is most effective. If group-work provides a whole range of potentialities it is more likely to be worthwhile to ask, in each of the various fields, which pattern of leader behaviours has been found to lead to what type of outcome. As Paul (1967) put it some time ago, in a discussion of research into psychotherapy, 'What treatment by whom, is most effective for this individual with that specific problem and under which set of circumstances?'

Assessment of programme outcome

The diverse origins of group-work are reflected in the manner in which protagonists of each of the various approaches seek to assess the success or failure of their endeavours. There is no doubt a broad consensus that some form of evaluation of effectiveness is required. However, while some fields have generated substantial numbers of quantitatively-oriented evaluation studies, others have generated more qualitative reports and case studies. In general the use of questionnaire measures and control groups has been restricted to those approaches stemming from the influence of Kurt Lewin and other social psychologists. This includes sensitivity training, encounter and organizational development. The sharpest contrast to this is provided by approaches deriving from the psychoanalytic tradition, concerning which rather few systematic reports are available.

The relationship between practitioners of group-work and researchers into the effectiveness of group-work has never been an entirely easy one, as might be anticipated. On the one hand practitioners are mostly committed to a spirit of open enquiry about groups and group behaviour. On the other, the existence of a separate research function within a group-work experience can be seen as implying that the researcher's perception of what occurs is somehow more valid than that of the group leader or members. The tension is that between subjective and supposedly objective modes of assessing what occurs. So long as the researcher's instruments detect changes which accord with the practitioner's perception of what occurs, all is well. But if the researcher's instruments indicate a null or negative outcome of training, scepticism about their validity tends to appear rather rapidly.

The usefulness of research data concerning group-work is thus not primarily as some form of objective or impartial evaluation; it is better seen as a form of feedback from researcher to practitioner. Like other forms of feedback in groups it may be self-serving or well-intentioned and it may be listened to or ignored, according to the circumstances under which it is provided.

The diversity of group-work has been touched upon. In light of this it makes little sense to ask of the research data whether groups *do* achieve a certain effect. A more answerable form of enquiry would be to ask whether they *can* achieve this particular effect. Review of the various studies reported in succeeding chapters may also help to indicate whether groups achieve certain outcomes with a good deal more regularity than others. In so far as they do, the case is strengthened for seeing group-work as a developing set of techniques for the creation of particular effects. If outcomes are more diverse, that view of group-work is enhanced which stresses the uniqueness of differing types of group experience.

The available evaluation data, particularly those reported in Chapter 2 show that group-work *can* achieve lasting measurable effects. Group-work continues to evolve, so further studies will be required to examine how far groups remain able to generate these effects. But the most pressing task is to examine with greater thoroughness the impact of groups in fields where they have so far been less studied, both to see whether the effects are similar or different and also to find clues as to why groups in the various fields may work out differently.

The management of hazards

In common with most other innovations in society, group-work has been castigated by its critics as dangerous to at least some of those who participate. The available studies have raised a good deal of controversy, which will be examined particularly in Chapter 3. Both critics and defenders of groups would however agree that there is an element of risk in participating in groups. The dispute concerns whether the level of risk entailed is any higher than that of participating in other frequent life experiences. Whether the risk be high or low, it is clear that practitioners have an obligation to explore ways of minimizing it.

Group leaders have available procedures for reducing risk at each step in the process of conducting group-work. For instance, they may institute selection procedures, they may design programmes in a manner which provides support to those who seek it, they may look for and respond to signs of distress during group sessions and they may make provision for continuity of support after the programme. Subsequent chapters will touch on what is known of the effectiveness of these various options in the different areas of group-work.

Provision for continuity

The definition of group-work adopted earlier incorporated the notion of its finiteness. Almost all group leaders would agree that the worth of a group should be assessed in terms of whether it produces some type of lasting change. The exception to this would be certain types of encounter leaders, who stress the playful aspect of group experience. In their idiom one might speak of having 'had a good group' in the same way as one would say that one had had a good holiday. Such an experience would be something that felt good at the time, but which was not expected to leave a lasting change in one's mood or state. The majority view requires something more than this, if the group is to be judged a success.

Basically the continuity of the group experience can be assured either by the continuing contact of group members, or by the internalization of personal learning by individuals. Continuing contact is available after many forms of organizational development and family therapy. The presence of this continuity provides one of the major points of reference for leaders in these types of groups. It may be that quite different styles of group leadership are required in the light of this.

In the remaining types of group-work, continuity of effect requires that the individual internalize what has been learned. Theorists have advanced a range of views as to how this is to be achieved, and this issue is addressed particularly in Chapter 4.

References

Back, K.W. (1972) *Beyond Words: The Story of Sensitivity Training and the Encounter Movement*. New York: Russell Sage.

Back, K. W. (ed.) (1978) *In Search of Community: Encounter Groups and Social Change*. Boulder, Colorado: Westview Press.

Bion, W. R. (1961) *Experience in Groups*. London: Tavistock.

Clark, J. (1978) Easter at El Escorial. *Group Relations*: 14–17.

Duck, S. (1977) *The Study of Acquaintance*. Farnborough: Saxon House.

Farson, R. (1978) The technology of humanism. *Journal of Humanistic Psychology 18* (2): 5–36.

Foulkes, S. H. and Anthony, E. J. (1957) *Group Psychotherapy: The Psychoanalytic approach*. Harmondsworth: Penguin.

Higgin, G. W. (1972) The Scandinavians rehearse the liberation. *Journal of Applied Behavioural Science 8*: 643–63.

Jones, M. (1953) *The Therapeutic Community*. New York: Basic Books.

Lieberman, M.A., Yalom, I.D. and Miles, M.B. (1973) *Encounter Groups: First Facts*. New York: Basic Books.

McLeod, J. (1977) *The Construction of Reality in the Basic Encounter Group*. Unpublished Ph.D thesis, University of Edinburgh.

Miles, M. B. (1964) On temporary systems. In M. B. Miles (ed.) *Innovation in Education*. New York: Teachers College, Columbia University.

Moreno, J. L. (1970) The Viennese origins of the encounter movement, paving the way for existentialism, group psychotherapy and psychodrama. *Group Psychotherapy 22*: 7–16.

Paul, G. L. (1967) Strategy of outcome research in psychotherapy. *Journal of Consulting Psychology 31*: 109–18.

Rogers, C. (1970) *Encounter Groups*. New York: Harper and Row.

Schutz, W. C. (1967) *Joy: Expanding Human Awareness*. New York: Grove Press.

Shaffer, J. B. P. and Galinsky, M. D. (1974) *Models of Group Therapy and Sensitivity Training*. Englewood Cliffs, New Jersey: Prentice-Hall.

Simon, S. (1978) Synanon: toward building a humanistic organisation. *Journal of Humanistic Psychology* 18 (3): 3–30.

2 The outcome of sensitivity training and encounter

Peter B. Smith

This chapter will review what we currently know of the effects of sensitivity training and encounter. The principal obstacle in the path of such a review is the diversity of current training practice. A willingness to innovate has always been a central value of sensitivity trainers; indeed the method only arose because of the willingness of a group of trainers to adapt their design in mid-programme. Such innovation has both strengths and weaknesses. Where trainers innovate in order to adapt a method to a new training goal or a new population of trainees there is much to be said for it. Where innovation seems to be more of an end in itself or an attempt to follow ephemeral fashions there may be less to say for it. Either way the rate of change means that if researchers are to make valid statements about the effects of groups, they must make clear what is and what is not included in a definition of sensitivity training.

Studies included in this chapter concern groups which involve the examination of interpersonal relations among those present, and extend their membership to include those *not* undergoing psychotherapy. Studies of other types of group are examined in subsequent chapters.

There is some evidence to suggest that whether a group experience is designated as sensitivity training, encounter, group therapy, organization development or what you will is not simply a matter of definition. It could very well be that the label by which an activity is designated will influence who actually volunteers to attend and what expectations they bring with them. For instance studies have shown that groups run by university counselling centres attract volunteers who are more disturbed than non-volunteers (Haase and Kelly, 1971; Olch and Snow, 1970). On the other hand groups run by university psychology departments show no such differences between volunteers and non-volunteers (Sheridan and Shack, 1970; Cooper, 1972a; Cooper and Bowles, 1973; Gilligan, 1973; Seldman and McBrearty, 1975).

Early studies

One of the earliest substantive studies of the effects of T-groups was that by Miles (1960, 1965). He studied the effects of a ten-day residential NTL programme on thirty-four elementary school principals. Two control groups were also employed. Respondents were asked to describe any changes they had noted in themselves eight months after the training. Job associates of trainees and controls were also asked to report on perceived changes. A system of content analysis was devised, based on scoring of 'verified changes', i.e. those reported independently by two or more respondents. Miles found verified changes for 72 per cent of trainees but only for 17 per cent and 29 per cent of his two control groups. The areas in which verified changes were most markedly greater for trainees were: 'the areas of increased sensitivity to others, equalitarian attitudes, skills of communication and leadership, and group and maintenance skills' (Miles, 1965).

The methods developed by Miles were employed by several subsequent investigators (Bunker, 1965; Boyd and Elliss, 1962; Valiquet, 1968; Moscow, 1971). Each of these studies found greater verified change among trainees than controls, with never less than 50 per cent of trainees showing change and never more than 37 per cent of controls. The types of change found varied somewhat from those reported by Miles, but were broadly similar. In reviewing these studies Campbell and Dunnette (1968) concluded that they provided the firmest evidence then available for the effectiveness of sensitivity training. As they pointed out, these studies do have some evident weaknesses. The most obvious of these is that the observers reporting on change know perfectly well who has attended training and who has not. Further difficulties are the unorthodox manner in which these researchers recruited their control groups and the use of measures collected only after training.

With the current availability of a broader range of studies, Smith (1975) has suggested ways in which it is now possible to be more demanding of research studies. In this way the risks should be reduced that misleading conclusions will arise from a review of the data. A first step in this direction is to examine only studies which utilize a measure both before and after training. The advantage of this procedure is that it obviates the problem that after training trainees may have forgotten how they were feeling before the programme. This might be the case particularly with studies using long-term follow-up such as the verified change studies. Such measures are required both from trainees and from untrained controls. A second step in making research more precise is to require that the training experience last for a sufficient length of time. Little is known about how long is in fact needed for the achievement of this or that training goal, but it is clearly unreasonable to compare groups lasting say ten hours with those lasting fifty hours without expecting some difference in outcome. In this review only studies of groups which met for at least twenty hours are included. Such meetings might of course be intensively focused as in the 'cultural island' model or they might equally comprise ten two-hour meetings on a once-a-week basis.

These limitations still leave almost a hundred studies for examination. The criteria employed by researchers have quite properly varied widely, since the types of group they have studied have also been diverse. In examining these studies one further distinction is important. Most of the studies have tested to see whether a particular effect is present immediately after training. A smaller proportion have then studied also whether such effects persist or not. The more numerous studies of immediate effects will be examined in the first part of each section, subdividing between a series of different types of measure.

Global measures of self-concept

Researchers have frequently studied whether or not participants feel more favourable toward themselves after a group experience. The most commonly used measures have been semantic differential rating scales. Significantly more positive self-ratings have been obtained in five studies (Cicatti, 1970; Larson, 1972; R. Lee, 1969; Lieberman et al., 1973; Miller, 1970), but not in three further studies (Krear, 1968; Sutherland, 1973; Parker and Huff, 1975). Two of these unsuccessful studies also included a measure of self-percept based on card sorting but this also showed no change.

Six further studies included ratings of self on a more restricted range of scales, and all showed more favourable self-image after the group was over (Alperson, Alperson and Levine, 1971; Berzon et al., 1969; Hewitt and Kraft, 1973; Insel and Moos, 1972; Solomon et al., 1970; Solomon et al., 1968). A slightly different procedure was used by Shapiro and Ross (1971) whose subjects were asked to select from a list of 171 adjectives those which best described them. After the group, trainees selected significantly more positive adjectives than did controls.

The evidence thus shows that after group experience, participants saw themselves more positively in twelve out of fifteen studies, whereas controls did not. Six of these studies also included follow-up measures testing whether this change persisted. Alperson et al. (1971) found that among high school volunteers, the effect had disappeared two months after a marathon group experience. Cicatti (1970) reports 'regression' of the changes found three months after student groups, but fails to mention on which measures this occurred. Solomon et al. (1970) worked with vocational rehabilitation clients, but they also found that the gain in self-evaluation had disappeared after six months. By contrast Lieberman et al. (1973) found that members of eighteen student encounter groups still evaluated themselves as more adequate than did controls six months after the groups ended. Likewise, Larson (1972) found that after six months, trainee Air Force non-commissioned officers still evaluated themselves more favourably than did controls. Furthermore Shapiro and Ross (1971) found that one full year after training, the differences between trained and untrained supervisors in a school for delinquent girls were still present. The loss of significantly enhanced self-evaluation at follow-up is apparently frequent but not inevitable.

Psychometric measures

A second group of studies concerning global measures of self-concept have preferred the use of psychometric instruments to the ratings so far discussed. Fourteen reports are available which used the Tennessee Self-Concept Scale (TSCS) of which only three detected any significant change. There is some difficulty in interpreting these studies since few of them make clear which of the various scale scores on TSCS were computed. Eleven studies (Vosen, 1967; Brook, 1968; Becker, 1971; Livingston, 1971; G. McFarland, 1971; H. McFarland, 1971; Scherz, 1972; Poe, 1972; Cirigliano, 1972; Norton, 1973; Sherrill, 1973) all found no effect. The three remaining studies also found no effect on the test's main score, referred to as 'total P'. Young (1970) found increases on seven subscales of TSCS after three-day groups for students. Follow-up data showed some lasting change, but this was most marked on the self-acceptance scale, which was not one of those which changed immediately after the group. Ware and Barr (1977) found increases on subscales entitled Self-criticism, Self-satisfaction and Personal Worth, but these differed significantly from controls only for one of two groups studied. Reddy (1970) found an increase on a scale entitled Number of Deviant Signs. Since this scale is usually used as an indicator of maladjustment, Reddy concludes that group members may have been adversely affected. Since Reddy's subjects showed no change on other scales entitled General Maladjustment, Personality Disorder, and Neurosis, this possibility is by no means established.

The TSCS studies contrast markedly with those using ratings and semantic differentials. It is unlikely that most of those choosing to use ratings were studying successful groups while most of those choosing to use TSCS were studying unsuccessful groups. A more plausible hypothesis would be that the TSCS, at least where only its 'total P' score is computed, fails to detect those changes which are picked up by rating scales. This could be because some of the items on TSCS refer to one's experience of self in specific settings outside of the group such as family, on which there would be no reason to expect change during a group. In contrast, semantic differential ratings are context-free and therefore more likely to reflect a person's feelings at the time of testing.

A number of other psychometric tests of self-concept have been employed, with mixed results. Rubin (1967a, b) measured self-acceptance through a sentence-completion procedure. Codings of sentence completions were significantly more self-accepting after training. Zullo (1972) used the Offer self-image questionnaire in assessing the effects of a three-day retreat for senior high school students. Significant changes were found on the scales for social relations and morals. The latter change was still present after four months. King (1976) measured self-acceptance among teacher-training students with the Lesser scale. Increases were found after a weekly group for a term and these were still present three months later. King et al. (1973) obtained a similar effect with undergraduate groups. Innis (1971) found no change on the Berger acceptance of self scale, and Lieberman et al. (1973) found no change on the Rosenberg self-esteem scale. This latter finding is particularly interesting because it was obtained from the same sample who *did* show significant increases in self-ratings of adequacy. This supports the view that some self-concept measures are better able to detect the changes which occur than are others.

Of the twenty studies using psychometric tests of self-concept, only seven have detected change. Three of these studies provide follow-up data and all of these give evidence for the persistence of change.

Self-ideal match

An alternative approach to the measurement of self-acceptance is to obtain separate ratings of self and ideal-self and study their convergence. Although some critics have pointed to difficulties in the interpretation of such convergence, a number of studies have used this method. Gassner et al. (1964) reported two studies of student workshops. In the first study enhanced self-esteem was found equally among trainees and controls; in the second no change occurred in either condition. W. Lee (1970) obtained a convergence of self and ideal Q sorts with two groups of elementary school teachers. The convergence differed from an untrained group, but not from a further control who received didactic instruction. Peters (1970) studied six groups attending a ten-day National Training Laboratories programme. Self and ideal ratings converged to a highly significant degree, whereas in a rather dissimilar control group they did not. Lieberman et al. (1973) found that self and ideal constructs tended to diverge in their sample, but the effect was not quite significant. Sigal et al. (1976) studied the effects of groups integrated within the school curriculum for tenth grade students. They found complex effects, using mostly the Miskimmins self-goal-other test. Divergence between self and goal tended to widen. On the other hand Shapiro and Gust (1974) did obtain convergence of self and ideal among counselling graduate students.

Three of the six studies do thus find convergence of self and ideal percepts. The effect can scarcely be seen as a reliable effect of group experience since two substantial studies showed movement in the reverse direction and two of the other studies found significant convergence among some of their controls. It seems likely that groups can influence not only trainees' feelings about themselves, but also the kinds of ideal self to which they aspire. The variability of the findings obtained could derive from the type of ideal different groups construct.

Of the forty-four studies which included some type of gobal self-concept measure, twenty-one detected change. Nine of these included follow-up measures among which six found persistence of change. The actual percentage of studies detecting change appears to depend more on the type of measure employed than the type of group studied. It is concluded that group members do rather frequently feel more positive or accepting of themselves after groups. These effects are most readily detected by ratings and by the Lesser self-acceptance scale. Whether or not these global feelings about oneself are associated with more specific changes will now be examined.

Specific aspects of self-concept

A wide variety of specific changes in self-concept have been antici-pated. The studies will be examined in a series of subsections which will focus on the self as locus of causality, prejudice and open-minded-ness, orientation toward participative behaviours and other aspects of personality.

The self as locus of causality

Participants in sensitivity training are frequently encouraged to take responsibility for their own actions, for instance by seeking out feedback or by caring for others in the group. Several measures have been employed which seek to assess whether trainees increase the degree to which they see themselves as active, causal agents in determining their behaviour rather than seeing themselves as pawns of others or of environmental pressures. The most widely used instrument of this type has been Shostrom's Personal Orientation

Inventory (POI). The POI was designed as a measure of self-actualizing behaviour and it yields two major scales, Inner-directed Support and Time Competence. The first of these derives rather directly from the conceptualization of oneself as the locus of causality and this scale comprises most of the items in the test. Increases in inner-directedness on POI have been reported in seven studies (Alperson et al., 1971; Lavoie, 1971; Trueblood and McHolland, 1971; Mitchell et al., 1973; Margulies, 1973; Kimball and Gelso, 1974; Gilligan, 1974). In a further ten studies there was either no increase in inner-directedness (Khanna, 1971; Bellanti, 1972; Poe, 1972; Klingberg, 1972; Shapiro and Gust, 1974; Pacoe et al., 1976; Ware and Barr, 1977) or else increases among both trainees and controls (Treppa and Fricke, 1972; Jeffers, 1972; Sherrill, 1973; White, 1974). In many of these studies there were also increases detected on one or more of the subsidiary scales of the test, but since the test items for many of the subscales overlap one another the statistical procedure employed by these investigators is not appropriate.

Among the studies using POI, seven included a follow-up measure. Alperson et al. (1971) noted that approximately half the change found was no longer present after two months. Lavoie (1971) found her significant effect was gone after one month. Both Kimball and Gelso (1974) and Gilligan (1974) found that after 4–6 weeks the changes they had detected were still present but that controls had meanwhile increased their scores so that the difference between trainees and controls was no longer significant. Treppa and Fricke (1972), Khanna (1971) and Bellanti (1972) continued to find no difference between trainees and controls on inner-directedness at follow-up. Khanna (1971) did however find a significant change on the other main POI scale, Time Competence, which was still present six months after training.

POI has proved a popular test with researchers into groups. However the frequency with which it shows increases among controls both during and after groups suggests that whatever it measures is somewhat volatile, easily appearing and as easily disappearing. The study by Jeffers (1972) used a Solomon four-group design, whereby half the subjects completed post-measures but no pre-measures. The findings supported the conclusion that changes on POI can be triggered simply by completing the test. This triggering might be particularly potent among those who attended groups, since the content of items is close to issues often salient in groups.

Some further studies have employed other measures also related to the conception of self as causal. Insel and Moos (1972) obtained responses to the question, Who am I? Responses were coded for external referents, defined as descriptions of oneself verifiable by reference to external sources and internal referents which are those only verifiable by reference to one's internal state. They found significantly more use of internal referents after a group for graduate students. Kassarjian (1965) found no increase on a measure of inner-directedness. His conception of inner-directedness appears to derive more from examination of the source of one's values, rather than Shostrom's emphasis on inner-directedness as self-awareness. Rotter's locus of control scale provides one further relevant measure. Diamond and Shapiro (1973) reported significant increases in perceived internal locus of control among students after group experience. Ware and Barr (1977) found no such changes in the student groups they studied. Katz and Schwebel (1976) found no change during a group-based management training programme but increases in internality among both trainees and controls subsequently. Katz and Schwebel also used the Harrison and Oshry Problem Analysis Questionnaire to measure how far managers saw their work problems as caused by themselves. Both trainees and controls showed significant increases. Rettig (1978) used a sentence completion test after a student group and found increased use of personal explanations of why one's behaviour works out as it does and decreased use of situational explanations.

The evidence presented in this section is less compelling than that in the previous section. Of twenty-four studies concerning the self as locus of causality, ten have detected increases not shown by controls. All of the seven follow-up studies are based on POI and only one or perhaps two of these gives evidence for persistence of change. It appears that an enhanced sense of personal causality, at least as measured in these studies does quite frequently occur but tends to be a transient effect. One possible reason for this might be that the tests employed mostly rest on *generalized* expectancies about personal control. If trainees learn in a group to exert increased personal control over their behaviour in some specific situation or with some specific person, these tests would most likely not detect the change.

Prejudice and open-mindedness

A number of investigators have hypothesized that trainees will become more 'open' to new experience and less prejudiced against the alien or unfamiliar. Such changes are difficult to define and still more difficult to measure. There is good reason to expect that group members will become more open to experiences similar to those which they experience in sensitivity training but less reason to expect them to become open to other types of novelty or change. If the changes to be expected depend on the nature of the trainee's specific experience we should expect rather low generality of the changes found. For instance one might anticipate that race prejudice might change in groups focused on inter-racial encounter but not in groups with other foci.

The more global measures used are examined first. Decreases on the California F scale are reported by Carron (1964), Khanna (1971) and Parker and Huff (1975). Kernan (1964) and Adams (1970) found no such changes. Carron's significant effect owed more to increases in his control group than to decreases among trainees. The trainees were supervisors in the chemical industry and the effect had disappeared seventeen months after training. Kernan's (1964) negative effect was based on engineering supervisors. His post-measure was not collected until ten weeks after training was over, so there is no conflict between this finding and Carron's. Khanna (1971) found that decreases in F scale scores of Tennessee schoolteachers were still present six months after training. On the other hand Adams's (1970) null finding was also obtained with schoolteachers. Parker and Huff (1975) report significant reductions in F scale scores after groups for students. Very few of these studies give actual mean scores for their samples, so it is impossible to judge whether the variability of the findings might be because some samples were initially much more prejudiced than others.

An allied measure, the Rokeach dogmatism scale, has been used in three further studies. Adams (1970) used the dogmatism scale and failed to obtain any effect. Poe (1972) also found no effect but H. McFarland (1971) reported significant decreases in dogmatism in groups of student teachers. However after the students had completed their teaching practice the change was no longer present. Insel and Moos (1972) reported no changes on the Wilson-Patterson measure of conservatism after a student group, whereas Parker and Huff

(1975) found that their student groups did show changes on this measure, as well as on the Breskin test of rigidity. Hoerl (1974) used the Flexibility and Tolerance of Ambiguity scales of the California Psychological Inventory, with members of three-week residential groups at the Center for the Study of the Person. No increases were found but Hoerl was interested to note that volunteers for the groups already scored far higher on these scales before the groups than did non-volunteers.

Haiman (1963) designed an open-mindedness scale which included many items from the F and Dogmatism scales but had half the items reversed to take account of responses set. He found significant increases among student groups. Weissman et al. (1971) predicted an increase in preference for novel, complex or ambiguous stimuli. A sharp increase was found after a student group, but an equally large effect occurred among controls.

One further global measure is the Marlowe–Crowne Social Desirability Scale, which measures the degree to which respondents seek to give conventional, socially desirable responses. Significant effects were obtained by Jeffers (1972) and Ware and Barr (1977) but not by Sutherland (1973). All of these investigators employed student groups. Katz and Schwebel (1976) also found change toward less socially desirable responses among management training groups, but these changes occurred equally for controls both at the end of training and two months later. There are thus fifteen studies which have used one or more global measures of open-mindedness. Seven of these have detected significant change. Only four of these studies included follow-up measures, one of which did find a persisting effect.

More specific measures of open-mindedness are those which are in some way designed to measure changes which might be anticipated as a result of a particular training design. Perhaps the most obvious such measure is that of attitude toward group training procedures. Miller's (1970) subjects rated the concept of sensitivity training more favourably on a semantic differential following training. They were also more favourable toward the concept of being praised. Lieberman et al. (1973) found more favourable attitudes toward the safety of encounter groups and also greater endorsement of the values which the investigators delineated as encounter group values. The principal change here was toward increased openness to making changes in one's own behaviour. Six months later neither of these changes had persisted, although the belief in the safety of groups approached significance.

Young (1970) predicted changes in trainees' conceptions of human nature. Using Wrightsman's philosophies of human nature scale, he found significant increases of the trustworthiness scale after student groups. Kleeman (1974) used the same scale, also with student groups, and obtained increases on the scales measuring strength of will, altruism and independence. Both of these studies included follow-up measures. Young found the effect no longer present, whereas in Kleeman's sample the differences between trainees and controls widened and changes on the trustworthiness scale were now also significant. Shapiro and Diamond (1972) reported increases in hypnotic suggestibility among three student groups. The tester was ignorant of which of the students he was testing had actually attended groups. Shapiro and Gust (1974) obtained a similar effect, but it was significant for only one of two populations of students studied.

Six studies have been reported which focus specifically on the effects of multiracially composed groups. Innis (1971) studied five groups in Texas, each of which had six white and two black members. Semantic differential ratings were made of a variety of concepts. The only significant change was on ratings of 'civil disobedience', but Innis fails to make clear in which direction the change occurred. Krear (1968) studied marathon groups in racially imbalanced schools. Semantic differential ratings became more favourable to the concepts of authority and family but showed no change on the concepts of community and racial integration. Rubin (1967a, b) studied eleven-day residential groups for professionals in New England. Eight of the fifty participants were black. Prejudice was measured by the Harding and Schuman human-heartedness scale. Control data were obtained by asking fourteen of the participants to complete the scale ten days before the course and again at the start. The remaining thirty-six trainees showed a significant decrease in prejudice after training. Hull (1972) found increases in 'world-mindedness' in student groups which also contained foreign students. Controls included both all-American groups and students who did not attend groups at all. Smith and Willson (1975) studied multiracial weekend workshops in England. One workshop comprised white teachers and black parents of children attending their schools. Interviews conducted before and three months after training indicated that teachers became more favourable toward the parents whereas the parents became more critical of the teachers. A second workshop, involving whites and Asians, showed no lasting effect.

Lieberman et al.'s (1973) study at Stanford University included four groups which were specifically set up as black-white encounters. The wealth of measures used in this study casts some light on the views advanced in this section. Lieberman et al. found no change on global measures of open-mindedness, either with the mixed groups or with the all-white groups. The measures used were the F scale and scales testing for suspiciousness of others and militancy. At the same time they *did* find significant changes in their four interracial groups on a questionnaire specifically oriented toward race questions. These changes were increased endorsement of black separatism and increased mistrust of the other race.

Significant changes are thus reported in ten of the twelve studies using more specific measures of openness. Five of these include follow-up measures, among whom three found persisting effects. Although every one of the studies of interracial groups detected significant effects, these effects were very diverse, ranging from greater acceptance to greater militancy. Since the measures were different one cannot be sure that these are opposed effects rather than different aspects of a more global change which occurred in all the multiracial groups. In interpreting these findings one should bear in mind that they mostly involved groups in which blacks were a small minority. Scores were usually not reported separately for the different racial groups and none of the studies included a control in which multiracial groups undertook activities other than sensitivity training. All of these points underline how little is yet known of the effects of multiracial encounter.

This section has shown that specific measures of openness to others or to new experience are much more likely to yield significant effects of groups. The changes found also appear much more likely to persist. There do appear to be some circumstances under which the more global measures also show change, but it is not possible to say whether this is due to some distinctive quality of the trainees in these studies or whether it derives from the training designs employed.

Orientation toward participative behaviours

Sensitivity training is frequently a participative rather than a passive process. One may expect that trainees would come to see their participation in group settings in a different light as a result of this.

Behaviours in the T-group are often construed in terms of leadership or control, expression of friendship, self-disclosure and so forth. This section is concerned with tests which reflect these aspects of the trainee's self-percept. The most widely used test has been Schutz's (1958) Fundamental Interpersonal Relationship Orientation – Behaviour (FIRO-B) which asks people to describe how they prefer to express inclusion, control and affection behaviours to others and how much of these behaviours they like to receive from others. Twelve studies have employed this test, of which nine have detected significant training effects. The changes reported are not homogeneous. Early studies in England (Smith, 1964; Cureton, 1968) found convergence between expressed and wanted scores on particular scales. More recent American studies (Terleski, 1971; G. N. McFarland, 1971; Zullo, 1972; Klein, 1973; Jacobson and Smith, 1972; O'Connor and Alderson, 1974) have all reported increases on some of the FIRO-B scales. Increases have been noted for: expressed affection (three studies), wanted affection (three studies), wanted inclusion (three studies), expressed inclusion (one study) and expressed control (one study). The remaining studies using this test have either presented their data in a manner which does not make clear whether changes attributable to training occurred (Schutz and Allen, 1966) or else found no effects due to training (Weissman, Seldman and Ritter, 1971; Lieberman et al., 1973; Kaye, 1973). Four of these studies included follow-up measures of which only one (Jacobson and Smith, 1972) found that the effects had persisted.

The overall impression given by the FIRO-B studies is that changes at least in recent groups are most strongly focused on the giving and receiving of affection. It is particularly interesting that the Lieberman et al. study, which detected change on many measures, showed no effect on FIRO-B. One possible explanation might be that changes detectable by FIRO-B are quite specific to the culture of particular groups. Thus a highly affectionate T-group might generate changes in FIRO-B affection scales, whereas a group with more conflict might not. The Lieberman et al. study included a much larger and more varied sample of groups than did the other studies using FIRO-B. It might therefore be that Lieberman et al.'s included groups showing moves in various directions on FIRO-B, yielding no overall change. In any event, the existing follow-up studies do not offer much confidence that the changes are much more than temporary adaptations to the culture of sensitivity training.

Another instrument which relates closely to matters of concern to T-groups is the Jourard self-disclosure questionnaire. This asks people to indicate to whom they disclose various kinds of information about themselves. Solomon et al. (1970) adapted the measure and found that group members reported increased willingness to disclose to others after a nine-day workshop. Cicatti (1970) found increases in self-disclosure to others outside the group during weekly student groups. Increases were in disclosure to best friend of the same sex and to closest faculty member. Gold (1968) found no overall change in self-disclosure. There was an increase in disclosure of 'personality' items, but this was no longer found after three months. Scherz (1972) also found no change after student groups. Walker et al. (1972) found that self-disclosure scores decreased after groups for women, many of whom were nuns. Drawing on material from follow-up interviews, the authors propose that there had been no actual decrease in self-disclosure but the women now construed their behaviour as less self-disclosing than before because they contrasted their usual behaviour with what had occurred in the groups. Hurley and Hurley (1969) have also shown that the Jourard questionnaire does not predict actual self-disclosure in groups. These studies are consequently perhaps best interpreted as measures of attitudes toward self-disclosure, rather than providing any very direct guide as to changes in self-disclosing behaviour.

T-group leaders exemplify a particular approach to group leadership. One might consequently look for changes in attitudes toward different styles of leadership. Carron (1964) found decreases on the initiating structure scale of the Fleishman Leadership Opinions questionnaire among chemical industry supervisors. This change was not found seventeen months later. Kernan (1964) found no change on the same test among engineering supervisors. W. Lee (1970) found changes toward more participative leadership on the Minnesota Teacher Attitude Inventory among elementary teachers. No effects occurred for untrained controls, but similar changes were found among teachers who took classes in human relations. Adams (1970) found no change on this test. Miles (1960) also studied schoolteachers, but obtained no change on the leader behaviour description questionnaire or a group participation scale. Gassner et al. (1964) reported highly significant changes on a democractic leadership scale after student workshops. Bolman (1970) found that managers attending group training showed increased endorsement of confrontation of 'interpersonal issues' and decreases on 'use of formal power' and 'endorsement of pyramidal values' (i.e. belief in hierarchical authority). These changes were still present four weeks later, but at this time the managers were still attending a course together and had not yet returned to their jobs.

This section has shown that measures of orientation toward participative behaviour do frequently change after groups. Of the twenty-four studies reviewed, sixteen detected favourable effects. Of the seven studies with valid follow-up data, only one found that the effects had lasted. The rather generalized tests employed in these studies thus appear to detect effects which are transient rather than lasting.

Other aspects of personality

The three preceding sections have examined changes in various aspects of self-percept. Further studies have been undertaken which do not fit readily into any of these sections. Leary's interpersonal checklist, which asks for self-ratings of various aspects of one's self-concepts has been used in four studies. Treppa and Fricke (1972) found an increased desire for dominance, whereas White (1974) found no change. Kaye (1973) found reductions in submissiveness and hostility, while controls became less loving. Each of these studies concerned student groups. Kaye's findings were still present eight months later. Khanna (1971) also obtained changes on the interpersonal checklist, but fails to indicate whether they were significant.

The groups of Filipino women studied by Lavoie (1971) saw themselves as more assertive, cheerful and venturesome on Cattell and Eber's Sixteen Personality Factors questionnaire and more sociable on the Gordon personal profile after training. These effects were gone after one month. Two studies using the California Personality Inventory (Flannigan, 1970; Vail, 1971) showed no change. Shapiro and Gust (1974) report enhanced scores on the Teachers counselling questionnaire and on the Taft experience questionnaire among counselling students. Kleeman (1974) found increases on self-ratings of self-determination, self-affirmation, self-motivation and empathy after student groups. The first two of these changes were still present after two months. Pfister (1975) found increased understanding of self as rated on the Edwards Personality Inventory among police attending groups. Martin and Fischer (1974) obtained ratings on the Adjective Check List after student groups in Canada. Trainees saw themselves as more dominant and heterosexual, but less suc-courant, deferent, abasing or unfavourably adjusted. Bloom (1975/6) conducted sensitivity training for the elderly. No change was found on two tests of mental ability and an index of activity level. In other studies no change was found on anomie (Rubin, 1967a, b) ego-strength (Kimball and Gelso, 1974; Adams, 1970), Bendig's scales of hostility (Uhes, 1971), the constructive personality change index (Solomon et al., 1968), the choice dilemma questionnaire (Poe, 1972), the Eysenck Personality Inventory (Insel and Moos, 1972), a The-matic Apperception Test, machiavellianism and the Guilford-Zim-merman Temperament Survey (Kernan, 1964).

Pollack and Stanley (1971) used a sentence completion test to assess students' ability to confront aggressive and sexual stimuli. Codings of responses showed improved coping after groups. A similar finding was that by Kuch et al. (1972) who obtained reduced 'unhealthy' responses to a forced-choice Rorschach test after a counselling group.

Lieberman et al. (1973) obtained several further measures as a part of their project. Group members reported significantly more growth experiences on a 'life-space' questionnaire after attending groups. They also rated more highly the level of their coping with their current personal dilemmas. Finally their descriptions of others changed in the direction of a factor which the authors term 'leniency'. None of these changes was sustained six months later.

The measures described in this section are diverse and it is not always easy to see why researchers selected some of them. Of the twenty-four studies mentioned, twelve did detect changes after training. Two out of four follow-up studies showed persistence of change.

Perceptions of others

The phrase *sensitivity training* implies that one of the major goals of training is that one should develop a more perceptive or accurate understanding of others. Surprisingly few studies have tested for such effects. Gassner et al. (1964) obtained ratings of the 'way others usually act' after student workshops. Such ratings were found to converge with self-percepts equally for trainees and controls. Innis (1971) found no change on Berger's acceptance of others scale after a one-week workshop.

These two studies contrast with others where the subject is asked to rate specific others. Lieberman et al. (1973) found no change in ratings of one's best friend or of the environment in which one lives after training. Hewitt and Kraft (1973) assembled four-person discussion groups of mixed trainees and controls before and after training. No change was found in perception of controls by trainees. Larson (1972) found a significant increase in semantic differential ratings by Air Force non-commissioned officers of their subordinates after the officers had attended training. This effect was still present six months later. Harrison (1962) found that one group of management trainees increased their use of interpersonal constructs to describe non-trainees. A second group did not differ from controls. Harrison's procedure was also used by Lieberman et al. (1973) who found no change after training.

Danish and Kagan (1971) developed an affective sensitivity scale, in which the subject is asked to infer the feelings of characters on videotape. Improved scores were found after a ten-day training programme, while controls showed no change (Danish, 1970). Norton (1973) also used this scale, working with student groups, but no effect was obtained.

This section provides very little support for the view that sensitivity training leads to changes in perceptions of others not present during training. Only three of the eight relevant studies showed any change. Two of these were undertaken within work organizations, while none of the studies which failed to find effects were located in organizational settings.

Perceptions of trainee behaviour by others

Changes in the behaviour of the trainee may be examined in two ways. Either one may create some kind of temporary test situation in which the trainee's performance is assessed, or one may ask the trainee's customary associates to report their perceptions of everyday performance. The first procedure can reduce observer bias, but the second offers a more direct test of whether changes are actually evident in everyday settings.

Performance tests

A number of the tests employed relate to the learning of communication skills. Heck (1971) asked teacher trainees to describe in writing how they would explain a problem to twelve-year-old. Responses by those who attended groups improved, as did those of others who undertook programmed tasks. Controls showed no change. Bellanti (1972) used a counselling simulation interview. After training, trainees were coded as higher on accurate empathy, unconditional positive regard and congruence. This effect was not found three months later. Elliott (1978) used a videotape version of the Carkhuff indices of communication and discrimination test. Scores on communication rose, while those on discrimination did not. Norton (1973) using the same test found increases on gross facilitation, empathic understanding and the discrimination of facilitative communications. Each of these studies used students. Pacoe et al. (1976) found increases on measures of both empathic communication and facilitative discrimination among medical students. These studies indicate increases on attributes such as empathy and listening skills, which are seen by Carl Rogers and others as prerequisites for effective helping of others.

Solomon et al. (1968, 1970) studied vocational rehabilitation clients. Ratings of rehabilitation progress were made of interviews before and after training. Increases were found, particularly on motivation to work. Dua (1972) compared individual counselling with group sessions. Ratings of anxiety within a group discussion fell for those attending groups. Argyris (1965) obtained codings of executives discussing case studies. Changes in rated behaviour were noted for those attending groups. Unfortunately Argyris indicates that the coder for the trainees' post-test was different, whereas the same coder continued to code the controls. The study must therefore by judged inconclusive, since the changes found could easily be due to the change in coder.

Becker (1971) found no change in the physical distance maintained by subjects while performing a task before and after training. Powell (1972) found no improvement on a decision-making exercise based on the film *Twelve Angry Men*. Finally Hewitt and Kraft (1973) brought trainees and controls together for a one-hour discussion before and after training. Controls saw no changes in trainees' behaviour.

The evidence from performance tests indicates that changes are frequently found on such tests. Of the eleven studies which permit a conclusion, eight found positive effects. Only one of these included follow-up data and this indicated fade-out.

Observation of everyday performance

Perceptions based on everyday performance are available from fifteen studies. Five of these concern teachers. Schmuck (1968) reports on an extensive programme which appears to have involved more than a hundred hours of training. Children in classes taught by sensitivity trainees showed increases in the influence they perceived themselves to have. Various other changes were also detected but these were found also among those who had other forms of training but no groups. G. N. McFarland (1971) found that after two and a half days of training for the teachers, children in their classes perceived a significant increase in attempts by the teacher to include them. Khanna (1971) asked students to use the Leary interpersonal check-list to describe their teachers. After training, the teachers were seen as less hostile and more accepting. W. S. Lee (1970) found no change in the manner in which teachers were perceived by parents and by administrators after the teachers had attended training.

Geitgey (1966) investigated sensitivity training for student nurses. The nurses were perceived more favourably by patients and by instructors. The instructors also rated the nurses' relations with patients more highly. Chambers and Ficek (1970) evaluated a marathon group for girls in a residential training centre. The girls were assigned to training or the control group by decision of their counsellors. One month after training the counsellors perceived more positive changes among trainees than controls. Since the counsellors were instrumental in assigning the girls to training in the first place, they might well have preferred to see more change among trainees than controls.

Larson (1972) obtained semantic differential ratings from the subordinates of non-commissioned officers in the Air Force. No changes were found after training. Pfister (1975) investigated the impact of sensitivity training for the police. Citizens involved in 'non-adversive' contacts with the police were asked to make ratings on the behaviour of the police officer they had dealt with. After training significantly higher ratings were found on confidence, warmth, sincerity, understanding, acting as a co-worker on a common problem and accepting the citizen as an individual. Controls did not show these changes. Cohen and Keller (1973) obtained data on the impact of a management development programme. Trainees' supervisors saw increases in 'human-relations behaviours' but these changes did not achieve significance overall. Significant effects were found only where the leadership climate was high on consideration and low on initiating structure, i.e. where human relations behaviour was to some degree already present. Katz and Schwebel (1976) obtained peer evaluations of middle managers in a management development programme. Peer evaluations increased equally for trainees and controls, both immediately after training and two months later.

R. E. Lee (1969) asked room-mates of students to complete the Barrett-Lenard relationship inventory as a description of trainees and controls. The students who attended groups were seen three weeks later as higher on empathy, unconditional positive regard and congruence. Cicatti (1970) also found change among students using the Barrett-Lennard measure, but fails to make clear who completed the instrument with regard to whom. Lieberman et al. (1973) as well as Parker and Huff (1975) also obtained ratings from close associates of students who attended groups but neither study detected changes. Cooper (1972a, b) compared health service consultation records of students who did and did not attend groups. No immediate difference was found, but controls saw doctors more frequently one year after the groups.

The studies based on observations of everyday performance provide some quite strong evidence for the visibility of sensitivity training effects. Eight studies showed significant effects while six did not. In addition the Cooper study found an effect which was assumed to be adverse and which occurred among controls but not trainees. Of the five studies including follow-up data three showed persistence of effect.

This section has indicated that of twenty-six studies involving observer perceptions of trainees, seventeen have found at least some effects favouring trainees. It should of course be remembered that in many of these cases the observers were well aware who had attended groups and who had not.

The current situation

The studies described in the preceding pages are impressively numerous, and offer some support to the enthusiasm of practitioners for these methods. A hundred and seventy-seven tests of immediate effects of training have been reported and of these ninety-six (54 per cent) detected significant effects. These tests are by no means independent of one another, since many studies employed several outcome measures. In fact the number of separate studies providing these tests is ninety-one. Twenty-eight of these studies included follow-up measures, which provided fifty-two tests of the persistence of effects. Seventeen measures (33 per cent) did show positive effects.

While the studies reviewed do employ somewhat more sophisticated research measures than those used in the early evaluation studies of groups, there continue to be numerous ways in which the findings could be misleading. Some of the most obvious of these sources of error are: perceptual biases in observers of trainees, the use of control groups which are not closely equivalent to trainees, the use of measures which do not reflect sufficiently closely what happens in groups, and the use of measures which are prone to test sensitization, i.e. effects attributable simply to the completion of the form within the training setting.

Although these sources of error are certainly present, there is little evidence that the more tightly controlled studies are any less likely to come up with positive effects than the less tightly controlled ones. In many ways the most systematically designed study has been that by Lieberman et al. (1973). These authors concluded that about two-thirds of participants showed positive effects at the close of the group, reducing to about one-third at their six-month follow-up. While these figures are expressed in terms of proportions of group members showing change rather than proportions of measures showing change, the conclusions accord well with the conclusions of this review: *A good deal of measurable change does occur after groups, but there is a substantial fade-out of these effects in subsequent months.*

The weight of data supporting this conclusion is now sufficient; what is required is not simply more data, but answers to a series of more specific questions. These questions centre on the need for clearer theorizing as to what occurs in groups. We need to know why the changes which occur in groups do occur. If this question could be answered, it should prove possible to make the effects of training more consistently predictable. We also need to know why the effects so frequently do not persist. Insight into this question might also imply different types of training design. Finally we need to know how far the mechanisms of effective sensitivity training are unique and how far they underly the widening range of other group-based training methods.

Note

This chapter is a revised and updated version of 'Controlled studies of the outcome of sensitivity training', 1975, *Psychological Bulletin 82*: 597-622, reproduced by permission of the American Psychological Association. This version also appears in Peter Smith (1980) *Group Processes and Personal Change* and is reproduced by permission of Harper & Row Ltd, London.

References

Adams, P. L. (1970) Experiential group counselling with intern teachers. *Dissertation Abstracts International 31A*: 605–6.

Alperson, B. L., Alperson, E. D. and Levine, R. (1971) Growth effects of high school marathons. *Experimental Publication System*, American Psychological Association *10*: Ms. no. 369–56.

Argyris, C. (1965) Explorations in interpersonal competence – 11. *Journal of Applied Behavioral Science 1*: 255–69.

Becker, J. L. (1971) The effects of instructional audiotape in self-directed encounter groups. *Dissertation Abstracts International 31B*: 4325–6.

Bellanti, J. (1972) The effects of an encounter group experience on empathy, respect, congruence, and self-actualisation. *Dissertation Abstracts International 32B*: 6668–9.

Berzon, B., Reisel, J. and Davis, D. P. (1969) An audiotape program for self-directed small groups. *Journal of Humanistic Psychology 9*: 71–92.

Bloom, S. (1975/1976) A study of the impact of sensitivity training on the elderly. *Interpersonal Development 6*: 150–2.

Bolman, L. (1970) Laboratory versus lecture in training executives. *Journal of Applied Behavioral Science 6*: 323–35.

Boyd, J. B. and Elliss, J. D. (1962) *Findings of Research into Senior Management Seminars*. Toronto: Hydro-electric Power Commission of Ontario.

Brook, R. C. (1968) Self-concept changes as a function of participation in sensitivity training as measured by the Tennessee Self-Concept Scale. *Dissertation Abstracts 29A*: 1700.

Bunker, D. R. (1965) Individual applications of laboratory training. *Journal of Applied Behavioral Science 1*: 131–48.

Campbell, J. P. and Dunnette, M. D. (1968) The effectiveness of T-group experience in managerial training and development. *Psychological Bulletin 70*: 73–104.

Carron, T. J. (1964) Human relations training and attitude change: a vector analysis. *Personnel Psychology 17*: 403–24.

Chambers, W. M. and Ficek, D. E. (1970) An evaluation of marathon counselling. *International Journal of Group Psychotherapy 20*: 372–9.

Cicatti, S. M. (1970) Comparison of three methods of facilitating encounter groups in a college environment. *Dissertation Abstracts International 31B*: 2954–5.

Cirigliano, R. J. (1972) Group encounter effects upon the self-concepts of high school students. *Dissertation Abstracts International 33A*: 2760–1.

Cohen, B. M. and Keller, G. (1973) The relationship between laboratory training and human relations growth in varying organisational climates. *Catalog of Selected Documents in Psychology 3*: 101–2.

Cooper, C. L. (1972a) An attempt to assess the psychologically disturbing effects of T-group training. *British Journal of Social and Clinical Psychology 11*: 342–5.

Cooper, C. L. (1972b) Coping with life stress after sensitivity training. *Psychological Reports 31*: 602.

Cooper, C. L. and Bowles, D. (1973) Physical encounter and self-disclosure. *Psychological Reports 33*: 451–4.

Cureton, L. (1968) T-groups and intergroups in teacher training. Unpublished M. Phil. thesis, University of Sussex.

Danish, S. J. (1970) The influence of leader empathy (affective sensitivity), participant motivation to change and leader-participant relationship on changes in affective sensitivity of T-group participants. *Dissertation Abstracts International 30A*: 5229–30.

Danish, S. J. and Kagan, N. (1971) Measurement of affective sensitivity: toward a valid measure of interpersonal perception. *Journal of Counseling Psychology 18*: 51–4.

Diamond, M. J. and Shapiro, J. L. (1973) Changes in locus of control as a function of encounter group experiences: a study and a replication. *Journal of Abnormal Psychology 82*: 514–18.

Dua, P. S. (1972) The effects of laboratory training on anxiety. *Journal of Counseling Psychology 19*: 171–2.

Elliott, G. R. (1978) The effects of T-group training on the communication skills of counsellor trainees. *Small Group Behavior 9*: 49–58.

Flannigan, M. W. (1970) A study of attitude changes through group processes. *Dissertation Abstracts 31A*: 2102.

Gassner, S. M., Gold, J. and Snadowsky, A. M. (1964) Changes in the phenomenal field as a result of human relations training. *Journal of Psychology 58*: 33–41.

Geitgey, D. A. (1966) A study of some effects of sensitivity training on the performance of students in associate degree programs of nursing education. *Dissertation Abstracts 27B*: 2000–1.

Gilligan, J. F. (1973) Personality characteristics of selectors and non-selectors of sensitivity training. *Journal of Counseling Psychology 20*: 265–8.

Gilligan, J. F. (1974) Sensitivity training and self-actualisation. *Psychological Reports 34*: 319–25.

Gold, J. S. (1968) An evaluation of a laboratory human relations training program for college undergraduates. *Dissertation Abstracts 28A*: 3262–3.

Haase, R. K. and Kelly, F. D. (1971) Characteristics of those who seek, those who complete, and those who drop out of sensitivity groups. *Counseling Center Research Reports* No. 26, University of Massachusetts.

Haiman, F. S. (1963) The effects of training in group methods on openmindedness. *Journal of Communication 13*: 236–45.

Harrison, R. (1962) The impact of the laboratory on perception of others by the experimental group. In C. Argyris *Interpersonal Competence and Organisational Effectiveness*. Homewood, Ill.: Irwin-Dorsey.

Heck, E. J. (1971) A training and research model for investigating the effects of sensitivity training for teachers. *Journal of Teacher Education 22*: 502–7.

Hewitt, J. and Kraft, M. (1973) The effects of an encounter group experience on self perception and interpersonal relations. *Journal of Consulting and Clinical Psychology 40*: 162.

Hoerl, R. T. (1974) Encounter groups: their effect on rigidity. *Human Relations 27*: 431–8.

Hull, W. F. (1972) Changes in world-mindedness after a cross-cultural sensitivity group experience. *Journal of Applied Behavioural Science 8*: 115–21.

Hurley, J. R. and Hurley, S. J. (1969) Toward authenticity in measuring self-disclosure. *Journal of Counseling Psychology 16*: 271–4.

Innis, M. N. N. (1971) An analysis of sensitivity training and the laboratory method in effecting changes in attitudes and concepts. *Dissertation Abstracts International 31A*: 6404.

Insel, P. and Moos, R. (1972) An experimental investigation of process and outcome in an encounter group. *Human Relations 25*: 441–7.

Jacobson, E. A. and Smith, S. J. (1972) The effect of weekend encounter group experience upon interpersonal orientations. *Journal of Consulting and Clinical Psychology 38*: 403–10.

Jeffers, J. J. L. (1972) The effects of marathon encounter groups on personality characteristics of group members and group facilitators. *Dissertation Abstracts International 32A*: 4153.

Kassarjian, H. H. (1965) Social character and sensitivity training. *Journal of Applied Behavioral Science 1*: 433–40.

Katz, S. I. and Schwebel, A. I. (1976) The transfer of laboratory training. *Small Group Behavior 7*: 271–86.

Kaye, J. D. (1973) Group interaction and interpersonal learning. *Small Group Behavior 4*: 424–48.

Kernan, J. P. (1964) Laboratory human relations training: its effect on the 'personality' of supervising engineers. *Dissertation Abstracts 25*: 665–6.

Khanna, J. L. (1971) Training of educators for hard-core areas – a success? Paper presented at 17th Congress, International Association of Applied Psychology, Liège.

Kimball, R. and Gelso, C. J. (1974) Self-actualisation in a marathon group: do the strong get stronger? *Journal of Counseling Psychology 21*: 38–42.

King, M. (1976) Changes in self-acceptance of college students associated with the encounter model class. *Small Group Behavior 7*: 379–84.

King, M., Payne, D. C. and McIntire, W. G. (1973) The impact of marathon and prolonged sensitivity training on self-acceptance. *Small Group Behavior 4*: 414–23.

Kleeman, J. L. (1974) The Kendall College human potential seminar model: research. *Journal of College Student Personnel 15*: 89–95.

Klein, R. S. (1973) The effect of differential treatments on encounter groups. *Dissertation Abstracts International 34B*: 415–16.

Klingberg, H. E. (1972) An evaluation of sensitivity training effects on self-actualization, purpose in life and religious attitudes of theological students. *Dissertation Abstracts International 32B*: 7312.

Krear, M. L. (1968) The influence of sensitivity training on the social attitudes of educational leaders of racially imbalanced schools. *Dissertation Abstracts 29A*: 1954–5.

Kuch, K., Harrower, M. and Renick, J. (1972) Observations on a time-extended group with campus volunteers. *International Journal of Group Psychotherapy 22*: 471–87.

Larson, J. L. (1972) The effects of a human relations workshop on personal and interpersonal perceptions in a military setting. *Dissertation Abstracts International 33A*: 2716.

Lavoie, D. (1971) The phenomenological transformation of the self-concept toward self-actualisation through the sensitivity training laboratory. *Interpersonal Development 2*: 201–12.

Lee, R. E. (1969) The relationship between the basic encounter group and change in self-concepts and interpersonal relations of college low achievers. *Dissertation Abstracts International 30A*: 2336–7.

Lee, W. S. (1970) Human relations training for teachers: the effectiveness of sensitivity training. *California Journal of Educational Research 21*: 28–34.

Lieberman, M. A., Yalom, I. D. and Miles, M. B. (1973) *Encounter Groups: First Facts.* New York: Basic Books.

Livingston, L. B. (1971) Self-concept change of black college males as a result of a weekend black experience encounter workshop. *Dissertation Abstracts International 32B*: 2423.

McFarland, G. N. (1971) The effects of sensitivity training utilised as in-service education. *Dissertation Abstracts International 31A*: 4013.

McFarland, H. B. N. (1971) An analysis of the effect of interpersonal communication group work on the dogmatism and self-concept of student teachers. *Dissertation Abstracts International 31A*: 6456.

Margulies, N. (1973) The effects of an organizational sensitivity training program on a measure of self-actualisation. *Studies in Personnel Psychology 5*: 67–74.

Martin, R. D. and Fisher, D. G. (1974) Encounter group experience and personality change. *Psychological Reports 35*: 91–6.

Miles, M. B. (1960) Human relations training: processes and outcomes. *Journal of Counseling Psychology 7*: 301–6.

Miles, M. B. (1965) Changes during the following laboratory training: a clinical-experimental study. *Journal of Applied Behavioral Science 1*: 215–42.

Miller, G. M. (1970) The effects of sensitivity training design and personality factors upon the attitudes of group participants. *Dissertation Abstracts International 30A*: 3836–7.

Mitchell, P., Reid, W. and Sanders, N. (1973) The human potential seminar at Muskegon Community college. *Michigan Personnel and Guidance Journal 4*: 31–7.

Moscow, D. (1971) T-group training in the Netherlands: an evaluation and a cross-cultural comparison. *Journal of Applied Behavioral Science 7*: 427–8.

Norton, B. E. (1973) The effects of human relations training upon teacher trainees' level of facilitative communication, self-concept and creativity. *Dissertation Abstracts International 33A*: 4094–5.

O'Connor, G. and Alderson, J. (1974) Human relations groups for human services practitioners. *Small Group Behavior 5*: 495–505.

Olch, D. and Snow, D. L. (1970) Personality characteristics of sensitivity group volunteers. *Personnel and Guidance Journal 48*: 848–50.

Pacoe, L. V., Naar, R., Guyett, I. P. and Wells, R. (1976) Training medical students in interpersonal relationship skills. *Journal of Medical Education 51*: 743–50.

Parker, C. C. and Huff, V. E. (1975) The effects of group counseling on rigidity. *Small Group Behavior 6*: 402–13.

Peters, D. R. (1970) Self-ideal congruence as a function of human relations training. *Journal of Psychology 76*: 199–207.

Pfister, G. (1975) Outcomes of laboratory training for police officers. *Journal of Social Issues 31*: 115–21.

Poe, B. J. (1972) The effect of sensitivity training on the relations between risk-taking and other selected behavior factors. *Dissertation Abstracts International 32B*: 6037–8.

Pollack, D. and Stanley, G. (1971) Coping and marathon sensitivity training. *Psychological Reports 29*: 379–85.

Powell, T. A. (1972) An investigation of the T-group and its effect on decision-making skills. *Dissertation Abstracts International 32A*: 6084–5.

Reddy, W. B. (1970) Sensitivity training or group psychotherapy: the need for adequate screening. *International Journal of Group Psychotherapy 20*: 366–71.

Rettig, S. (1978) Active and reactive states of being. *Small Group Behavior 9*: 7–13.

Rubin, I. M. (1967a) Increased self-acceptance: a new means of reducing prejudice. *Journal of Personality and Social Psychology 5*: 233–8.

Rubin, I. M. (1967b) The reduction of prejudice through laboratory training. *Journal of Applied Behavioral Science 3*: 29–50.

Scherz, M. E. (1972) Changes in self-esteem following experimental manipulation of self-disclosure and feedback conditions in a sensitivity training laboratory. *Dissertation Abstracts International 33B*: 1805–6.

Schmuck, R. A. 1968) Helping teachers improve classroom processes. *Journal of Applied Behavioral Science 4*: 401–35.

Schutz, W. C. (1958) *FIRO: A 3-Dimensional Theory of Interpersonal Behavior*. New York: Rinehart.

Schutz, W. C. and Allen, V. L. (1966) The effects of a T-group laboratory on interpersonal behavior. *Journal of Applied Behavioral Science 2*: 265–86.

Seldman, M. L. and McBrearty, J. F. (1975) Characteristics of marathon volunteers. *Psychological Reports 36*: 555–60.

Shapiro, J. L. and Diamond, M. J. (1972) Increases in hypnotisability as a function of encounter group training. *Journal of Abnormal Psychology 79*: 112–15.

Shapiro, J. L. and Gust, T. (1974) Counselor training for facilitating human relationships. *Counselor Education and Supervision 13*: 198–206.

Shapiro, J. L. and Ross, R. L. (1971) Sensitivity training for staff in an institution for adolescent offenders. *Journal of Applied Behavioral Science 7*: 710–23.

Sheridan, K. and Shack, J. R. (1970) Personality correlates of the undergraduate volunteer subject. *Journal of Psychology 76*: 23–6.

Sherrill, J. D. (1973) The effects of group experience on the personal-vocational development of vocationally undecided college students. *Dissertation Abstracts International 34A*: 573.

Sigal, J., Braverman, S., Pilon, R. and Baker, P. (1976) Effects of teacher-led curriculum-integrated sensitivity training in a large high school. *Journal of Educational Research 70*: 3–9.

Smith, P. B. (1964) Attitude changes associated with training in human relations. *British Journal of Social and Clinical Psychology 3*: 104–12.

Smith, P. B. (1975) Controlled studies of the outcome of sensitivity training. *Psychological Bulletin 82*: 597–622.

Smith, P. B. and Willson, M. (1975) The use of group training methods in multiracial settings. *New Community 4*: 1–14.

Solomon, L. N., Berzon, B. and Davis, D. (1970) A personal growth program for self-directed groups. *Journal of Applied Behavioral Science 6*: 427–51.

Solomon, L. N., Berzon, B. and Weedman, C. W. (1968) The self-directed therapeutic group: a new rehabilitation resource. *International Journal of Group Psychotherapy 18*: 199–219.

Sutherland, S. H. (1973) A study of the effects of a marathon and a traditional encounter group experience on self-esteem, defensive behavior and mood. *Dissertation Abstracts International 33B*: 3963.

Terleski, D. R. (1971) The relationship between unstructured and structured sensitivity group experiences of group members and self-perceived changes. *Dissertation Abstracts International 31A*: 5139–40.

Treppa, J. A. and Fricke, L. (1972) Effects of a marathon group experience. *Journal of Counseling Psychology 19*: 466–7.

Trueblood, R. W. and McHolland, J. D. (1971) Measures of change toward self-actualization through the human potential group process. Unpublished manuscript, cited in R. R. Knapp and E. L. Shostrom (1976) POI outcomes in studies of growth groups: a selected review. *Group and Organisation Studies 1* (2): 203–22.

Uhes, M. J. (1971) The expression of hostility as a function of encounter group experience. *Psychological Reports 28*: 733–4.

Vail, J. P. (1971) The effect of encounter tapes for personal growth on culturally disadvantaged negro girls. *Dissertation Abstracts International 31A*: 5141.

Valiquet, M. (1968) Individual change in a management development program. *Journal of Applied Behavioral Science 4*: 313–25.

Vosen, L. (1967) The relation between self-disclosure and self-esteem. *Dissertation Abstracts 27B*: 2882.

Walker, R. E., Shack, J. R., Egan, G., Sheridan, K. and Sheridan, E. P. (1972) Changes in self-judgements of self-disclosure after group experience. *Journal of Applied Behavioral Science 8*: 248–51.

Ware, J. R. and Barr, J. E. (1977) Effects of a nine-week structured and unstructured group experience on measures of self-concept and self-actualization. *Small Group Behavior 8*: 93–101.

Weissman, H. N., Seldman, M. and Ritter, K. (1971) Changes in awareness of impact upon others as a function of encounter and marathon group experiences. *Psychological Reports 28*: 651–61.

White, K. R. (1974) T-group revisited: self-concept change and the 'fishbowling' technique. *Small Group Behavior 5*: 473–85.

Young, J. R. (1970) The effects of laboratory training on self-concept, philosophies of human nature and perception of group behavior. *Dissertation Abstracts International 31B*: 3696–7.

Zullo, J. R. (1972) T-group laboratory learning and adolescent ego-development. *Dissertation Abstracts International 33B*: 2799.

3 Studies of the processes and dynamics within experiential groups

W. Brendan Reddy
and Kathy M. Lippert

The origins of the T-group method have been referred to in Chapter 1. Since 1947 sensitivity training and its many offshoots have experienced a wide range of criticisms and attacks as have all educational, personal and interpersonal learning movements and interventions. The 'laboratory experience', as it is sometimes called, has also had strong advocates and supporters. Sensitivity training, in its purest form, has already reached its zenith. If sensitivity training groups are being conducted in large numbers, they certainly are not being researched or written about in the same numbers. However, laboratory training is well entrenched as a prime learning mode and is alive and well in business, government, schools, organizations, and volunteer groups.

The early fantasy of a communist take-over, followed by reports of high casualty rates, has all but disappeared. In general, the research has never been of the highest quality, but then the limitations and difficulties in conducting small group research are legion. Indeed, one major piece of research (Lieberman et al., 1973) has been challenged, and rightly so, on methodological grounds (Schutz, 1975; Smith, 1975a; Rowan, 1975). When it first appeared, the study was hailed as the definitive answer to whether personal growth groups 'worked', whether they precipitated casualties, and which group leaders were effective or ineffective.

In 1978, Russell reanalysed the Lieberman et al. (1973) data and found that 33 per cent of the trainers had minimal or no previous experience in leading encounter groups. In addition, the reanalysis supported either no difference between traditional group psychotherapy and the type of encounter methods outlined in Chapter 1, or a slightly greater effectiveness of the encounter group methods. Russell reaffirmed Bergin's (1971) contention that some leaders (trainers, facilitators, therapists) contributed to positive change in participants and other leaders contributed to negative change or no change.

The question is not whether group-work carries the label, 'may be dangerous to your health'. Like any human treatment involving change, of course there will be those participants who under given circumstances will exhibit adverse effects (Hartley et al., 1976). However, the deleterious effects seem to be minimal (Smith, 1975a) and the experience less stressful than university examinations or experiments on perceptual isolation (Cooper, 1975). Cooper (1974) reported that some T-group participants saw themselves and were seen by others as disrupted by the experience. He also reported that the same participants saw themselves and were viewed by others (family and friends) as coping better, developing better relationships with significant others, communicating more effectively, and happier. Moreover, Hogan (1974), in his definitive work on legal aspects of group-work, maintains there is simply not enough evidence of corruption in the field and subsequent adverse effects to warrant stringent measures such as licensing.

We do now have ample evidence that participants change for better or for worse (Smith, 1975b, see also Chapter 2; Cooper and Mangham, 1971; Campbell and Dunnette, 1968). What need to be examined at this point are the micro-level processes and group dynamics. We have become more knowledgeable and sophisticated in conducting groups, but studies of intra-group dynamics and processes are anecdotal or scattered in the literature. As practitioners and as researchers, we simply need to know what has been learned in the past few years that can enhance our own effectiveness in the laboratory setting. Our objective in this chapter is to present the research in areas which we believe to be critical in producing positive or negative changes in participants.

We will focus on six areas: (a) characteristics of participants, (b) structure and design of laboratories, (c) group composition, (d) phases of group development, (e) trainer influence, and (f) feedback.

Studies which are of particular importance are discussed in detail; others are presented in summary.

Characteristics of participants

The consumers

Can we be aware who are the consumers of group-work and how they behave under particular circumstances? While a number of authors (Reddy, 1970, 1972; Peters, 1973) have suggested screening procedures for the more extreme behaviour problems or the psychologically disturbed, what do we know of the 'typical' group participant, some thirty-two years after National Training Laboratories (NTL) conducted the first T-group session in Bethel, Maine, in 1947?

Epps and Sikes (1977) surveyed 757 volunteers who participated in personal growth groups. The research question was: 'Do the selected variables indicate the likelihood of a person (a) attending a group, and (b) having a positive or negative reaction to the experience?' While several variables were selected for examination, we will summarize the most relevant to practitioners:

(1) Participants originally became interested in a personal growth group because someone told them about it.

(2) The 'higher' one's education, occupation, and income, the greater the probability they would participate in a personal growth group.

(3) The 35–44 age group was the most likely to participate in a personal growth group.

(4) Divorced and separated persons participated in larger numbers than others.

(5) Females were more likely to participate than were males.

(6) Religiously affiliated persons participated in greater numbers than those who were not affiliated.

(7) Persons in the 45–54 age group were the most likely to have a negative experience; yet they were twice as likely to participate as compared to expected frequencies.

(8) If participants liked 'closeness felt' most about the experience, they were most likely to report a totally positive experience.

(9) Persons whose goal was learning about themselves were most likely to have a negative experience.

(10) Those who indicated that they were seeking a chance to experiment with new behaviour were both least likely to have a positive experience and most likely to have a negative experience.

Epps and Sikes concluded that at least for T-group volunteers from the Kansas City area, sociological differences did account for divergent results in personal growth groups. While the study is limited because all participants were from the one area, it nevertheless gives some insight into the characteristics and motivations of personal growth group volunteers.

Mitchell (1975) found that persons who changed most as a result of sensitivity training had a high degree of achievement, responsibility, vigour, dominance, and endurance. Nurturance, succourance, autonomy, and cautiousness seemed to hinder positive change. The author felt his findings were consistent with those of Harrison and Lubin (1965) whose results suggest that person-oriented individuals are less challenged by their group learning experience than work-oriented persons.

Fromme et al. (1974) provided intensive, one-week experiential group training to fifty-three male and thirty-eight female community educators who were from a highly conservative population. Scores on the pre/post-measures, the California Psychological Inventory and the Tennessee Self Concept Scale, showed that these participants became more inhibited, cautious, defensive, disorganized, and emotionally upset as a result of their experience. However, on scales that best reflected the goals of the experience (sharing feelings, feedback), participants showed positive changes. The authors suggest that the negative changes may be characteristic of a population that is task-oriented rather than interpersonally-oriented and is resistant rather than open to ideas of personal change.

Rather than using typical workshop designs with conservative populations, the Fromme et al. data suggest experimenting with new structures, designs, and trainer styles. If disorientation and emotional upset are again the result, experiential training may be counterindicated, or some form of pre-training designed to aid participants in coping may be advisable.

View of the change centres

It stands to reason that the view and perception of the *place* of change may influence who chooses to participate in a programme. Lieberman and Gardner (1976) studied 426 participants attending encounter workshops at personal growth centres, 108 participants in sensitivity training, 89 psychotherapy patients, and, from a national sample of 1500, 200 participants in women's consciousness groups. Prior to entering the growth centre, participants completed a questionnaire designed to elicit degree of stress, symptomatology, and self-perceived goals. The results indicated that the participants in all these groups had higher scores on stress and symptoms than a normative population.

Most participants attended for 'psychotherapeutic purposes'. The authors report that the major difference they found was not in participants' goals but in their view of the change process. Growth centres and sensitivity training do not focus on traditional change induction methods nor on the painful aspects of these methods, and consciousness-raising groups emphasize the supportive aspects. Conversely, clinic patients do not expect to experience pleasure with change; they expect pain. However, regardless of the anticipations, in actuality participants in all change groups (clinic patients and growth group participants) experience pain. Participation in a help-giving system was integral to members' life-styles. Moreover, growth centres were found to be in addition to traditional psychotherapy and not an alternative. Some 80 per cent of the sample went to both rather than one or the other. Interestingly, in the participants' view, the institutions were not seen as different from each other in their offerings, goals, or length of process.

Volunteer v. non-volunteer

The most obvious difference in experiential training is between those that volunteer to attend groups and those who do not volunteer to participate.

Seldman and McBrearty (1975), using the California Psychological Inventory and the Edwards Preference Schedule investigated 367 volunteers for marathon groups and 814 non-volunteers from among university students. Volunteers had a lower sense of well-being but a greater need for independence than did non-volunteers.

While Kuiken et al. (1974) found no differences in histories of self-disclosure in college students who volunteered for T-groups versus non-volunteers, they did find that volunteers, especially males, were lower in authoritarianism. The females in the study indicated that they were less satisfied with their interpersonal competence and that they spent less time with others than did the non-volunteers. The authors suggest that male participants may have volunteered because their liberal socio-political views were compatible with the views implied by the T-group. Conversely, the volunteer women may have made their choices on the basis of their concerns about personal and social relationships.

In a study using the Personal Orientation Inventory (POI), Noll and Watkins (1974) explored the differences between thirty-nine males and forty females who participated in encounter groups and forty males and forty-four females who declined to participate. Among women, participants rated themselves more self-actualized than did non-participants. However for men this pattern was reversed. Both male and female participants had a greater capacity for intimate contact than did the non-participants.

Olch and Snow (1970) used the California Psychological Inventory in examining thirty-nine undergraduates who volunteered for T-groups and sixty-two who did not volunteer. Volunteers saw themselves as less well adjusted, less self-assured, less mature and less socially skilled than non-volunteers. Hoerl (1974) found that encounter group volunteers were already more flexible than people who did not volunteer.

Based on Schubert's (1964) contention that volunteers for psychological experiments are strong 'arousal seekers', Stanton (1976) hypothesized that encounter group participants would be a comparable group. Using the Zuckerman et al. (1964) Sensation-Seeking Scale, Stanton tested forty-two female and sixty-six male education students. The volunteers were significantly higher on the Sensation-Seeking Scale than were non-volunteers.

Pre-training

One area which has received attention in psychotherapy but minimal attention in experiential group training is pre-training (Goldstein,

1971). Zarle and Willis (1975) completed one of the few studies in preparing participants for encounter groups. The authors explored a pre-group training procedure for encounter group participants to develop specific coping behaviours in response to stressful situations. The treatment subjects received individual induced-affect training in four fifty-minute sessions during the two weeks prior to the encounter group experience. They then participated in a leaderless encounter group experience conducted by using an audiotaped procedure. One control group received induced-affect training only and a second control group received audiotape encounter only. The hypotheses that participants who did not receive the induced-affect pre-group training would demonstrate significant increases on the Neuroticism Scale of the Eysenck Personality Inventory, and that group members who did receive the training would not show such increases, were supported.

While the study has methodological limitations and the groups were not led by trainers, the results nonetheless indicate an alternative to the difficulties of screening, an alternative that warrants serious exploration and research.

Summary

The consumers of experiential group-work are usually not tightly screened, but the data show that casualties are minimal. We have the diagnostic tools to screen out extreme cases and to create conditions in the small group to enhance learning. While it seems appropriate, as it always has, to screen participants, there is also no question but that it is difficult to develop an effective screening process. It requires additional time (and money) and has legal implications when someone is not accepted. Since many practitioners run groups for profit, they are interested in increasing the number of participants rather than in procedures which might reduce the number of participants. Still another reason is that some practitioners view any screening procedure as anathema to their values and to their helping orientation. It is also our impression that many practitioners see writing or research as part of traditional psychology and again antithetical to the values of the small group.

Participants have sociological and demographic similarities that create a unique, although broad, population. In general, small group participants are 'people' rather than 'task' oriented. They attend primarily for 'psychotherapeutic' or remedial purposes. They seem to have a lowered sense of well-being, are mildly sensation-seeking, and have concerns about their interpersonal skills. However, volunteer participants appear more liberal and flexible, more interested in self-actualization, and are less authoritarian than non-volunteers.

Many participants enrol with the intention to deal with what they perceive as personal deficits and want to do so in a relatively painless and speedy manner. The probability, of course, is that neither of those goals is realistic. The research on personal change is clear – it is painful and lengthy.

We infer from the evidence we have reviewed that working with conservative groups in particular might be enhanced by conducting pre-workshop training to ensure more effective induction.

Both as practitioners and researchers, we need to develop more specific and focused programmes in order to be responsive to all participants. At the same time, we should continue to educate the public that experiential group training is not the most effective way to resolve many psychological problems.

Structure and design

An issue which has long been debated by practitioners and theorists alike is whether the design or structure of the small group experience has much impact on the learning and experience of the participants. There are those who argue, 'the looser the better', and those that counter 'the tighter the better'. The former proponents contend that in non-structured settings anxiety is generated and in order to reduce and manage that anxiety, participants behave so as to permit opportunities for feedback, self-confirmation or disconfirmation, new behaviours, and thus new learnings. However, the structuralists maintain that the anxiety is often unmanageable and therefore unproductive. Thus, learning is limited.

In an attempt to shed some empirical light on the controversy, Levin and Kurtz (1974) investigated participants' perceptions following human relations training. Three structured and three unstructured groups, with each of three trainer teams conducting one group under each of the two formats, were included in the design. The structured groups were based on a sequence of structured exercises introduced by the trainers. Participants completed a Group Opinion Questionnaire at the final (twelfth) session. Subjects and trainers were students. The trainer pairs varied in amount of experience.

The results supported the superiority of structured exercises in generating more positive perceptions of the experience versus the non-structured groups. The authors suggest that greater ego-involvement and unity occurs in structured groups because all members are in a sense required to participate. In the unstructured setting, participants can remain marginal or outside the group. Greater perceived behaviour change may arise from the feeling of a more designed opportunity for the practice of new behaviours.

Ware and Barr (1977) examined the effects of nine-week structured and unstructured group experiences on measures of self-concept and self-actualization in comparison to untrained controls. The authors found positive change in both experimental groups. What is vague in this study, however, is the definition and design of structure and non-structure.

A study by Kinder and Kilmann (1976), using a 23-hour marathon format is noteworthy because the authors investigated the interaction between participants' scores on the Rotter locus of control scale and high and low degrees of leader structure as related to outcome. The Rotter scale differentiates between 'internals' who see events as amenable to one's personal control, and 'externals' who see events as controlled by factors outside of oneself.

Subjects were randomly assigned to one of five groups:

Beginning	Later phases	No. of Ss
(1) unstructured	structured	11
(2) structured	unstructured	10
(3) unstructured	unstructured	9
(4) structured	structured	9
(5) no treatment	no treatment	8

Ss were forty-seven male and female college students. The leader (male) was the same in all groups. He defined his leadership role in the structured sessions and initiated and controlled the sequence of exercises. In the unstructured sessions he made no statements unless requested, and unlike the structured sessions, he did not request feedback or inputs from any specific group members. Three independent judges rated perceived structure and unstructure of the leader from videotape samples. Change in self-actualization was measured on the Time Competence and Inner Directedness scales of the Personal Orientation Inventory (Shostrom, 1966).

The major finding was that the optimum sequence for changes in the Time Competence and Inner Directedness scales for persons favoring external locus of control was high leader structure early in the group followed by less leader structure during later phases.

In another study of a marathon group, Kilmann and Sotile (1976) found that 'internals' (on locus of control) in an unstructured group rated the leader and the group more positively than did 'externals'. In the structured group the finding was reversed.

These studies suggest that at least among those favouring external locus of control, participants in structured groups are more comfortable and show greater increases in measures of self-actualization than do participants in unstructured groups. Cooper and Bowles (1974/75), however, raise some cautions about groups based on structured exercises and the psychological conditions of learning. The authors found the structured groups in their sample (v. unstructured) had more negative changes on personality measures and also the highest number of peer-rated casualties. Cooper and Bowles, supported by the work of Argyris (1967), contend that in the structured setting participants are unable to develop their own personal goals, objectives, and behavioural experimentation. The structure provided may not have been conducive to psychological success but rather to psychological failure. Moreover, as in other studies of this kind, what may be interpreted as increased pathology may instead be seen as a losing of defences or a willingness to disclose more personal information. The population for this study were middle to senior level managers from different industrial organizations and the findings might not prove generalizable to all groups.

Although we have participants' reactions and perceptions at the termination of the group, there are few studies to test for changes in back-home job satisfaction and performance as related to structure, design, and trainer style. Ivancevich and McMahon (1976) studied managers undergoing training and found that a directive and structured training style had a greater influence on group development than did a facilitative or less directive style. There was also evidence that a majority of participants with a directive and structured trainer reported significant improvements in satisfaction and performance increases. However, the impact of training deteriorated over time in the back-home setting.

Summary

The evidence on structure and design is counter to experiential training lore, namely, that structure is anathema to effective learning. Structured groups seem more satisfying to some participants and contribute to positive change. There is some support for the view that persons favouring an internal locus of control are more comfortable with less structure. A limitation of excessive structure, however, is that it may reduce the opportunity for the development of personal goals and objectives.

What remains unknown is the impact of specific designs on learning or even the relative merits of various components of designs over one another.

Composition

Research on group composition has been conducted for many years. The results are conclusive. By manipulating the 'type' of participants in the experiential group setting, and thus the interaction, the outcome will be affected. Curiously, while the evidence may be compelling, few trainers seem to use the information in planning their work.

Reddy (1977) reviewed the literature and found that most studies focused on experiential groups and minimally on task groups. In this chapter we will discuss only that model of group composition which has the greatest support for positive outcome in experiential groups.

Several authors (Reddy, 1977; Smith, 1974; Harrison and Lubin, 1965) have proposed that when group membership consists of some persons who are high on a particular need and others are low on that same need, then the probability that positive change will take place is increased. These authors propose that some degree of need incompatibility is a precondition for change. Both Reddy (1977) and Smith (1974) have empirical support for this model.

Reddy (1972) placed forty participants into four sensitivity training groups according to their pre-measured interchange compatibility for affection as measured by the FIRO-B measure (Fundamental Interpersonal Orientation Inventory – Behaviour, Schutz, 1958). Two groups (A and B) each had ten participants. Within each group five members had high need for affection scores (and were therefore compatible with each other) and five members had low need for affection scores (also compatible with each other). The compatible subgroup A was thus incompatible with subgroup B. A second two groups (C and D) were each composed of ten members who had moderate combined affection scores. Trainers were assigned according to how closely their own scores approximated the group affection norm. The laboratory was five days long and residential.

Reddy hypothesized that groups A and B whose members had affection needs which were compatible with some members of the group and incompatible with others would make greater positive gains in self-actualization than groups C and D which were composed of persons all of whose affection needs were compatible. Self-actualization was measured by the Personal Orientation Inventory (POI). The hypothesis was strongly supported. The author concluded that groups A and B engaged both in confrontation (because of their incompatibility) and support (because of their compatibility). This led to greater change. Members of the compatible groups (C and D) were neither stimulated nor conflicted enough to seek alternative behaviours.

Smith (1974) also showed that quite different processes occurred when climates were confronting, supportive, or both confronting and supportive. He used group composition as an operational expression of Kelman's (1958) social influence modes. Smith hypothesized that compliance in groups would be highest where the composition was maximally confronting; identification where composition was supportive; and internalization where both confrontation and support were present. The hypotheses were tested in sixteen one-day sensitivity training groups. Each group consisted of three men, three women, and a male trainer. Group composition was manipulated on the basis of FIRO-B affection and control scores. All three hypotheses were supported. That is, the differences in behaviour found in groups of different compositions were consistent with the differences predicted by Kelman's theory.

In summary, research on compatibility has already yielded much material and still is an area in need of continued investigation. When participants are placed in groups based on FIRO-B scores (particularly affection scores) in such a way as to maximize both support and confrontation, we can expect a greater probability of positive change on a variety of interpersonal and self-actualization measures.

Phases of group development

The theoretical work on phases of group development has been extensive. Indeed, there are several excellent reviews (Tuckman, 1965; Hare, 1973; Hill and Gruner, 1973; Braaten, 1974/75; Shambaugh, 1978). What has been absent in the area until recently is empirical research. Tuckman and Jensen (1977) reviewed the published research on small group development over the past ten years that constituted an empirical test of Tuckman's (1965) phases of group development, namely, forming, storming, norming, and performing. Of the twenty-two studies reviewed, only one set out directly to test the phases.

While it has been very difficult to compare and contrast all the theories, there are some major common areas. Lundgren (1977) analysed the developmental trends in sensitivity training groups by exploring the sequence of interpersonal issues or problem areas which emerged at different periods in the life of the group. He assumed that there is a meaningful and orderly sequence in the emergence and salience of interpersonal issues in T-groups and that, over time, the issues would be reflected in the content and interaction among the participants.

Drawing from theory and research on the stages of group development, Lundgren hypothesized five general stages: '(1) the initial encounter, (2) intermember conflict and confrontation of the trainer, (3) group solidarity, (4) exchange of interpersonal feedback, and (5) termination – separation' (p.181).

The data were gathered from five T-groups in a two-week residential laboratory. Each group had from ten to twelve members, with a total of twenty-eight male and thirty female participants. There was one male trainer to each group.

Using an observational coding system, Lundgren found that issues of control, which were expected to be central in trainer-member relationships, were of low salience in comparison with openness and solidarity. Moreover, group interaction was heavily and consistently member-centred rather than trainer-centred. This is in direct contrast with Slater's (1966) contention that the course of group formation is contingent upon changes in members' orientations toward the trainer. Lundgren suggests that what may be operating is the unique population in his sample. That is, the samples in past research have been either with college students in academic settings where group leaders were older and had faculty status, or with management personnel unfamiliar with T-group experience. It may well be that the authority/control issues were not as salient in the population which Lundgren studied.

Another finding was that openness was the primary issue with which participants dealt from the beginning of the groups. It was only during the latter half of the second week that concerns about solidarity became more central. Consistent with the Bennis and Shepard model (1956), which suggests that participants must first deal with issues of authority and then with interpersonal ones, control and solidarity were the two areas which showed most systematic change over time in this study. Although they were not particularly salient at any time, themes of control were more central during the first week and those of solidarity more salient during the second week.

Schutz (1958) suggested that the key issues in group development are inclusion, control and affection, and that these develop in temporal sequence and are repeated over time. However, at the group's end, the problems occur in the reverse order, the sequence being affection, control, and inclusion. Lundgren suggests that while there is some overlap of themes within a single session, the overall trends do show a high degree of correspondence with Schutz's model. However, Schutz's model does not take into consideration the 'openness' theme suggested by Lundgren.

In a second report, Lundgren and Knight (1978) conducted the largest test to date of a set of hypotheses derived from the theoretical and anecdotally-based literature on sequential stages of group development. The information was gathered from twenty T-groups during six two-week Basic Human Interaction Laboratories conducted by the NTL Institute at Bethel, Maine, in 1972. The twenty T-groups included 137 males and 85 females. It is interesting to note that 45 per cent of the participants were employed in the helping professions and 31 per cent were from educational settings. Approximately 50 per cent of the participants had had prior laboratory experience. Using the same developmental stages as in the previous study – the initial encounter, intermember conflict and confrontation of the trainer, group solidarity, exchange of interpersonal feedback, and termination – Lundgren and Knight tested a number of indices and found that their results could best be interpreted in terms of a three-stage model. In Stage One, 'The Initial Encounter', trainers did not play an active role; however, the low number of references to the trainer by the members indicated that they overtly accepted that style. Members also tended to avoid personal issues, presented themselves in a positive light, and provided each other with support-ive feedback. In sum, the initial encounter is characterized by restraint and the development of psychological safety which in turn facilitates more direct problem-solving activity later.

In Stage Two, 'Interpersonal Confrontation', there was consider-able 'work' activity with a more intense focus on individuals and increased negative feedback among members. As might be expected, the high involvement and direct confrontation put the groups into crises and led to little expression of identification with the group.

Stage Three, 'Mutual Acceptance', was characterized by decreas-ing focus on task and a high degree of acceptance among members. Members became more positive and relaxed as the 'work' lessened; they managed or resolved earlier conflicts and confrontations. There was also evidence of gradual withdrawal and separation as members prepared for the end of the programme.

Lundgren and Knight did not find a period during which the trainer was confronted, as hypothesized in a number of theories of phases of group development. As Lundgren indicated in his earlier study, the group composition may account for this. That is, in the sample being discussed, the trainer/participant differences in age, education, and professional status were less marked and a majority of the participants had previous experience in laboratory training. The authors concluded that a period of intense concern with issues about authority is by no means inevitable in the formation of a group.

Again, contrary to popular belief, the evidence did not support the view that a period of high group cohesion preceded effective task performance. Lundgren and Knight did find, however, that a period of positive and harmonious member relationships, as evidenced in Stage Three, followed the intense 'work-oriented' stage.

The authors conclude that the 'findings provide support for the general contention that T-groups show regular, systematic patterns of change over time'(p.221).

Farrell (1976) also studied phases of group development. He used three groups with an analytically-oriented leader, each of which met for two hours per week for a term. Two groups of twenty had all males and a third group of thirty was mixed. Each group was a class and the course requirements included: attendance, readings, listening to tapes, and writing papers. Farrell isolated five 'boundary' issues that he felt are critical 'in the formation and maintenance of the cultural identity of the group and the personal identity of individuals in groups' (p.529). These issues are: (a) authority, (b) individuation, (c) expression, (d) intimacy, and (e) work. He defines a phase as 'a period of time during which the group members show a predominant concern with one cluster of issues' (p.531).

Using a content analysis system developed for the study, Farrell found regularities across the three groups in terms of the sequence in which they confronted the boundary issues.

The phases are as follows:

Phase 1: Authority – restoration v. revolution
Phase 2: Transition from authority to intimacy
Phase 3: Intimacy – close v. far
Phase 4: Transition from intimacy to authority
Phase 5: Confrontation and consolidation of group culture
Phase 6: Work
Phase 7: Separation – emergence of unresolved issues and group disintegration

Like Lundgren, Farrell found common and stable phases in groups over time. While some of the phases are consistent with Lundgren's, there is, in Farrell's work, a much greater focus on authority issues. This may have to do with the impact of Farrell's analytic leaders and the fact that it was a student population in a course setting.

Summary

The work on phases of group development does show common issues and phases with one notable exception, the variability of concern with authority. We need to know and test the specific composition of the groups and understand the culture and population from which they are drawn and then look again at the phases. We may then see different or more consistent phases of group development in these populations.

Trainer behaviour

The most systematic research on trainer–member influence is that of Lundgren and his students at the University of Cincinnati.

In an early study, Lundgren (1975) found that T-group members accurately perceived trainers' attitudes toward the group and that the participants' own attitudes corresponded closely with their perceptions of trainers' attitudes. Perhaps most important, at an early time-point in the life of the group, senior trainers' self-attitudes did not match their perceptions of participant attitudes toward themselves. Their less experienced co-trainers showed low positive correlations with their perceptions of members' attitudes towards themselves. At a late point in the laboratory, both groups of trainers' perceptions of participants' attitudes toward themselves were significant and positively correlated – yet these perceptions did not relate to *actual* member attitudes. Lundgren concluded that trainers consistently and strongly *underestimate* the favourability of participants' attitudes toward themselves. 'Thus, the primary agents of influence were characterized by inaccuracy in their social judgments, while the objects of influence showed a high degree of accuracy' (p. 765).

Lundgren (1976a) found a significant tendency for participants in a weekend human relations workshop to be most attracted to individuals holding more negative attitudes towards the trainers than their own. However the styles of the three sets of co-trainers in this workshop were unstructured and non-directive, and this style may account in part for the findings.

In two studies on interpersonal needs, trainer style, and member attitudes, Lundgren (1975) and Lundgren and Knight (1977) found that members expressed positive attitudes toward the trainer and the group to the extent that their own needs for control and affection (as measured by FIRO-B) were similar to that of the trainer. It did not matter if members' control or affection scores were high or low. Comparable trends were also shown with affection needs and attitudes toward the group.

In a third study, using a larger sample in a long-term residential laboratory, Lundgren and Knight's (1977) findings of trainer/participant compatibility were not supported. They did find, however, that trainers low in both control and affection elicited the most negative reactions later. The authors note that over 50 per cent of their sample were in the helping professions and had previous T-group experience. Lundgren and Knight speculate that the trainer behaviour conformed to participants' expectations early in the group's life and reduced anxiety. However, as time passed and participants wanted closer relationships, affectional behaviours were not forthcoming from the trainers.

Babad and Melnick (1976) examined the validity of the belief that in order to make positive gains in T-groups members must actively participate, must be emotionally involved in the process, and must be receptive to feedback from fellow members. The authors also studied the effect of the T-group as a function of trainers' differential liking for each member.

As was expected, the perceived effect of the group was a function of members' emotional involvement, the reception of feedback, and the trainer's liking for each participant. The process was clearly interactive between members and trainers. Members showing 'good member behaviour' were liked by the trainer and reinforced for the behaviour. This reinforcement, of course, increased the probability of 'good member behaviour'.

While authors have used a number of measures and questionnaires to understand the trainer/member interaction, Rory O'Day (1973, 1976) has constructed an empirically derived typology of individual training styles. The training style has three major components: definitional, behavioural, and affective; these correspond to issues attended to, form of the intervention, and trainer's expressed feelings. The major components are further divided into twenty-five definitional categories, seventeen behavioural categories, and sixteen affective categories.

Using this typology (O'Day, 1976), coders examined the individual training styles of four trainers in four two-week stranger T-groups. One trainer was perceived more positively by members than were the others. The major difference in his style was that he more frequently encouraged and accepted the direct expression of members' hostility toward himself. The single female trainer was perceived as least successful. O'Day characterized her style as having to be in control of the group's proceedings; he also points out that she was leading a group whose members were disappointed and angry at having a female trainer. While this experience is talked about obliquely among professionals and it is acknowledged that female trainers may have a more difficult time being accepted and perceived as competent by group members, no systematic investigations have been reported in this area.

In his reanalysis of the Lieberman et al. (1973) data, Russell (1978) concluded that two major variables were characteristic of leaders who brought about positive change in experiential small group partici-pants: (a) a warm supportive relationship, and (b) emotional stimu-lation. Russell maintains that these characteristics are consistent with Bierman's (1969) theory that two dimensions, affection and activity, are related to positive outcome in psychotherapy.

Table 3.1   Relationship between therapist dimensions of affection and activity

		Affection	
		High	Low
Activity	High	Produces strong positive results	Produces strong negative results
	Low	Produces mild positive results	Produces mild negative results

Derived from Bierman (1969)

Table 3.1 illustrates the relationship between the two variables. Affectionate/active therapists produce strong positive change; affec-tionate/inactive therapists produce mild positive change; unaffec-tionate/active therapists, strong negative change; and unaffection-ate/inactive therapists, mild negative change.

It seems, according to Russell (1978), that Lieberman et al.'s (1973) data support these same dimensions in reference to facilitative and non-facilitative experiential group leaders. Lieberman et al.'s own conclusions are only partly consistent with Bierman's model. They contend that the most effective leaders showed a high level of caring and of 'meaning attribution' but only a moderate level of emotional stimulation and of 'executive function'. That is, Lieberman et al., in contrast and in addition to Bierman, stress the importance of the leader providing meaningful concepts and explaining individ-ual and group behaviour.

Summary

The research results are contradictory. The following is a summary of the findings presented in this section.

Trainers, for all their experience, are not accurate in their social judgements regarding participants.

Participants express positive attitudes toward the trainer and the group to the extent that their own needs for control and affection are similar to those of the trainer. Participants are most attracted to those members who hold more negative attitudes towards the trainers than their own.

Trainers low in both control and affection elicit the most favourable response from participants early in the life of the group. The same trainers elicit the most negative reactions at a later stage of the group.

The perceived effect of a T-group is a function of participants' emotional involvement, the reception of feedback and trainers' liking for each participant.

Trainers increase the likelihood of their being perceived positively by group members when they encourage and accept the direct expression of members' hostility.

Two major variables are characteristic of leaders who bring about positive change in experiential groups; a warm supportive relationship with members, and emotional stimulation of the group members. In addition, it is important in the learning process that the leader provides cognitive and conceptual links for the small group participants.

Little is known about how female trainers are perceived or the impact they have on group members. There is some suggestion that female trainers are not readily accepted by male participants.

Feedback

The term feedback is used in group-work to refer to mutual sharing of perceptions of one another's behaviour in the group. Although the concept is central in group-work, surprisingly little research has been conducted in this area. That which has been done, however, particularly by the West Virginia group, is of very high quality. We will examine these studies shortly.

It has long been assumed, and still is by many, that feedback which is well timed, direct, and given with emotion, is always desirable. While a number of authors (Golembiewski and Blumberg, 1970; Argyris, 1970; Harrison, 1962) support the importance of feedback, the focus is primarily on the general aspects of effective feedback, e.g. the need for it to be non-evaluative, descriptive, and recent, and not on the specifics of delivery.

Adelson (1976) has shown that feedback changes during the development of the group. Rating feedback according to four dimensions (evaluative, specific, cognitive or emotional, direct or indirect), Adelson found that feedback increased as the group developed and that, at least with his sample, there was a predominance of non-evaluative, specific feedback which the author felt reflected both the focus and nature of the group. It was also noted that direct feedback to the trainers increased as the group developed.

Lundgren and Schaeffer (1976) also studied the development of the feedback process in sensitivity training groups. Their feedback units were rated on eight dimensions: (a) here-and-now versus there-and-then; (b) positive versus negative; (c) expressive versus non-expressive; (d) non-directive versus directive; (e) concrete versus abstract; (f) two-way versus one-way; (g) supportive versus confronting; and (h) descriptive versus interpretive.

Lundgren and Schaeffer found that, over time, member feedback became more expressive and less focused upon here-and-now events, while trainer feedback became more non-directive. During the early sessions of the training group, trainer feedback was less expressive, less focused upon self–other relationships, less related to the here-and-now, more negative and confronting, more abstract, and more interpretive than member feedback. These differences did diminish by later sessions, however. The authors found no significant differences between male and female feedback senders. Not surprisingly, group differences strongly outweighed their similarities.

Lundgren and Schaeffer speculate on the shift in member feedback away from a strong here-and-now focus. They note that in an earlier study, Lundgren (1968) found that increases in the accuracy of members' perceptions of others' reactions to themselves were greatest in T-groups with the *least* here-and-now focus. In a similar way, Lieberman, Yalom, and Miles (1973) found that positive member change tended to be low in encounter groups where norms most strongly supported here-and-now confrontation.

The West Virginia group has systematically examined the specific delivery and sequencing of feedback in the small group setting. A review of the feedback research is well presented in Jacobs and Spradlin (Jacobs, 1974). In summary, Jacobs et al. (1973a, b, 1974) and Schaible and Jacobs (1975) have found that situations which provide for a greater exchange of feedback among small group participants than would take place spontaneously will lead to superior outcomes. Subjects rated positive feedback as more accurate than they rated negative feedback. Perhaps more important, positive feedback was rated as more desirable, affecting subjects more than negative feedback and promoting a greater intention to change. Negative *behavioural* feedback (i.e. that which describes the other person's behaviour) was more credible than negative *emotional* feedback (i.e. that which describes one's own feelings). Thus, unlike trainers' frequent advice to share feelings as well as behavioural descriptions, the research suggests that for maximum impact this should be done only for positive feedback. With negative feedback, behavioural description alone is more credible.

In terms of sequencing, Jacobs et al. (1973) found that positive behavioural feedback was rated as most credible and negative feedback as least credible under conditions of anonymous delivery. Positive and negative emotional feedback were not significantly different in credibility when the identity of the deliverer was not given.

Finally, Schaible and Jacobs (1975) present results which suggest that the delivery of positive feedback first will increase the probability of acceptance of negative feedback later in an intervention.

Summary

We have explored two major aspects of feedback, the spontaneous development of feedback and the specific delivery and sequencing of feedback in the small group setting.

Feedback to both participants and trainers increases over the life of the group. To the former, feedback becomes more expressive and less focused upon here-and-now events; to the latter, feedback becomes more non-directive. A here-and-now focus does not seem to lend itself to positive member change.

In terms of specific delivery and sequencing, superior outcomes can be more readily attained when feedback situations are provided by the trainers rather than left to develop by chance.

Positive feedback is rated by subjects as more accurate than negative feedback, more desirable, more influential, and promoting greater intention to change. Negative behavioural feedback is more credible than negative emotional feedback. Positive feedback delivered first, followed by negative feedback, is more effective than the reverse sequence. Anonymous delivery of positive behavioural feedback is rated as most credible and negative feedback as least credible.

It is our impression that little use has been made of the above feedback information by trainers in T-groups. We think there is a need to use and experiment with these data in experiential group designs.

General summary

To recapitulate, we have both the body of knowledge and the expertise to enhance positive learning and change in experiential groups by manipulating group processes and dynamics. When there are pre-workshop data about participants, groups can be composed in such a way as to ensure support and confrontation between participants, and thus to increase the probability of personal learning. With knowledge of group development phases, trainers can more readily determine when to make appropriate interventions and when to time, present, and sequence specific feedback.

The experiential group field has matured and has become more sophisticated. It still suffers, however, from too many trainers who seem to be unaware of, or who choose not to use, the results of research. Practitioners in the experiential group field, seemingly more than in other professions, lack opportunity for advanced training and development.

The research, while contributing much to the field, does have its limitations. As we have seen, the research has been conducted primarily on college students, and we know less of other populations. Well controlled studies are too infrequent. Estimates of trainer expertise are typically based on years in the field, rather than on the types and number of groups the trainers have conducted. The results of studies of trainers are based on a small number of participants or groups and the unique conditions of the laboratory may not permit the results to be generalized.

Researchers need to focus on homogeneous populations, such as individuals in specific adult stages of development. For example, we have little data or experience with small group work for the elderly.

Much of the research has been done on groups with male trainers. There does seem to be an increase in the number of female trainers in the field, particularly on internal organization training staffs. Their impact on and relationships with participants are likely to be quite different from those of male trainers. We can make no assumptions, only open the area to investigation.

Knowledge and an understanding of the processes and the dynamics within experiential groups have advanced; we still have a long way to go.

References

Adelson, J. P. (1976) Feedback and group development. *Small Group Behavior 6*: 389–401.

Argyris, C. (1967) On the future of laboratory education, *Journal of Applied Behavioral Science 3*: 153–83.

Argyris, C. (1970) *Intervention Theory and Method*. Reading, Mass: Addison-Wesley.

Babad, E. Y. and Melnick, I. (1976) Effects of a T-group as a function of trainers' liking and members' participation, involvement, quantity and quality of received feedback. *Journal of Applied Behavioral Science 12*: 543–62.

Bennis, W. F. and Shepard, H. A. (1956) A theory of group development. *Human Relations 9*: 415–37.

Bergin, A. E. (1971) The evaluation of therapeutic outcomes. In A. E. Bergin and S. L. Garfield (eds) *Handbook of Psychotherapy and Behavior Change*. New York: John Wiley.

Bierman, R. (1969) Dimensions of interpersonal facilitation in psychotherapy and child development. *Psychological Bulletin 5*: 338–53.

Braaten, L. J. (1974/75) Developmental phases of encounter groups and related intensive groups. *Interpersonal Development 5*: 112–28.

Campbell, J. P. and Dunnette, M. D. (1968) Effectiveness of T-group experiences in managerial training and development. *Psychological Bulletin 70*: 73–104.

Cooper, C. L. (1974) Psychological disturbance following T-groups:

relationship between Eysenck Personality Inventory and family/ friends' judgements. *British Journal of Social Work 4*: 39–49.

Cooper, C. L. (1975) Experiential learning groups: a substitute for therapy? *Bulletin of the British Psychological Society 28*: 337–41.

Cooper, C. L. and Bowles, D. (1974/75) Structured exercise-based groups and the psychological conditions for learning. *Interpersonal Development 5*: 203–12.

Cooper, C. L. and Mangham, I. L. (eds) (1971) *T-groups: A Survey of Research*. Chichester: John Wiley.

Epps, J. D. and Sikes, W. W. (1977) Personal growth groups: who joins and who benefits? *Group and Organizational Studies 2*: 88–100.

Farrell, M. P. (1976) Patterns in the development of self-analytic groups. *Journal of Applied Behavioral Science 12*: 523–42.

Fromme, D. K., Jones, W. H. and Davis, J. O. (1974) Experiential group training with conservative populations: a potential for negative effects. *Journal of Clinical Psychology 30*: 290–6.

Goldstein, A. P. (1971) *Psychotherapeutic Attraction*. New York: Pergamon Press.

Golembiewski, R. T. and Blumberg, A. (eds) (1970) *Sensitivity Training and the Laboratory Approach*. Itasca, Ill.: F. E. Peacock.

Hare, A. P. (1973) Theories of group development and categories for interaction analysis. *Small Group Behavior 4*: 259–304.

Harrison, R. (1962) Defenses and the need to know. *NTL Human Relations Training News 6*: 1–4.

Harrison, R. and Lubin, B. (1965) Personal style, group composition, and learning. *Journal of Applied Behavioral Science 1* (1): 286–94.

Hartley, D., Roback, H. B. and Abramowitz, S. I. (1976) Deterioration effects in encounter groups. *American Psychologist 31*: 247–55.

Hill, W. F. and Gruner, L. (1973) A study of development in open and closed groups. *Small Group Behavior 4*: 355–81.

Hoerl, R. T. (1974) Encounter groups: their effect on rigidity. *Human Relations 27*: 431–8.

Hogan, D. B. (1974) Encounter groups and human relations training: the case against applying traditional forms of statutory regulation. *Harvard Journal of Legislation 11*: 659–701.

Ivancevich, J. M. and McMahon, J. T. (1976) Group development, trainer style and carry-over job satisfaction and performance. *Academy of Management Journal* 19: 395–412.

Jacobs, A. (1974) The use of feedback in groups. In A. Jacobs and W. Spradlin (eds) *The Group as Agent of Change*. New York: Behavioral Publications.

Jacobs, A., Jacobs, M., Cavior, N. and Burke, J. (1974) Anonymous feedback: credibility and desirability of structured emotional and behavioral feedback delivered in groups. *Journal of Counseling Psychology* 21: 106–11.

Jacobs, M., Jacobs, A., Feldman, G. and Cavior, N. (1973) Feedback II: The 'credibility gap': delivery of positive and negative and emotional and behavioral feedback in groups. *Journal of Consulting and Clinical Psychology* 41: 215–23.

Jacobs, M., Jacobs, A., Gatz, M. and Schaible, T. (1973) Credibility and desirability of positive and negative structured feedback in groups. *Journal of Consulting and Clinical Psychology* 40: 244–52.

Kelman, H. C. (1958) Compliance, identification and internalization. *Journal of Conflict Resolution* 2: 58–60.

Kilmann, P. R. and Sotile, W. M. (1976) The effects of structured and unstructured leader roles on internal and external group participants. *Journal of Clinical Psychology* 32: 848–56.

Kinder, B. N. and Kilmann, P. R. (1976) The impact of differential shifts in leader structure on the outcome of internal and external group participants. *Journal of Clinical Psychology* 32: 857–63.

Kuiken, D., Rasmussen, R. V. and Cullen, D. (1974) Some predictors of volunteer participation in human relations training groups. *Psychological Reports* 35: 499–504.

Levin, E. M. and Kurtz, R. R. (1974) Structured and nonstructured human relations training. *Journal of Counseling Psychology* 21: 526–31.

Lieberman, M. A. and Gardner, J. R. (1976) Institutional alternatives to psychotherapy: a study of growth center users. *Archives of General Psychiatry* 33: 157–62.

Lieberman, M. A., Yalom, I. D. and Miles, M. B. (1973) *Encounter Groups: First Facts*. New York: Basic Books.

Lundgren, D. C. (1968) *Interaction process and identity change in T-groups*. Doctoral dissertation, University of Michigan. Ann Arbor: University Microfilms No. 68-13.

Lundgren, D. C. (1975) Interpersonal needs and member attitudes toward trainer and group. *Small Group Behavior* 6: 371–88.

Lundgren, D. C. (1976a) Member attitudes towards the leaders and interpersonal attraction in short-term training groups. *Group Process* 6: 141–8.

Lundgren, D. C. (1976b) Trainer-member influence in T-groups: one-way or two-way? *Human Relations* 27: 755–66.

Lundgren, D. C. (1977) Developmental trends in the emergence of interpersonal issues in T-groups. *Small Group Behavior* 8: 179–200.

Lundgren, D. C. and Knight, D. J. (1977) Trainer style and member attitudes toward trainer and group in T-groups. *Small Group Behavior* 8: 47–64.

Lundgren, D. C. and Knight, D. J. (1978) Sequential stages of development in sensitivity training groups. *Journal of Applied Behavioral Science* 14: 204–22.

Lundgren, D. C. and Schaeffer, C. (1976) Feedback processes in sensitivity training groups. *Human Relations* 29: 763–82.

Mitchell, R. R. (1975) Relationships between personal characteristics and change in sensitivity training groups. *Small Group Behavior* 6: 414–20.

Noll, G. A. and Watkins, J. T. (1974) Differences between persons seeking encounter group experiences and others on the Personal Orientation Inventory. *Journal of Counseling Psychology* 21: 206–9.

O'Day, R. (1973) Training style: a content-analytic assessment. *Human Relations* 26: 599–637.

O'Day, R. (1976) Individual training styles: an empirically derived typology. *Small Group Behavior* 7: 147–82.

Olch, D. and Snow, D. L. (1970) Personality characteristics of sensitivity group volunteers. *Personnel and Guidance Journal* 48: 848–50.

Peters, D. R. (1973) Identification and personal learning in T-group. *Human Relations* 10: 33–5.

Reddy, W. B. (1970) Sensitivity training or group psychotherapy: the need for adequate screening. *International Journal of Group Psychotherapy* 20: 366–71.

Reddy, W. B. (1971) Selection and screening of encounter group participants. In L. Solomon and B. Berzon (eds) *Encounter Groups: Issues and Applications*. San Francisco: Jossey-Bass.

Reddy, W. B. (1972) On affection, group composition, and self-actualization in sensitivity training. *Journal of Consulting and Clinical Psychology 38*: 211–14.

Reddy, W. B. (1977) Interpersonal affection and change in sensitivity training: a composition model. In C. L. Cooper (ed.) *Theories of Group Processes*. New York: John Wiley.

Rohrbaugh, M. (1975) Patterns and correlates of emotional arousal in laboratory training. *Journal of Applied Behavioral Science 11*: 220–40.

Rowan, J. (1975) Encounter group research: no joy? *Journal of Humanistic Psychology 15*: 19–28.

Russell, E. (1978) The facts about 'Encounter groups: first facts'. *Journal of Clinical Psychology 34*: 130–7.

Schaible, T. D. and Jacobs, A. (1975) Feedback III: Sequence effects enhancement of feedback acceptance and group attractiveness by manipulation of the sequence and valance of feedback. *Small Group Behavior 6*: 151–73.

Schubert, D. S. P. (1964) Arousal seeking as a motivation for volunteering. MMPI scores and central-nervous-system-stimulant use as suggestive of a trait. *Journal of Projective Techniques and Personality Assessment 28*: 337–40.

Schutz, W. (1975) Nonencounter and certainly not facts. *Journal of Humanistic Psychology 15*: 7–18.

Schutz, W. C. (1958) *FIRO: A 3-Dimensional Theory of Interpersonal Behavior*. New York: Rinehart.

Seldman, M. L. and McBrearty, J. F. (1975) Characteristics of marathon volunteers. *Psychological Reports 36*: 555–60.

Shambauch, P. W. (1978) The development of the Ssall group. *Human Relations 31*: 283–95.

Shostrom, E. L. (1966) *Personal Orientation Inventory Manual*. San Diego: Educational and Industrial Testing Service.

Slater, P. E. (1966) *Microcosm: Structural, Psychological and Religious Evolution in Groups*. New York: John Wiley.

Smith, P. B. (1971) Correlations among some tests of T-group learning. *Journal of Applied Behavioral Science 7*: 508–11.

Smith, P. B. (1974) Group composition as a determinant of Kelman's social influence modes. *European Journal of Social Psychology 4*: 261–77.

Smith, P. B. (1975a) Are there adverse effects of training? *Journal of Humanistic Psychology 15*: 29–48.

Smith, P. B. (1975b) Controlled studies of the outcome of sensitivity training. *Psychological Bulletin 82*: 597–622.

Stanton, H. E. (1976) Hypnosis and encounter group volunteers: a validation study of the Sensation-Seeking Scale. *Journal of Consulting and Clinical Psychology 44*: 692–5.

Tuckman, B. W. (1965) Developmental sequence in small groups. *Psychological Bulletin 63*: 384–99.

Tuckman, B. W. and Jensen, M. A. C. (1977) Stages of small-group development revised. *Group and Organization Studies 2*: 419–27.

Ware, J. R. and Barr, J. E. (1977) Effects of a nine-week structured and unstructured group experience on measures of self-concept and self-actualization. *Small Group Behavior 8*: 93–100.

Zarle, T. H. and Willis, S. (1975) A pregroup training technique for encounter group stress. *Journal of Counseling Psychology 22*: 49–53.

Zuckerman, M., Kolin, E. A., Price, L. and Zoob, I. (1964) Development of a Sensation Seeking Scale. *Journal of Consulting and Clinical Psychology 28*: 477–82.

4 Theories of personal learning in groups

Keith Oatley

To be open to one's experience is to be affected by it, to be open to change. In groups (such as those defined in Chapter 1) people can begin to experience themselves and others in ways which are not necessarily familiar to them outside the group setting. These experiences can be the seeds of new directions and personal growth for people in their ordinary lives.

Freud (1930) expressed the view that we are equipped, from our infancy and evolutionary past, with various motives of a not altogether prepossessing kind. Society then provides a set of injunctions to constrain the individual in ways which might be more convenient for others than for himself or herself. In so far as this view is true, part of the purpose of therapy or personal growth is to discover from one's own experience what it is to be human, what it is to relate to others, feel with them and for them, rather than to act out of some set of handed down roles, rules and injunctions. From our own experience we can construct for ourselves as adults a sense of ourselves and of others which is rooted in our own personal learning rather than in historically derived scripts and externally implanted conventions, oughts and musts.

This kind of learning is called experiential. It is fundamentally different from the learning usually available in places of education, or from the learning of skills by apprenticeship.

In schools learning typically includes a syllabus defined by acknowledged experts in a subject. A body of knowledge is passed from these experts to students, and it is sufficiently well defined to be recognizable when it is expressed, for instance in an examination. This mode of learning seems to have existed in one form or another in most societies, perhaps beginning with the oral traditions in which history and ways of seeing the world were passed on by elders. The knowledge is predominantly verbal, at least in its transmission. It tends to be knowledge 'about' things, rather than 'of' them. It is culturally defined and since the invention of writing it has grown prodigiously, because with printed books and libraries, although retrieval becomes difficult, nothing is forgotten.

In a skill, on the other hand, learning is defined primarily by the exigencies of the environment and the nature of the task, rather than by any consensus interpretation of the world by society. The end product is easily recognizable by the master, and relatively easily by the apprentice: the well-baked loaf, the properly built brick wall, or whatever. Here one learns from one's mistakes, which are displays of the differences between aspirations and actual performance, and these lead to modifications of performance. In turn the modifications are compiled into more effective procedures for carrying out the task. The master offers perceptions of mistakes, and advice about procedures.

In both these kinds of learning there are recognizable external criteria: the 'correct' conceptualization of verbal knowledge, or the well executed performance. For learning about perceptions of interpersonal events and our own feelings, the situation is rather different. Although attempts are made to cast such matters into the conventions of cultural consensus, e.g. 'you ought to love your parents', or into the framework of skill-learning with role models, social skills training and the like, the issue is better seen as being to do with internal criteria.

In experiential learning, therapists or facilitators often disclaim knowing what their clients should learn. Rather they aim to provide a setting in which clients can learn. Instead of giving advice about (for example) how to conduct relationships, they will take part in relationships with their clients in such a way as to allow them to learn their own potentialities for relationship. In this way the client or the member of a group creates internal criteria and conceptions of himself or herself in relation with others: criteria and conceptions founded upon personal experience.

It is with the theoretical bases of attempts to create this experiential kind of learning and personal change that this chapter is concerned.

One-to-one therapy and groups

Obviously one-to-one psychotherapy has something in common with groups. Both enable people to extend their experience of relationship; and they do this principally through the greater deliberateness with which the experience is pursued. There is an explicit or implicit contract that people taking part in the relationship will deliberately pay attention to themselves, to each other, and to what is going on between them, and will try and make sense of that.

'A community of two or more is therapeutic when we care for, and are attentive to one another.' So says the 1979 brochure of the Philadelphia Association. And that seems a good place to start. In one-to-one therapy a therapist can realistically come to care for his or her client (as well as giving attention). A paradigmatic demonstration of attentive caring in one-to-one therapy is given by Bergin (1971). He reports an anonymous study where two therapists A and B saw respectively fifteen and thirteen adolescent boys who were, at the time of first being seen, very disturbed and closely similar in major diagnostic characteristics. Later, as adults, four of A's patients were classified as schizophrenic, five not schizophrenic but socially inadequate, and six of the fifteen were classified as socially adequate. Meanwhile eleven of B's patients were classified as schizophrenic in adulthood and the other two while not schizophrenic were classified as socially inadequate. Bergin reports that from the analysis of the case notes it emerged that 'Therapist A consistently devoted more time to those cases that later turned out to be more disturbed: B did the opposite. That is when A perceived greater disturbance in a child, he devoted more time to him ... A was very obviously interested in, liked, and had respect for the boys.'

Just as in Winnicott's (1971) words most mothers can be 'good enough mothers' to give their children a sense of themselves and enable them to grow with some continuity of experience, so some therapists like A, while not being omnipotent, can be good enough therapists. Evidently one of the crucial issues is whether the therapist actually does care about or – to use a term which is not in polite academic usage – love his or her client. As Truax and Mitchell (1971) point out, it seems that about a third of therapists are of this kind, and two-thirds are either ineffective or 'psychonoxious': not good enough therapists. At the same time, different clients may benefit from different therapists.

Most groups are time limited, so there is not usually the opportunity for sustained relationships. But if time for the kind of knowing that will enable love to occur is not really available, there is at least in groups the opportunity for liking and for being attentive to one another.

Effects of group experience and their relation to theories of change

It is clear that to have a theory of personal learning or change it must be demonstrable that such learning occurs. There are now many studies on this with adequate methodology and these are comprehensively reviewed in Chapter 2. The conclusions of this review will be taken as a starting point for considering the kinds of personal learning that do occur in groups.

First it is clear that demonstrable changes, both in how people feel about themselves and in how others see them, do occur as a result of attending a group. The changes are sometimes on the small side, and they tend to fade over a few months. Thus a group can sow a small but significant seed of new experience, and with cultivation this seed may grow and new directions of experience of oneself and others may emerge. As pointed out above, groups in this respect are unlike the more sustained (and sustaining?) effects of longer-term personal therapy.

From among the effects of groups reviewed in Chapter 2 I will for the purposes of this chapter select two main sets. First there is the set of changes having to do with the participants' own feelings: in general people acquire more favourable views of themselves, and feel more in control of their own actions. Secondly there is the set of changes having to do with perceptions of and interactions with others, such as greater ability to give and receive affection, more openness, a greater degree of acceptance of others, and improved communication.

These changes are of course quite congruent with the ideology of groups, and with the goals of leaders and other participants. But the issue of how they might occur is not solved as simply as that. What is it about the group experience that promotes these changes?

Prerequisites of group experience

Though the procedures adopted by group leaders vary widely, there are a few procedures which are very common. While not necessarily creating the group experience, they set the stage for it. Here follow three such procedures or ground rules. (Many others are also in use, and they vary with the style of group. See, for instance, Shaffer and Galinsky (1974) for an excellent account of a range of group theories and procedures.)

The cultural island

Group leaders arrange for a group to meet for a finite time, in a specific place, isolated from the outside world and free of interruptions. The participants commit themselves to stay on this island for the course of the group.

This procedure has a number of advantages. If people are to have an experience which is somewhat different from that of the ordinary world, it is sensible to create a setting apart from the ordinary world and to make it easy for people to devote their full attention to it. In a new setting fewer rules and roles will be imported from the outside, and the opportunities for experiments on oneself, on new kinds of feelings and behaviour, will be increased. In such settings the people present will also be able to create their own unique group culture – itself an exciting experience.

In Chapter 1 Smith suggests a less obvious result of this procedure. It is typical that during the group people come to feel warmly and affectionately towards each other. By committing oneself to the cultural island for the time of the group, the usual means in society for inhibiting increase in liking (i.e. withdrawal or failure to arrange further meetings) cannot be used. There is moreover an understanding in the group that feelings expressed at the time do not necessarily imply commitments beyond the temporal boundaries of the island. This warmth, liking and trust are part of the strong power of groups. They are important ingredients of change; one would find it hard to learn anything positive or constructive with people one didn't like and trust, and these feelings of acceptance seem especially important prerequisites for significant experiential learning to occur.

Abdication of leaders from the usual 'leadership' role

This is perhaps the most famous manoeuvre of group leaders. One method is that of Bion (1961), the founder of the Tavistock group. At the start of a group he simply sits and says nothing for a good long time, until the opportunity occurs for him to make his first interpretation, i.e. that the group seems to be waiting for him to do something. At the other end of the scale some encounter and Gestalt group leaders might begin with exercises of one kind or another. Typically group leaders would not apply an agenda in the way that chairmen or teachers might. This provides the opportunity for each person to be his or her own chairperson, rather than depending on another to structure the world. Again this is relatively obvious in its effects of encouraging autonomy and the taking of responsibility for oneself.

In most groups it is axiomatic that people's feelings are among the important subjects for attention. Even if group members (particularly those who had not been to a group before) didn't come in with any very strong feelings, they are likely to have some as a result of the abdication procedure. It is moreover an event shared by the whole group, and their experience and reactions to it become part of the material on which the group will begin to work.

Experiential emphasis

The previous procedure of abdication can be seen as the leader refusing to act as a teacher in either the school-learning or apprenticeship training models outlined on p.86 by avoiding giving either lectures or advice. Instead the leader focuses the attention of the members on their own experience in the group. Leaders with different styles will use different means for achieving this. Leaders of psychoanalytic or Tavistock groups tend to rely on interpretation, for example Bion's interpretation that the group seemed to be waiting for him to do something. Others make interventions such as asking someone how she feels about some person or event. Still others make such more direct suggestions or injunctions with a view to shifting the person's focus from the distancing to the immediate and personal, e.g. 'Talk in the first person: say "I" rather than "they".'

Leaders often act as role models and can do so by themselves being self-disclosing, honest, trusting, and non-defensive, paying attention to whoever is talking and to whatever is going on in the group, emphasizing feelings over ideas and so on. Group members do then start to experience themselves and others in ways that are not usual outside the group, and this is a major prerequisite of experiential learning. Without the new experience there is not likely to be much change. I will turn now to how this change might be conceptualized, and how the observed changes in people's feelings and interpersonal behaviour might come about.

A cognitive theory

Though there are many ways of conceptualizing mental life I shall present here a cognitive theory based on the idea of the mental schema as adumbrated by Bartlett (1932) and Piaget (1974). A virtue of this theory is that it makes clear the relation between the data that are presented to our senses and the representations and procedures within the mind which we bring to bear on those data in the interpretive 'effort after meaning'.

The important idea is that of the schema (to use Bartlett's term). A schema consists of an internal representation or model of the world (in Craik's 1943 formulation), and the mental processes of inference which act upon it. It is from schemata that we generate sequences of purposeful action. Evidently the more knowledge we have represented in our internal model and the better organized it is, the more appropriate our behaviour will be for our own purposes and the exigencies of the world. Lest this sounds too cold and analytical, let me put it in a slightly different way by drawing on the writings of Horney (1942). She proposed that as children we start to compile a life strategy, or implicit theory, about our relation to others in the world. This implicit theory which will go on being elaborated throughout life is the schema or mental model. Within this implicit theory we make inferences about ourselves in relation to others, construct expectations, and plan actions.

As an illustration of how such schemata arise, Horney compares what a child might do to cope with a mother of a particular kind and what an adult might do to cope with a boss with a similar character. 'The child Clare ... has a self-righteous mother who expects the child's admiration and exclusive devotion ... Both mother and boss are complacently self-admiring, are arbitrary, favour others unfairly and tend to become hostile if what they regard as due homage is not paid them or if they sense a critical attitude.' Horney points out that one can imagine that if one were an employee of such a boss and needed to keep the job, one would 'more or less consciously evolve a technique for handling the boss'. One would 'refrain from expressing criticism; make a point to appreciate explicitly whatever good qualities there are ... agree with the boss's plans regardless of one's own opinions; let suggestions of one's own appear as if the boss had initiated them' and so on. In other words one would compile some conception of this person's plans and a set of corresponding plans to fulfil one's own purposes of keeping one's job and maintaining a tolerable atmosphere.

The child presumably has a similar problem: she must compile a similar strategy, but has much less chance either to leave or to see outside the world that surrounds her. Whereas an adult might evolve this schema more or less consciously and be able to discard it under other circumstances the child will evolve it unconsciously. Moreover this schema is likely to lay the foundations for her schemata of subsequent social relationships.

Horney argues that these kinds of strategies are distortions of the healthy growth process. However it seems better (within the terms of the theory being developed here) to assume that everyone evolves some implicit theories based on innate predispositions and on their interactions with significant others in their early lives. Fortunately these implicit theories are capable of a good deal of modification thereafter. In other words, on the basis of one's earliest relationships one compiles a model or schema of relationship in general. The experience of interacting with others gets compiled into an implicit (and largely unconscious) theory of interaction. Like any theory it will make predictions of certain kinds – i.e. it will generate expectations. And like any theory it will always be incomplete, inadequate in some respects, and capable of improvement.

Personal learning is (within these terms) the extension or modification of an implicit theory. And the question about how change occurs becomes 'How do we change our implicit theories about ourselves and others?' An answer that emerges from groups is that change occurs by means of certain experiences (personal experiments?) which have the quality of enabling the theory to improve, the schema to accommodate.

Feelings

One of the consequences of relating to the world by means of mental schemata is that our perception and understanding of what goes on in the world is always a matter of interpretation. We make interpretations of the world in terms of whatever implicit theories we have at our disposal. Clearly if our schema and the external evidence match closely we can easily make sense of events; in other words our schema can assimilate the evidence. However, if schema and 'reality' do not match then two things occur. One of them, as has been pointed out independently by two cognitive theorists (Weir, 1975 and Katz, 1978), is that feelings or emotions are generated. The second is that the discrepancy could be an invitation for the theory to be improved.

The idea that emotions can be understood as discrepancies between significant personal schemata and actuality is an important one. Katz's insight was that if we conceive of emotions in this way we can understand a good deal more of their phenomenology than might otherwise be possible. Thus we can see that they have a tense according to whether our schema is being applied to something in the present or the future. If we apply a representation of an important goal (e.g. having an interesting job) to some mental simulation of the future and a discrepancy occurs, we experience worry or anxiety. Applying the same goal to a present state we might experience not anxiety but discontent. Another set of emotions is generated where instead of applying goals in the form of things we want, we apply goals in the form of how we ought to be. Guilt and shame arise when our schema of ourselves as we ought to be is not matched by our actual behaviour. Pleasant feelings arise either as nice surprise, discrepancies due to things wanted but not anticipated, or as mismatches which have been resolved (e.g. 'at last I've found the person I want to marry'). Further subdivisions can be made where a person focuses on the different causes of a discrepancy. Katz gives an example of a man whose wife says she no longer loves him. If he focuses on his wife's perfidy he will experience anger, if on 'the other man' then jealousy, if on his own loss of her then grief, if on his wanting her back then longing, if on what the neighbours might think then embarrassment, and so on.

Feelings arise therefore from the meanings we give to events and from interpretation of discrepancies. It follows that to pay attention to these feelings allows us to understand the meanings we place on events, and allows the possibility of getting in touch with our implicit theories. Not to pay attention to them, or to disown them, clearly would have the opposite effect. It can also easily be seen that discrepancies may induce revisions of our implicit theories. Thus the man in Katz's example might revise his implicit theory by deciding that all women are hurtful and therefore to have no more to do with them, or by deciding to try better next time, and so on.

Often in groups the relation of feelings to change seems straight-forward. It is common for instance that group members should have misgivings about the advisability of personal disclosure. To disclose anything very personal about themselves might lead to rejection of one kind or another. It comes as a pleasant surprise that typically a self-disclosing statement has the opposite effect of inviting warm and accepting feelings towards the person concerned.

Although in a scientific theory a discrepant observation provides disconfirmation of a theory and hence an invitation to change, it is by no means clear how this effect might occur in the case of our personal, implicit theories. The argument from therapy is that to accept and own feelings is therapeutic and promotes change, and that seems intuitively clear within this formulation. But how the change occurs is another matter. Presumably it is not simply as a result of having strong feelings. Lots of people have all kinds of feelings which are strong (and even distressing) but they may experience the feelings simply as happening to them. Rather than changing, some people often feel swept about or locked interminably in the rigid grip of these feelings.

It seems as if feelings arising from discrepancies could be the initiators of change, but only in circumstances where the feelings themselves, or the changes that might occur, are not too frightening, and also are not prohibited – either by some external agency (such as a repressive parent) or by its internalized heir. With a 'good enough' mother, or a therapist who can express care and attention for clients while letting them be, or in the atmosphere of supportive-ness and trust that occurs in many groups, we have the necessary atmospheres of acceptance in which feelings are allowed and there-fore changes can occur. Presumably, also, personal change does not occur simply by consciously and deliberately deciding to take a different view about oneself and the world. If this were the case, new year resolutions would be more successful than they are. Rather it needs an acknowledgement of who one actually is and an ownership of what one feels, thereby allowing one's experience to touch one instead of disowning, denying or idealizing it and so removing it from contact with oneself or the world.

This theory makes some sense also of why intellectual insight is not enough for therapeutic change to occur. 'Intellectual' here means some understanding of a discrepancy in one's implicit theory, but an understanding which is somehow disconnected from the feelings that usually accompany such discrepancies.

By owning what one feels and does one also regains a sense of agency and autonomy. Instead of feelings and events just happening to one there is the sense of acting and being – and this links strongly to the finding that group members discover an increased sense of agency and autonomy.

Empirical testing of learning from discrepancy

How might one test this idea that personal change arises for a group member when, in an atmosphere of trust, owned discrepancies from expectations occur? Smith (1980) has recently addressed this problem in two studies of residential training groups.

Suppose some people go to a group and after a while feel accepted and encouraged by the warmth and cohesion in the group. They might well find themselves behaving somewhat differently from usual. Smith points out that as yet there is 'no attributional dilemma for participants – their behaviour differs because this is an exceptionally nice bunch of people'. But if one or more participants challenge other participants, either overtly or perhaps even simply by doing something which others would like to be able to do but cannot, then although a state of trust and safety will be present (set up by some of the prerequisites of the group discussed on p.89), so too will disconfirmation or discrepancy. Smith argues that people cannot now attribute what goes on simply to the nice people and warm atmosphere in the group. It becomes harder to see one's behaviour just as a product of external circumstances; it becomes more a matter of choice and personal agency.

Taking the idea further Smith uses Kelman's (1963) distinction between different types of social influence. First there is compliance, where one acts because another has the means of control over one (the example of early schema learning from Horney (1942) quoted above, is of this kind). Secondly there is identification. If one likes someone, one might go along with that person's preferences so as to maintain a rewarding relationship with the attractive person. Changes of behaviour brought about by both these influences are externally caused. The third type of change described by Kelman is called internalization. This is where, although someone might derive the idea for making a change from another (maybe by example or maybe by a more overt challenge), the person makes the change for his or her own reasons. The learning is experiential. It involves some revision of implicit theory, perhaps to start with simply by risking a new type of behaviour; and it is prompted in an atmosphere of trust by some mismatch or discrepancy.

In Smith's two (1980) empirical studies he classified group members as externalizers (people showing compliant and identifying patterns) and internalizers. This was done on the basis of correlations between the extent to which each member judged other people in the group to have influenced him or her, to be attractive to him or her, and to have made him or her feel tense. (Tension was the measure used for being challenging.) For instance people were classified as internalizers if influence, liking and tension were all positively correlated. Notice how tension would be an indication of a feeling arising from discrepany in Katz's formulation described on p.93. In both studies Smith found that internalizers showed ratings of benefit which lasted longer than those of externalizers. In the second study where measures of personal agency were also taken, internalizers showed increased perceptions of personal agency that were significantly greater than those of externalizers.

Thus in these studies not only do we begin to have a sense of how outcome is related to events within the group but we can perceive this within the framework of a set of ideas about how, in the benign climate of warmth and acceptance on the cultural island of the group, disconfirmation of implicit theories leads to change.

Interaction with others

The second main region in which groups have been found to promote personal change is in communication with others. The ideology is that groups promote increased sensitivity to what is going on both in one's own and others' relationships in the group. It is clearly difficult to measure this, since it is not easy to acquire any very objective view of what goes on in any relationship. But it seems clear that people's perceptions of others in the group and their feelings toward others do change. Their communications with others also tend to improve, even outside the group, as judged by people who were not in it.

Before discussing people's changes of perception, I will make some observations about the general nature of our perceptual processes. One of the most productive views to take about perception of inanimate objects is that it involves a process of unconscious inference (Helmholtz, 1866). Patterns on the retina are interpreted as betokening the existence of things in an outer world. It is helpful to think of the mental constructions which we create, our inner perceptual models of the outer world, as being generated by perceptual schemata. (See for instance the account by Oatley, 1978.) We are highly certain about our perceptions of things in the physical world, and can usually easily agree with others about them. Helmholtz argued that this is because seeing physical objects is like doing certain kinds of experiments in physics. We experiment with a number of different viewpoints of a table, for instance, and form a schema of that object. We infer, says Helmholtz, that the table has an 'existence independent of our observation, because *at any moment we like* simply by assuming the proper position with respect to it, we can observe it' (italics in original).

Helmholtz might have gone on to say (though he did not) that this is very different from perceiving people. Although the bodies of people exhibit roughly the same problems of perception as other physical objects, we are not (except in jokes) only interested in people for their bodies. What we really want to know are their intentions (particularly towards ourselves), their motives, their attitudes, their plans and so forth. We have no completely reliable opportunity to carry out the kind of systematic experimentation in the social world that Helmholtz describes in the physical world. Rather we are observers who can look sporadically without being able to vary the conditions. And though this deficiency might seem to be made up by the fact that we can ask questions, the social constructions of reality which we will thereby elicit are not always dependable. Indeed when we forget that people have quite different purposes from each other and from ourselves, we easily make mistakes. As children most of us were offered the notion 'bedtime' as something supposedly of benefit to us. Only later did we realize its main function was to allow parents to get us out of the way.

One of the important things that goes on in groups – it is indeed the thing that caught the imagination of Lewin and the other founders of the T-group (see e.g. Back, 1972) – is that we can begin to make some systematic observations, for ourselves, in the social domain. Here is a culture in which it is perfectly acceptable to solicit several people's perceptions of an event, thus finding that people do not necessarily all see the same thing. Also when inferring an intention it is acceptable to ask the actor if what we infer actually is what he or she had in mind. And one can get valuable feedback too in perceptions of oneself. Many of these things come as surprises (discrepancies). Moreover quite a few of them, contrary to people's anxieties, are quite pleasant surprises, leaving them with an affirmed sense of themselves.

We can take this matter further by enquiring what our schemata for other people and for personal interaction consist of. How might schemata represent plans, intentions and the like?

Max Clowes, Don Langridge and I have been developing one answer to this in terms of 'role-themes'. Deriving the term from the work of Schank and Abelson (1977), we argue that a role-theme is an interpersonal schema containing a role for oneself and one or more other actors. Each role consists of a set of interrelated goals, a set of scripts which are habitual plans for achieving them, a means for generating planned actions based on a repertoire of possible actions, on the perceived state of the world, and on the known plans of other actors. Within this theory 'role-theme' is the name given to an interpersonal schema. It serves in each person to generate purposeful action sequences. In our perception of others it is the basis for our understanding of them. Horney's patient Clare for instance might generate plans to satisfy her important goal of being accepted – by her mother and perhaps subsequently by others in her life. Her habitual plans or scripts for achieving this were to be modest, unassertive, admiring, and so on. If we were to perceive her in an interaction we might see her as eager to please, or even as a bit of a sycophant.

Berne (1974) has used the term script as a name for a compulsive life theme in which a person might be embedded. Clearly his work has a close relationship with these ideas though I wish to take a somewhat different direction from the transactional analysis of scripts which he began. The current idea of the role-theme allows us to distinguish a number of modes of relating with others.

First there is the mode of basic social relations. For instance if I speak, you must remain silent, waiting for some verbal or non-verbal cue signalling that it is your turn to talk. Both speaker and listener fill roles in each other's scripts and need elaborate knowledge of social conventions to carry on a conversation successfully. With some people during psychotic episodes one can be struck by the fact that even at this level of reciprocity two people's scripts may not interact properly.

Secondly there is the level of the life strategy which is the level at which both Horney and Berne are talking. Here we have in our themes available role categories for one or more other actors – and the plot continues if the other can be induced to fill the complementary role. This kind of relationship is sometimes referred to as 'projective identification'. This means that whole aspects of oneself are projected into another. One might imagine Clare (in Horney's example) joining the circle of her mother's devoted admirers, projectively identifying onto her mother those aspects of her own self which were admirable. She in turn felt unworthy, and felt herself to be essentially unlikeable. Main (1975) points out that these kinds of projective identifications involve the loss of valuable parts of oneself, as well as causing sometimes inappropriate intrusions into the life of the recipient. Thus a man acting in a timid and cowardly way can almost force another to act aggressively towards him. The recipient may feel uncomfortable and resentful about this role, while at the same time finding it hard not to feel superior in the face of the weakness of the projector. The projector meanwhile has lost all power of assertive action. Main asserts that such 'disturbances affect all pair relationships more or less'. And they certainly appear in groups, often starting with a series concerning the role of the leader.

The third mode of operation of role-themes is one which might be called empathetic identification – a means by which instead of simply relating to people as actors in rather highly rehearsed scripts of our own, we use our perceptual and emotional resources to perceive them as they are. Basing the argument on perceptual theory one would argue that just as to perceive a physical object one needs appropriate object schemata, so to perceive a person one would need appropriate person schemata, i.e. scripts and themes.

Recently Humphrey (1977) has put forward an idea for the basis of abilities to perceive people. He argues that the significance of introspection is that it enables us to inspect our own intentions and feelings and, using these, to identify with another person. That is to say, a schema or script which we use to understand what another is feeling or intending is our own set of feelings when we imagine ourselves to be in the other person's situation. Humphrey puts a number of convincing arguments as to why we might use ourselves as a basic personal schema in this way, rather than building up some abstract representation as we do for inanimate objects.

In order then for perception of a person to be accurate, it is clear that we must first be able to discern the cues and context of his or her situation. Secondly we must have at our disposal a range of feelings, intentions, etc. to choose from. We must ourselves know what it is to love, hate, grieve, be happy, sulk, etc. If we have not ourselves had some version of the experience of which another is speaking, we will probably not be able to recognize it. Similarly if we are too preoccupied with strong feelings of our own, we will not so easily be able to mobilize feelings in empathy with the other. If we do not pay attention to the cues of what the person is actually saying or doing, we might run our schematizing process relatively free of any data (a bit like dreaming) and simply assume that the other person thinks and feels as we habitually do: that is to say we have no real idea of who he or she distinctively is at all.

Groups give both the opportunity to extend our own personal emotional experience, and to practise, with the benefit of feedback and comparison with others' perceptions, this perceptive identification with others. It is surely significant too that Rogers (1957) in his proposal that accurate empathy is itself of therapeutic value is arguing for the importance of being perceived in this way by the other person. Thus in offering a perception of another, we can contribute to that person's sense of themselves, affirming their perception of who they are and what they feel.

The fourth mode of operation of these interpersonal schemata is that of getting to know someone as an individual. This means that as well as being able to perceive the other, or get some sense of his or her themes (aspirations, ways of going about things, etc.), we gradually build up a model of the other as an individual on the basis of a longish sequence of shared experience which allows us to make corrections to our basic model of the other. In groups it is unlikely that there is time for this kind of knowledge to develop, and as I have argued above, this is one of the differences between groups and sustained individual therapy.

However, with the framework of these four modes of interacting in mind it is possible to say something about what one might realistically expect from groups.

Primarily we might conceive groups as allowing people to gain some insight into what they and other people are up to when operating in modes one and two of the role-theme interactions described above, and also to gain some opportunity to practise mode three. For instance in mode one it comes as a pleasant surprise that it is possible to listen to someone attentively and not simply be waiting for one's own turn to talk. In mode two when we cast ourselves and another into a highly rehearsed role, it is often helpful to have others' perceptions of that, since we may be unaware of it. In mode three, being attentive to others and also introspecting our own feelings, we discover that we can make inferences about the possible feelings and intentions of others and that these perceptual intuitions can be checked by asking the people concerned.

Groups can start to enable us to understand some of our strategies of interpersonal encounter, and to provide some testing for those of our perceptions of others which could be labelled as projections, or projective identifications. Projection as defined by Freud (1911) is a defensive mechanism whereby a person having feelings which he or she disowns experiences these feelings outside themselves, usually in another person. For instance in a group Alfie might say to Betty that he felt frightened of her. But after they have talked about it for a bit it might emerge that Betty was not really being threatening. Rather Alfie was feeling angry at her for some reason, but was not very aware of his anger and had projected it onto Betty, thus seeing her as angry and hence frightening. One can imagine that in growing up we might not always be sure which feelings belonged to us and which to others. Sometimes older and more powerful people have reasons for telling children what they feel and what they ought to feel, and sometimes they are dishonest. 'No, of course I'm not cross with you. It's just that it's your bedtime.' So we might easily be confused about what we were actually feeling. Though the process might be slow and even painful, the commitment in groups to being open about one's feelings and intentions offers some hope of sorting some of these matters out.

A number of styles of group leadership pay particular attention to the problems both of projection and projective identification. In the

Tavistock and psychoanalytic group models projections are interpreted by the leader. In Gestalt groups dramatizations of parts of oneself are used instead, and a person may be asked to 'be' different characters or objects in a dream she has had, and to stage conversations between them. (A dream might be the role-theme process running free.) Or a husband might be asked to play the role of his wife (not present in the group), alternatively talking to her as if she were there and then playing her part, talking to him. In Gestalt work the object is to become aware of one's roles and of the roles played by parts of oneself, and so, by reowning these split and projected parts, become (paradoxically) more spontaneous and freer of some of the restrictions imposed by these roles.

Research data on how effective some of these specific techniques are in making people's personal relationships more direct and honest are sparse. However it is possible to imagine research designs comparing (say) T-group ground rules, these same ground rules plus Gestalt dramatization, and these same ground rules plus interpretation of projections.

In the interpersonal domain the group gives an opportunity to carry out some of the experimentation that might facilitate our social perception. Clearly no social situation could allow the kind of experimentation and consequent certainty that Helmholtz described for the physical world, but groups do allow us the opportunity for some important kinds of interpersonal discovery. And the research evidence is consistent with the idea that people do take this opportunity.

Conclusion

I have moved in this chapter from the prerequisites for groups, via the issue of learning from discrepancies which challenge existing schemata and thereby give rise to feelings, to discussing interpersonal perception and relationship. In a similar way many groups move through stages having to do with acceptance and trust, via a phase of trying out new things and a different sense of agency, towards the establishment of relationships among members of the group. (It is a sequence which itself echoes Freudian stages of development.) With a series of events of this kind taking place, and perhaps with different members being most concerned with different issues, or with the whole group either concerning itself with one of these phases or progressing through several, it evidently becomes unrealistic to ask in research designs simply 'do groups promote change?' Rather what seems to be needed is theoretically guided research relating outcome for particular individuals to the kinds of group experience with which they have been involved. Only thereby will we be able to see clearly how groups can sow a seed which can then grow into a recognizable form.

Note

This paper is dedicated to Berel Schiff who in a conversation about cognitive theories of therapeutic change once said to me, 'But if people are to change the way they think, you must change their experience'. I am grateful to Peter Smith and Heather Wood for reading a draft of this manuscript and for making helpful suggestions.

References

Back, K. W. (1972) *Beyond Words: The Story of Sensitivity Training and the Encounter Movement*. New York: Russell Sage Foundation.

Bartlett, F. C. (1932) *Remembering*. Cambridge: Cambridge University Press.

Bergin, A. E. (1971) The evaluation of therapeutic outcomes. In A. E. Bergin, and S. L. Garfield (eds) *Handbook of Psychotherapy and Behavior Change*. New York: John Wiley.

Berne, E. (1974) *What Do You Say After You Say Hello?* London: André Deutsch.

Bion, W. R. (1961) *Experiences in Groups*. London: Tavistock.

Craik, K. (1943) *The Nature of Explanation*. Cambridge: Cambridge University Press.

Freud, S. (1911) Psychoanalytic notes on an autobiographical account of a case of paranoia (Dementia Paranoides). *Standard Edition of the Complete Works of Sigmund Freud*, vol. 12. London: Hogarth Press (1955).

Freud, S. (1930) *Civilization and Its Discontents*. London: Hogarth Press.

Helmholtz, H. von (1866) *Treatise on Physiological Optics*, vol. 3. Ed. J. P. C. Southall (1962). New York: Dover.

Horney, K. (1942) *Self-Analysis*. London: Routledge and Kegan Paul.

Humphrey, N. K. (1977) *Nature's psychologists*. Paper based on the Lister Lecture delivered to the British Association for the Advancement of Science, September 1977: to be published in B. Josephson and V. S. Ramachandran, (eds) *Consciousness and the Physical World*. Oxford: Pergamon Press.

Katz, J. M. (1978) Discrepancy, arousal and labelling: towards a psycho-social theory of emotion. Paper presented to the World Congress of Sociology, Uppsala, Sweden, August 1978.

Kelman, H. C. (1963) The role of the group in the induction of therapeutic change. *International Journal of Group Psychotherapy 13*: 399–432.

Main, T. (1975) Some psychodynamics of large groups. In L. Kreeger (ed.) *The Large Group: Dynamics and Therapy*. London: Constable.

Oatley, K. (1978) *Perceptions and Representations*. London: Methuen.

Piaget, J. (1974) *The Child and Reality*. London: Frederick Muller.

Rogers, C. R. (1957) The necessary and sufficient conditions of therapeutic personality change. *Journal of Consulting Psychology 22*: 95–103.

Shaffer, J. B. P. and Galinsky, M. D. (1974) *Models of Group Therapy and Sensitivity Training*. Englewood Cliffs, New Jersey: Prentice-Hall.

Schank, R. C. and Abelson, R. P. (1977) *Scripts, Plans, Goals, and Understanding: An Inquiry into Knowledge Structures*. Hillsdale, New Jersey: L. Erlbaum Associates.

Smith, P. B. (1980) An attributional analysis of personal learning. In C. P. Alderfer and C. L. Cooper (eds) *Advances in Experiential Processes*, vol. 2. Chichester: Wiley.

Truax, C. B. and Mitchell, K. M. (1971) Research on certain therapist interpersonal skills in relation to process and outcome. In A. E. Bergin and S. L. Garfield (eds) *Handbook of Psychotherapy and Behavior Change*. New York: John Wiley.

Weir, S. (1975) The perception of motion: actions, motives and feelings. In *Progress in Perception*. University of Edinburgh, Department of Artificial Intelligence Report No. 13.

Winnicott, D. W. (1971) *Playing and Reality*. London: Tavistock.

5 The usefulness of groups in clinical settings

Peter B. Smith, Heather Wood and Gerald G. Smale

The distinction between the use of groups in clinical and non-clinical settings is an essentially arbitrary one. The development of the types of group-work surveyed in Chapter 1 has progressively blurred the boundary between group-work which is remedial in intent and group-work which seeks to enhance the skills or experience of someone who can already cope adequately with everyday experience. The focus of the present chapter will thus overlap themes already explored, but will be restricted to groups overtly labelled as therapeutic.

The term 'group psychotherapy' has been in use for several decades, but it is employed to describe a rather wide variety of procedures, ranging from long-lasting types of dynamically-oriented 'insight' therapies to much briefer periods of group discussion or instruction as favoured by some behaviour therapists. Consequently it is unlikely to be fruitful to enquire whether or not group therapy 'works'. A more promising line is to analyse 'what treatment, by whom, is most effective for this individual with that specific problem, under which set of circumstances?' (Paul, 1967). A substantial range of empirical studies is available through which to seek answers to these questions. While many of them employ levels of measurement which leave a good deal to be desired, the abundance of studies of group therapy does make it possible initially to adhere to the criteria employed in Chapter 2 whereby studies are only included if they utilized control groups and a repeated measures design. In some later sections of this chapter it is not possible to sustain these criteria. In certain parts of the field studies are also becoming available which contrast the effectiveness of different types of group or individual therapy with equivalent groups of clients.

Group psychotherapy with children

Abramowitz (1976) discusses forty-two empirical studies of group therapy with children. Of these, seven lacked control groups or were not specifically for clients with problems, and a further sixteen are available only as unpublished dissertations. The remaining nineteen will be discussed here. The nineteen studies report a total of twenty-six different therapeutic treatments in comparison with controls. Of these, among the most frequent were those derived from behavioural techniques. Tosi et al. (1971) worked with reticent sixth and seventh-graders. Increases were found in the frequencies of speaking in class and of raising one's hand for those who attended behaviour modification groups, but not for controls who saw a film. Hansen et al. (1969) set up behaviour modification groups for sociometrically isolated sixth graders. Increases in sociometric status were found, particularly where the groups had contained high status children as well as isolates. Clement and Milne (1967) as well as Clement et al. (1970) worked with socially withdrawn 8–9 year olds referred by the teacher. In both studies the most effective treatment was found to be a form of play therapy which incorporated tangible reinforcements. Improvements were found on a Behaviour Problem Checklist and from classroom observation. Follow-up measures showed that the effects of play therapy with reinforcement did persist. Ritter (1968) treated adolescent snake phobics by a form of systematic desensitization undertaken in groups. Significant effects were found on a behavioural test of snake avoidance.

Hinds and Roehlke (1970) ran behaviour modification groups for third to fifth graders referred by the teacher for disruptive classroom behaviour. Behaviour observations showed increased adaptive behaviours and decreased disruptive behaviours. These were not found for those who attended a 'placebo' group or others who remained in the classroom. Randolph and Hardage (1973) utilized 'classroom behaviour management' with fifth and sixth grade potential drop-outs, but no treatment effects were detected. Kelly and Matthews (1971) used behaviour modification with fifth and sixth graders who were identified by the teacher as a discipline problem, but no clear effects were found.

Of the behavioural studies, six out of eight did find significant effects (75 per cent). This approach appears effective in increasing social skills and reducing specific fears. The two failures suggest that it may be less effective in treating discipline problems, particularly among older children.

The other most frequently employed form of group psychotherapy with children is less clearly delineated, but is variously described as verbal therapy or group counselling. The principal activity in this type of group is likely to be discussion of one's problems and of how they may be overcome. Thombs and Muro (1973) found improved sociometric scores among isolated second graders, but McBrien and Nelson (1972) found no such effect among isolated first to third graders. Barcai et al. (1973) worked with under-achieving fourth to fifth graders. Improvements were obtained on intelligence and on story completion measures, but these effects were also found in other groups who simply received extra teaching. Winkler et al. (1965) also worked with under-achieving fourth graders, but no effects were found. McCollum and Anderson (1974) found increased vocabulary among 'learning-disabled' children after group counselling.

Barcai and Robinson (1969) employed group therapy with fifth and sixth graders with discipline or achievement problems. Teachers rated their subsequent classroom performance as more improved than controls. Taylor and Hoedt (1974) obtained a similar effect with teacher ratings of anxiety among elementary children with behaviour problems. However Tolor (1970) obtained a mixture of positive and negative effects in a similar population. Randolph and Hardage (1973) found improved grades but decreased involvement among potential drop-outs.

The studies of verbal group therapy or counselling show five positive outcomes and four mixed or null (55 per cent). These approaches appear able to generate positive outcomes on an equally broad front to those achieved by behaviour modification, but apparently with less reliability. This could be because it is not so easy to create the right circumstances for effective use of these methods, but equally it could be because they have been employed in more difficult circumstances. The only study in which both approaches were directly compared showed them to be equally ineffective (Randolph and Hardage, 1973).

Activity or play therapy provides a third possible approach, particularly with younger children. This approach lays less stress on discussion and more on the resolution of difficulties through play or through some form of symbolic representation. Fisher (1953) obtained improved reading skills among retarded 10–13 year olds in a home. Moulin (1970) reported gains in non-verbal intelligence and psycholinguistic abilities among under-achieving first to third graders. Irwin et al. (1972) found no change in eight-year-old clinic patients after activity therapy, but increases in Rorschach scores and semantic differential ratings after psychodrama. Thombs and Muro (1973) found play therapy superior to group counselling in raising sociometric scores, whereas McBrien and Nelson (1972) found both equally ineffective. Clement and Milne (1967) and Clement et al. (1970) found play therapy less effective than the treatment they also employed which incorporated tangible reinforcement. There were also no lasting effects of play therapy.

Activity or play therapy yields four successful outcomes and five mixed or null (45 per cent). Direct comparisons (Clement and Milne, Clement et al., Irwin et al.) suggest that more structured approaches are more effective, but there is no way of knowing whether this is always so. Both group counselling and play therapy may vary widely in the degree to which the leader structures events.

Overall, the studies of group psychotherapy with children show that significant effects are quite frequently obtained. The data do not at present provide a firm basis for a preference for one method over another. Very little information is available as to the magnitude or durability of the effects obtained. Most probably whether or not they persist will depend upon a host of factors, both within the school and in the family, which are explored at other points in this volume.

Group psychotherapy with severely disturbed patients

The various types of groups which have been used with severely disturbed patients have reflected changes in psychiatric thinking particularly about schizophrenia. Early approaches focus on hospitalized patients and are more concerned with patients' ward adjustment than with their possible discharge. For instance Tucker (1956) found reduced soiling among chronic psychotics after groups, with no change among controls. Sacks and Berger (1954) found that chronic schizophrenics attending groups were more likely than controls to be transferred to less disturbed wards. Kraus (1959) found less disturbed scores on the MMPI among psychotics attending groups as well as enhanced ratings of ward behaviour by ward physicians. Not all such studies showed positive effect. Feifel and Schwartz (1953) found no difference in ratings of improvement among psychotics attending groups and controls. Boe et al. (1966) found no change in those who attended groups, while controls saw themselves as more assertive and more pompous.

The authors of these early studies do not provide very precise descriptions of the type of group experience patients received. The groups in the various studies may well have ranged from a primarily social focus to an intensively therapeutic one. Thus a wide variety of possible explanations remain as to why the groups were sometimes more effective than at other times. Baehr (1954) provided patients with either group therapy, individual therapy or both. Greatest improvement on ratings of discontentment by the patients was found for those receiving both forms of therapy. Semon and Goldstein (1957) compared group-centred and leader-centred groups for schizophrenics. Both types of group showed improvements on some sections of the Palo Alto Hospital Adjustment Scale which were not found among controls. Anker and Walsh (1961) compared group therapy and a form of drama therapy for schizophrenics. Those involved in the drama therapy showed greater gains in hospital adjustment. These studies imply that hospital adjustment may be enhanced by a variety of procedures through which the patient gains more attention or involvement in activities, one instance of which would be some kind of group.

Further studies show that some kinds of group experience are more effective than others in achieving such effects. Pattison et al. (1967) found that after analytically-oriented therapy patients showed less improvement than controls. Coons (1957) compared a warm, permissive type of group with a 'benign authoritarian' focus on insights into one's problems, i.e. a leader who provided supportive interpretations. Members were mostly schizophrenics. The warm, permissive groups showed increase on intelligence and on ratings of adjustment made by coders who were unaware who had attended which group. These changes were not shown by controls or those in the insight groups. This study was taken further by Roback (1972), who showed that groups receiving both the warm, permissive focus and the insight focus were superior to either one alone or to controls. Cadman et al. (1954) assessed the effects of 'round-table' group therapy, i.e. therapy with no therapists present, but in which different group members were 'primed' before each meeting. Much higher improvement rates were found after one year than among controls. These three studies all suggest that it is supportive non-analytic therapy which may be most appropriate with this population.

Advocates of drug therapy would argue that the positive effects that some types of group can achieve are more readily obtained through appropriate courses of drug treatment. For instance Cowden et al. (1956a, b) compared the impact of group therapy with that of drugs such as chlorpromazine and reserpine. The effect of the drugs was marked, but the addition of group therapy did not further reduce disturbed behaviour. King (1958, 1963) found that chlorpromazine plus weekly groups also had no greater effect than the drug alone in controlling symptoms and discharge rates. On the other hand, Borowski and Tolwinski (1969) did find that groups in addition to chlorpromazine had additional effects. Delusional thinking lessened among 61 per cent of those in groups plus drugs, but only 14 per cent of those on drugs alone. Williams et al. (1962) compared the effects of a 'group living' programme for schizophrenics with controls who received insulin therapy, ECT and drugs. The programme included daily group therapy, co-operative work and recreation and weekly psychodrama. The group living patients showed much more extensive changes than controls, including reduced pathology, greater involvement with others and changes in the type of hospitalization required.

The current emphasis on seeking early discharge of patients means that the usefulness of groups must now be judged by their effectiveness in making patients ready for discharge or sustaining them subsequent to discharge. A difficulty with some of the studies is that they fail to make clear whether or not drugs were also employed along with the groups. This is true for instance of an otherwise impressive study by Fairweather et al. (1960). These authors compared the effectiveness of four types of treatment with long-term psychotics, short-term psychotics and non-psychotic patients. The treatments studied were group therapy, group living, individual therapy and a control condition. Follow-up indicated various significant effects of therapy, of which the most marked was that those receiving any form of therapy were more likely to be in work. Those receiving group therapy and the controls were discharged soonest, whereas those in individual therapy stayed in hospital almost 50 per cent longer. There were however marked interactions between these effects and patients' diagnostic category. Long-term psychotics in therapy tended to get worse rather than better, so that the positive effects reported must be due to the non-psychotics and short-term psychotics. Further follow-up (Fairweather and Simon, 1963) showed that only those receiving group therapy continued to be significantly more likely to be in work and out of hospital.

Vitalo (1971) compared a training programme in interpersonal skills to group therapy and controls. Those in group therapy showed greatest decrease in pathology while those in the training programme scored higher on interpersonal skills. Both showed improved ward behaviour. Olson and Greenberg (1972) contrasted group therapy with incentive therapy and controls. In the incentive therapy patients were rewarded with tokens for appropriate behaviour. Nurses perceived greatest improvement in the group therapy condition, but incentive therapy showed greater benefits on measures such as number of days spent out of hospital. This study illustrates how treatments which encourage patients to work toward discharge from hospital may not be rated highest by those hospital staff not directly involved in the training. Lipton et al. (1958) found no difference in discharge rates for those receiving group therapy and those who did not. Haven and Wood (1970) obtained a similar result.

The studies evaluating groups in terms of discharge rates are at best equivocal. This may well turn out to be because discharge rates are influenced by differences both between and within studies in other more potent variables such as types of medication employed and the degree of initial pathology of those in the study. Almost all the most recent studies have examined the use of groups *after* patient discharge. This is no doubt because many hospitals now see this as the appropriate time for therapeutic support. O'Brien et al. (1972) compared discharged patients who subsequently received group or individual therapy. Those in groups were seen by independent raters as better adjusted than those in individual therapy. However these differences were not reflected in differential readmission rates to hospital. No difference in readmission rates was also reported by Levene et al. (1970), Herz et al. (1974) and Claghorn et al. (1974). In contrast, Prince et al. (1973), Purvis and Miskimmins (1970) and Shattan et al. (1966) all found that those in groups were less likely to be readmitted to hospital. The successful studies appear to be those in which the groups were more community-based and more likely to be led by social workers than psychiatrists.

In addition to examining readmission rates a number of these studies include further data on patients' adaptation after release. O'Brien et al. (1972) found that despite there being no differences in readmission rate in their sample, patients attending groups were rated by independent observers as improving on a psychiatric rating scale and as more socially effective. In a similar manner Herz et al. (1974) found that while an equal amount of resources went into individual and group treatments, the therapists strongly preferred the group treatment. On the other hand, Levene et al. (1970) found more improvement on individually treated patients. Claghorn et al. (1974) found that those in groups moved toward seeing themselves as less dominant and affiliative and others as more so. They argue that this constitutes a positive change in so far as it constitutes a more realistic appraisal of one's disability. There do therefore appear to be some detectable effects of after-care groups, but these are not always sufficiently substantial to affect readmission rates. No separate analyses are provided showing the relative utility of group and other treatments for those patients who are *not* readmitted.

Groups for severely disturbed patients have thus been extensively studied. It appears that groups within the hospital setting do at least sometimes have marked effects on adjustment. The evidence appears particularly good for supportive types of group-work. On the other hand there is little compelling evidence that groups are particularly effective in enhancing discharge or in preventing readmission. It may well be that these more substantive changes are not achievable within the format of therapy groups meeting so briefly, in some studies only once monthly. More sustained endeavours are considered in the later section of this chapter which considers therapeutic communities.

Group psychotherapy for neurotics

As Parloff and Dies (1977) note, the frequency with which group therapy is employed with neurotics is not reflected by the number of available research studies. This may perhaps be because analytically-oriented therapists who are strongly represented in this field see less need of designs employing control groups. Alternatively it might be that control groups are much less easy to come by than is the case with hospitalized patients, or that therapists in this field are less favourably oriented toward research.

Luria (1959) compared students in out-patient group therapy with controls attending classes. Those in groups became more favourable toward themselves and rated themselves as more relaxed and more potent. Controls did not change. Swarr and Ewing (1977) also studied student therapy groups. Their controls were on a waiting list for treatment, but since therapy lasted on average 144 days and the waiting period was only eighteen days the comparison is a weak one. Group members showed increased self-esteem, motivation and inter-personal functioning as well as decreases in anxiety and excessive achievement needs. A similar study by Piper et al. (1977) used a better-matched waiting-list control group. Group members and controls both showed substantial change but those in the groups showed a greater reduction in their ratings of the difference between how they saw themselves and how they wished to be. Donovan and Marvit (1970) found that out-patients attending brief group therapy showed reduced ratings of alienation not shown by controls.

Two studies have reported on the use of groups in the in-patient treatment of neurotics. Haven and Wood (1970) found that after group treatment seventeen out of twenty-one patients (81 per cent) were discharged and not readmitted, whereas four out of twelve controls (33 per cent) met this criterion. Bovill (1972) reports one of the few British studies in this section. In-patients received four hours per week of group therapy and were free to continue this after discharge. Follow-up over two years showed that group members were readmitted for an average of three days, whereas for controls the average was twenty-one days. After ten years (Bovill, 1977) these figures stood at ten and twenty-seven days respectively. This impress-ive finding unfortunately leaves some ambiguity as to how it was achieved. The group patients not only attended groups but also had relaxation classes, were in the care of Bovill rather than her colleagues (who provided the controls) and had more extended after-care.

A number of researchers have compared group therapy with other forms of treatment for neurotics, particularly various behavioural treatments which have come to the fore in recent years. Imber et al. (1957) compared group and individual therapy. They found that gains on a scale of social ineffectiveness varied not so much by type of therapy as by amount of contact with the therapist. Barron and Leary (1955) found changes on MMPI for those in both group therapy and individual therapy to be no greater than those shown by controls.

Lazarus (1961) employed group desensitization (a form of behaviour therapy based on relaxation) in the treatment of phobics. He found that of eighteen phobics receiving group systematic desensitization, thirteen recovered. Of another seventeen phobics who attended therapy groups with an interpretive therapist, only two recovered. The remaining fifteen were then treated by group systematic desensitization and a further ten recovered. Paul and Shannon (1966) undertook a more detailed and better controlled study of systematic desensitization for chronically anxious students. They found that nine sessions had equally strongly positive effects whether undertaken individually or in groups. Positive effects included substantial improvements in students' subsequent grades. Controls' grades got worse, while those in insight therapy showed a lesser amount of favourable effect. Gelder et al. (1967) compared group therapy and systematic desensitization in the treatment of phobics. Desensitization achieved a quicker effect. At the end of treatment the figures still favoured desensitization, but the difference was no longer significant. Dawley and Wenrich (1973) used group implosive therapy (a form of behaviour therapy in which one is encouraged to confront one's fears) in the treatment of test anxiety in students. Test anxiety scores declined after five sessions spread over several weeks and remained low one month later. Smaller, non-significant changes were obtained for controls and a placebo condition.

Obler (1973) compared systematic desensitization and group therapy for sexual disorders. The behavioural treatment showed a variety of positive effects, while fifteen hours of analytically-oriented group therapy did not. Auerbach and Kilmann (1977) studied the effectiveness of group systematic desensitization on penile erection failures in men. Eight students who were treated for eighteen sessions showed improvement in their self-reported sexual performance subsequently. Controls showed no change. Follow-up data were collected three months after treatment was complete. Solyom et al. (1973) compared behavioural treatments and group therapy in the treatment of fear of flying. Behavioural treatments were most effective, but after one year the group therapy clients also showed some positive effect.

Studies such as these have indicated the potential of group forms of behaviour therapy. Little evidence exists that there is any difference in the impact of group behaviour therapy and individual behaviour therapy. A weakness which both group and individual forms of behaviour therapy share with other approaches already reviewed is the lack of substantial follow-up studies. One field which illustrates the necessity of such studies is the treatment of obesity, in which group approaches have been frequently employed. Murray et al. (1975) review thirteen previous studies of group-based behaviour therapy for obesity, many of which showed significant treatment effects. However none of these studies had follow-up measures more than a month or two after treatment. In Murray et al.'s study, group treatment of nine obese women which included self-control training and the eating of low-calorie food together did achieve weight loss which was sustained twelve weeks later. However after twenty-four weeks the effect was no longer present. Bornstein and Sipprelle (1973) compared three group treatments for obesity, with a six-month follow-up. A group in which group members' anxiety about obesity was deliberately induced proved superior to a group in which this was not done. Kingsley and Wilson (1977) compared group behaviour therapy, individual behaviour therapy and a group treatment in which members placed social pressure upon one another to sustain weight loss. Obese volunteers were followed up for a year. The group treatments included a 'booster' session every three months. Group behaviour therapy achieved the greatest weight loss and this increased over the subsequent year. Individual behaviour therapy achieved a lesser loss and this loss decreased over the subsequent year. This decrease may of course have been because the individual treatment clients received no booster sessions.

It is very likely the case that some specific behaviour problems are much more prone to relapse than others. Just because those with eating problems frequently relapse it need not necessarily be the case that phobics do likewise. None the less the potential utility of group behaviour therapy is unlikely to be clarified until more follow-up studies are available. Where group behaviour therapy and equivalent individual treatment are shown to be equally effective, there is in any event an economic argument in favour of group treatment.

Group therapy has also been found (Teahan, 1966) to enhance the grades of high ability low-achieving students. Felton and Biggs (1972, 1973) report enhanced internality on the Rotter scale of locus of control after Gestalt-type group therapy for academic low achievers.

Falloon et al. (1977) undertook social skill training groups for out-patients. Modelling, rehearsal and homework assignments appeared to enhance effectiveness, but all conditions showed substantial change and there was no untreated control. Waldman and Reiser (1961) found vocational readjustment clients more likely to be placed in work after group therapy. Knox (1974) found that groups for army veterans in a 'domiciliary restoration' programme enhanced patients' anxiety levels but controls showed equally large increases.

This section has reviewed diverse applications of group therapy. An encouraging number of studies do report favourable outcomes of treatment. However control groups in this area often also show substantial improvement, so that caution is necessary in ensuring that those in groups not only change but that they change more than do the controls. In this field the issue is becoming increasingly not whether group therapy can be effective, but for which conditions it can be as quickly and economically effective as some forms of behaviour therapy. Group administration of behaviour therapy is in any case serving to blur the boundary between the two treatments. In the case of very specific behaviour problems it may well be that brief forms of group behaviour therapy can be effective. In the case of the much more frequently occurring general anxiety or disorders, the answer is much less likely to be positive.

Group psychotherapy with social deviants

Group therapy has been frequently employed with some types of social deviant, particularly those who are children and those who are in residential institutions, whether these be hospitals or prisons. Many of the studies reported in this field are not methodologically rigorous (Slaikeu, 1973), but some interesting results have been noted.

Snyder and Sechrest (1959) compared the effect of group therapy based on strongly directive group leadership with a placebo condition and no treatment for groups of defective delinquents. They found that the directive group therapy achieved most favourable ratings in 'housing reports' completed by those in authority. Feder (1962) found that group therapy for delinquent adolescent boys achieved greater 'therapeutic readiness' as shown by a self-concept measure based on card sorting than did no treatment. Persons (1966) also compared group therapy with no treatment among delinquent adolescents. He found reduced anxiety on the Manifest Anxiety scale and less pathological scores on MMPI after the groups. Although these studies yield promising results, none included follow-up measures and none of those measures which were used derive directly from the behaviour which led the adolescents to be classified as delinquent in the first place.

Truax et al. (1966) studied the effect of Rogerian group therapy on delinquent adolescent girls. Marked improvements in self-concept were found. Follow-up showed that after one year those in groups had on average spent 54 per cent of time outside the institution compared with 40 per cent of time for controls. These differences were highly significant. A similar study by Redfering (1973) found improved ratings of self, parents and peers. After one year the proportion of girls attending groups who had been released, placed on parole or were living with their parents were all significantly higher. Taylor (1967) found improved behaviour and scores on various personality tests among delinquent girls after six months of analytically-oriented group therapy. The recidivism rate was however no different from controls, possibly because of individual variance in a rather small sample. Adequate studies of group therapy for delinquent boys are less numerous. However, Sarason and Ganzer (1973) found lasting effects for two forms of structured group therapy, one involving structured discussion, the other role-playing. After three years recidivism in the treated groups was 17 per cent, compared with 34 per cent for controls.

Results for adult offenders are much less impressive. Bailey (1970) found no effects of therapy among women prisoners. Jew et al. (1972) found that an extensive programme of groups with a large sample of disturbed male prisoners showed a lower rate of reimprisonment after one year, but not after two or four years. Within the much more specifically defined area of sex offenders, Peters et al. (1968) did obtain positive effects. Those who attended groups were less frequently rearrested either for sex offences or for other offences.

Treatment for addictions also frequently employs group methods. Kilmann and Auerbach (1974) studied marathon groups for narcotics addicts. After these, the group members were less anxious and rated themselves higher on self-control and achievement. Controls saw their behaviour as more externally controlled. Willett (1973) found no effect of group treatment among heroin addicts. Ends and Page (1959) studied group therapy for hospitalized alcoholics. Enhanced self-concept was found, and it was shown in an earlier study (Ends and Page, 1957) that this effect was most marked where the groups were Rogerian in orientation. McGinnis (1963) found that group therapy enhanced alcoholics' ego-strength as measured by MMPI. In a field where problems of relapse are frequently encountered, none of these studies included follow-up measures of any kind. Conclusions can thus be no more than tentative.

Whilst mental retardates are not typically thought of as social deviants, there are also some studies testing the use of groups in enhancing the hospital adjustment of retardates. Wilcox and Guthrie (1957) found positive effects of groups on adjustment, while Wilson et al. (1967) did not. However the Wilson sample was so small (N = 6) as to virtually preclude a significant effect.

The use of groups with social deviants does appear to hold some promise, particularly in the case of adolescents. The most notable successes were achieved through Rogerian and directive approaches, rather than an analytic one. In view of the firmness with which many socially deviant behaviours are rooted in the offender's social context, it is particularly important that studies in this area include relevant follow-up measures. One might speculate that group treatments with deviants will prove lastingly effective only if they can either replace the client's support network or trigger changes in it. It is with forms of group therapy which seek to do just this that the remaining sections of this chapter are concerned.

Therapeutic communities

Since the term 'therapeutic community' was coined by Main in 1946 it has been used liberally, leading to some confusion about its precise definition. D. H. Clark (1965) differentiates between the 'therapeutic community approach', which refers to attempts to create a humane and stimulating hospital environment, and the 'therapeutic community proper'. The distinguishing feature of the 'therapeutic community proper' is that the community itself, and its constituent groups and members, are seen as the principal agents of therapeutic change.

Thus the social environment is not the context within which treatment is conducted, but the treatment itself. It is in this sense that the term 'therapeutic community' will be used here.

The principles of therapeutic community treatment are expounded by Jones (1953, 1962) and Rapoport (1960). Rapoport summarizes therapeutic community ideology as comprising four themes: democratization, permissiveness, reality confrontation, and communalism. In practice this generates a programme of therapeutic groups which employ a range of methods to effect change, and administrative groups which control the organization of the community. Daily community meetings provide a forum for the discussion of topical issues. Whilst the majority of therapeutic communities are residential units, some offer a day hospital programme. In both cases the therapeutic programme occupies a substantial proportion of the patient's time each day.

The focus of this review is those studies which evaluate the efficacy of therapeutic community treatment, and the means by which these effects are achieved. Since research in this area is not extensive, no studies have been excluded because of methodological flaws. Many of the findings cited should therefore be regarded as tentative rather than conclusive.

Comparisons with traditional psychiatric treatment

Caine (1965) and Caine and Smail (1969) report a comparative study of chronic neurotic patients from two therapeutic communities, and from two mental hospitals and a neurosis unit. Patients completed a battery of personality tests and a problem check-list on admission, and at intervals during and after treatment. Significant differences were found for the therapeutic community sample on all measures one year after discharge, which were maintained four years later. In contrast, the main significant differences for the comparative treatment group were only on the problem check-list, and eighteen months after discharge on the depression scale of the MMPI. Caine and Smail suggest that this latter improvement may be attributable to supportive drug treatment in the comparative sample.

D. H. Clark, Hooper and Oram (1962) compared discharge rates on a women's convalescent ward before and after conversion to a therapeutic community ward. Patients stayed in the community ward for a shorter period of time, and there were fewer transfers to long-stay wards. Moreover, the readmission rate was no greater for patients treated by this method.

Miles (1967, 1969) compared the social relationships of psychopathic patients in a therapeutic community unit with those of similar patients in a traditional ward. In the therapeutic community ward the number of isolated patients decreased substantially over time, while the number of reciprocated choices on sociometric measures increased. Although patients in the control group became more accepting of each other, there was no increase in reciprocated choices and the frequency of mutual rejection hardly declined.

Studies of communities with schizophrenic patients have yielded more ambiguous results. Murray and Cohen (1959) compared schizophrenic patients in a therapeutic community ward and a traditional psychiatric ward with patients in a non-psychiatric control ward. Sociometric measures revealed that social organization in the therapeutic community ward resembled that in the control ward, whereas in the traditional ward there were many isolated patients. The authors take this as evidence that community therapy can reverse the deterioration in social relationships which accompanies mental illness. Myers and Clark (1972) compared disturbed schizophrenic patients treated in a traditional ward with others treated by therapeutic community methods. A higher proportion of community patients showed an improvement in the severity of symptoms, and an increase in spontaneous interaction while on the ward. A greater number of patients were also discharged from the community.

In contrast, Letemendia et al. (1967) report a comparative study with chronic schizophrenic patients with less favourable results. Over a two-year period, administrative changes were made throughout a hospital, including attempts to improve communication and the abolition of locked wards. The hospital was then split into two divisions, employing therapeutic community and more traditional 'eclectic' methods. Neither the administrative nor the treatment changes appeared to affect improvement or discharge rates.

Fairweather et al.'s (1960) study has been discussed above. The group living condition is not explicitly described as a therapeutic community, but bears sufficient resemblance to this method to warrant consideration. Together with individual therapy, this condition yielded the highest percentage of employed patients at follow-up, and was more economical than individual therapy in requiring less time in treatment and personnel. However, long-term psychotics responded variably to this treatment, some improving while others deteriorated. In less intense therapeutic situations, these patients tended to stabilize at 'marginal' levels of adjustment.

Thus results with schizophrenic patients tend to be equivocal. Although Murray and Cohen (1959) do not specify the precise diagnosis of their patients, it may be that acute schizophrenics are more likely to respond well to the treatment than chronic patients. This might account for the disparity between the findings of Myers and Clark (1972), and Fairweather et al. (1960) and Letemendia et al. (1967). In general, the above studies provide some evidence for the efficacy of therapeutic community treatment when compared with traditional psychiatric methods, at least with chronic neurotic, convalescent, psychopathic and disturbed schizophrenic patients.

While the two methods of treatment have differing goals, it is questionable whether a single outcome criterion provides an adequate measure of the changes effected by each method. If therapeutic communities aim to effect enduring personality change and improved social relations while traditional hospitals are primarily concerned with symptom relief, then any comparative study should examine change in both domains. Several of the studies reported fail to comply with this stipulation, and employ measures which are likely to favour either therapeutic community methods (e.g. Murray and Cohen, 1959) or traditional methods (e.g. Letemendia et al., 1967). This may account for some variability in the results. Nevertheless, studies of individual differences in response to treatment provide results which are consistent with those reported above.

Individual differences in response to treatment

At the Henderson Hospital, Rapoport (1960) found that 25 per cent of the psychotics improved, compared with 45–75 per cent of those with personality disorders, and 77 per cent of those diagnosed neurotic. Patients were then grouped according to the extent of their incapacity with work, criminality, alcoholism or addiction, and relationships with friends. Employing this index a significant, inverse relationship was found between severity of disorder and improvement in the unit. They were also classified according to the number of 'acting out' disturbances they were involved in each month. Highest improvement rates were found among those who were involved in some disturbance, but less than once a month. Rapoport suggests that patients are more likely to benefit if they take some advantage of the unit's permissiveness, rather than conforming or acting out to an extreme.

Studying the same community, Whiteley (1970) compared the characteristics of those who did not relapse within two years of discharge with those who had a further psychiatric admission or conviction in this time. Positive prognostic indicators were pre-hospitalization social adjustment and affective symptomatology, in contrast to 'thought disorder' or 'action' syndromes; negative indicators were largely concerned with the severity of the previous criminal record, and childhood institutionalization. Whiteley concludes that a degree of emotional maturity is necessary if patients are to benefit from therapeutic community treatment.

This is consistent with A. W. Clark's (1967a) finding that the treatment was more successful with patients whose behaviour was less extreme and disturbed. He considers that these patients are more amenable to social influence processes than patients who are grossly withdrawn or aggressive. Almond et al. (1969b) found that those who became acculturated to a therapeutic community ward entered the hospital admitting to considerable subjective distress and acknowledging their problems. Those who failed to acculturate tended to be older, admitted to the least subjective distress on admission, denied their problems, and hid behind 'conventional facades'.

Thus it appears that some capacity for social involvement without excessively defensive behaviour is a necessary precursor of full therapeutic participation. To some extent this may coincide with psychiatric diagnoses; chronic schizophrenics are most likely to be impaired in this respect, while neurotic patients would probably be the least disabled. However, an understanding of group therapy is only advanced if we appreciate the significance of these diagnoses. They appear to be of relevance inasmuch as they relate to the patient's ability to become involved in therapy. Studies which examine the process of therapeutic community treatment demonstrate the relationship between involvement and improvement.

The relationship between value-change and improvement

The value-system of the therapeutic community has been consciously and deliberately formulated, with the intention of facilitating the process of therapeutic change rather than the administration of an organization. Communication, permissiveness and co-operation are

advocated, while secrecy, authoritarian attitudes and role-differenti-
ation are discouraged. There are two ways in which these values may
affect the patient: the adoption of some values may be therapeutic in
itself, while others may enable the patient to become more involved
in therapy, and hence derive benefit from the community. If individuals assume greater responsibility for themselves and their own
destiny they may become less passive and apathetic; if they learn the
value of self-expression they may benefit more from therapy. Such
considerations have prompted researchers to examine the relationship between the adoption of therapeutic community values and
improvement.

Ferguson and Carney (1970) found that an enthusiastic attitude
towards the treatment was clearly associated with good prognosis.
However, evaluations were made one year after discharge; it is
possible that retrospective impressions of the treatment were
influenced by the benefit which patients had experienced.

A. W. Clark (1967a) related scores on a sixteen-item scale, the
Personality and Social Network Prognosis Scale, to ratings of improvement. Both ratings were made by clinicians. Two items on the
Prognosis Scale were concerned with the extent to which each patient
accepted the theories and practices of the unit at an emotional and
an intellectual level. There were significant correlations between
scores on these two items and ratings of improvement, whereas there
was no association between improvement and the extent to which
patients were rated by the clinicians as assuming a 'front' of
acceptance of unit ideology.

A. W. Clark and Yeomans (1969) found that those who improved
became more favourable towards the unit during treatment, whereas
there was no shift in the attitudes of those who failed to improve.

Rapoport (1960) devised a fourteen-item values questionnaire to
measure a single dimension, from traditional treatment values to
therapeutic community values. Of those whose values shifted during
treatment in a pro-unit direction, 60 per cent improved, compared
with 28 per cent of those whose values did not shift in this direction.
Rapoport suggests that the 40 per cent of those with favourable
attitudes who did not improve may have been providing compliant
responses.

Almond et al. (1968) used multiple methods to assess the value-
system of a therapeutic community ward. A questionnaire was
devised and responses factor-analysed. The principal factor to emer-

ge was labelled 'Social Openness and Ward Involvement', which was seen to epitomize the values of the ward. In a subsequent study (1969a), patients completed the questionnaire at repeated intervals during treatment. Over time, they manifested an increased belief in personal responsibility and the desirability of exposing personal problems. They rejected the denial of problems, and social isolation and withdrawal.

Almond et al. (1969b) also studied the relationship between acculturation and improvement. Staff provided ongoing ratings of the patients' involvement and behaviour, and retrospective ratings of improvement. In general, ratings of improvement were significantly correlated with acculturation, whereas behavioural indices were not. The authors performed 'cross' correlations, correlating behaviour at admission with values at discharge, and values at admission with behaviour at discharge. The former correlation was significantly greater than the latter. Almond et al. therefore suggest that initial values are not a critical determinant of behaviour change, but rather that role-playing of approved behaviour will lead to subsequent value-change and improvement. This appears to conflict with Rapoport's suggestion that compliant responders, who have not genuinely adopted unit values, will be less likely to improve. However, Almond et al. were concerned with compliance which preceded value-change, whereas Rapoport was referring to those who never fully accepted unit values. It is possible that initial compliance with therapeutic norms is constructive, whereas sustained compliance will preclude any enduring therapeutic benefit.

These studies indicate that there is some relationship between the adoption of therapeutic community values and improvement, although the direction of causation remains unclear. Attitude research is characterized by methodological problems. Ratings of another's values (e.g. A. W. Clark, 1967a) must be inferential, and are probably not a valid index, while self-report measures (e.g. Rapoport, 1960) are open to the influence of social desirability. Behavioural measures of participation may therefore provide a more reliable and valid index of the patient's involvement in the community.

The relationship between participation and improvement

Therapeutic community ideology allows considerable variation in the extent to which patients participate in the treatment. The therapy is not dispensed, but is there for them to make use of if they choose or are able to do so. If it is potentially effective, then those who participate more actively in the community should gain the greatest benefit.

Whiteley (1970) assessed patients' involvement in a community from case records, and compared this with outcome as assessed at follow-up interviews. There was a tendency for the better outcome group to have been more positively involved in the community, whereas the poor outcome group were negatively involved or indifferent.

Gillis (1960) found a significant correlation between clinicians' ratings of patients' participation and improvement. He does not argue that there is a causal relationship between the two, but rather that participation is a legitimate index of clinical condition.

Such a conceptualization does, however, neglect the possible therapeutic function of participation. Daniels and Rubin (1968) compared ratings of participation in community meetings with clinical condition and subsequent outcome. There was a low correlation between chronicity and degree of participation, but this alone did not account for the obtained relation between participation and improvement. Daniels and Rubin therefore propose a simple positive feedback model, in which the patient gets better because he participates, and participates more as he improves. A. W. Clark (1967b) provides a more elaborate model of this process. Five surveys were conducted at four-monthly intervals, when all members of the unit rated each other on measures of involvement and improvement. The two were significantly correlated, and scalogram analysis indicated that participation followed a trend over time. Patients initially became involved in social activities and dyadic relationships, adopted a favourable attitude toward the unit, became fully involved in group therapy, and then improved. Clark therefore suggests that participation precedes improvement in time, although there is no definite evidence of a causal relationship between the two.

Participation in a therapeutic community therefore seems to be both a sign of social adjustment, and a precursor of therapeutic change. Again, these findings suggest that those with some capacity for social involvement will be more able to use and benefit from therapeutic resources.

Therapeutic components of the programme

Given that there seems to be some relationship between participation in a therapeutic community and improvement, then it is important to consider what aspects of the programme effect therapeutic change.

Comparing patients in a therapeutic community with those in traditional hospitals, Caine and Smail (1969) found that the former attributed change to relationships within the hospital and to meeting others like themselves, while the conventional treatment group cited drugs and the rest and relief from responsibility which hospitalization offered.

Steinfeld and Mabli (1974) employed Yalom's (1970) Curative Factor Q-sort to assess the benefits accruing from various aspects of a therapeutic community programme. The fundamental aspects of the programme's philosophy, responsibility, insight and honesty, were verbalized by residents as being most important. One problem with Yalom's measures is that values are confused with therapeutic mechanisms. It is impossible to ascertain whether these values had the role of curative factors, or whether this is simply a study of acculturation.

Krausova and Hemsley (1976) questioned patients at discharge about the relative usefulness of the various helping agencies in the community. Patients evaluated the doctor as the most helpful, with groups and occupational therapy perceived as less important. Rapoport (1960) found that the majority of patients cited a senior staff member as the most helpful person, and those who identified with a senior staff member were more likely to improve.

In contrast A. W. Clark and Yeomans (1969) found that patients who improved valued group therapy most highly at discharge, while those who failed to improve valued doctors more highly. On admission, patients had generally expected themselves and doctors to be the most important sources of treatment. In Ferguson and Carney's (1970) study, patients found nurses the most helpful staff members. In this community, nurses represented the constant core group of staff, with others serving only a peripheral function. This suggests that patients' preferences can only be understood with respect to the specific social context. Status does not guarantee therapeutic efficacy, particularly if doctors do not have sustained contact with patients. Patients' preferences may change over time, and this would be obscured by cross-sectional studies.

Evaluating the various groups within the community, Rapoport (1960) found that staff and patients agreed about the utility of 'small' groups, and this finding was replicated by Manning (1976) in the same community. These groups were led by doctors, and emphasized verbal communication. Manning infers that this is indicative of a subversion of therapeutic community ideology and the replacement of sociotherapy by psychotherapy. While the ideology advocates communalism and the flattening of the status hierarchy, it seems that patients still value intensive interaction with staff members. It is important to acknowledge that groups may need leaders and experts, and that the notion of a leaderless community might be naive. However, it may be that small groups represent a salient aspect of the therapeutic programme, but that other activities are a necessary precursor of full therapeutic participation, as A. W. Clark's (1967b) study suggests.

There is some evidence that friendships with other patients play a role in the therapeutic process. A. W. Clark (1967a) found that positive ties with other patients and acceptance by other patients were correlated with improvement. Rapoport (1960) found that 28 per cent of those with no friends improved, compared with 80 per cent of those with one or two friends and 95 per cent of those with three or more friends. In addition, 74 per cent of those whose best friend improved, also improved themselves, compared with 48 per cent of those whose best friend did not improve. Although friendships may simply reflect a patient's level of adjustment, it is possible that they also contribute to the gains which are derived from the community.

Therapeutic community treatment appears to compare favourably with traditional psychiatric treatment, at least for those patients who already have some capacity for social involvement. Those patients who adopt the community ideology, participate actively in the community, and form close relationships, are those who improve. This presupposes an initial level of social adjustment which may be lacking in severely withdrawn, disturbed, or aggressive patients.

While involvement is related to improvement, Rapoport's (1960) study offers a cautionary observation: patients must eventually negotiate the transition from the community to the social world, and some fail to maintain the benefit they have derived and to generalize the effects of therapy to other social relationships. Kennard et al. (1977) found that patients who had little or no contact with a community after discharge saw themselves, and were seen by others, as less 'pleasant' but also less 'ill' than those who continued more regular contact. The intensity of such a programme may enhance its therapeutic potential, but it also poses problems when patients must leave. If an individual is to establish his autonomy, he may need temporarily to reject the community and be seen as less pleasant. For some, this may be a hazardous process.

Family therapy, in working with natural social groups, may diminish this particular problem.

Family therapy

Family therapy has developed as a method of intervention over the last three decades. Its sources include the application of psychoanalytic concepts to the patient's family network (Skynner, 1976), attempts to develop a new understanding of schizophrenic behaviour by analysing the communication patterns within the patient's social context (Laing and Esterson, 1964; Bateson et al., 1956; Lidz et al., 1965), and attempts to find ways of working with disadvantaged minority groups (Minuchin et al., 1967). Guerin (1976) and Skynner (1976) provide histories of the development of the various schools of practice. Many social workers have always seen the family as the central focus of their efforts to facilitate change. Some workers, probation officers for example, have had statutory obligations to be involved in the client's home background. Indeed, working with the whole family is a central premise of the philosophy of the Seebohm Report upon which the current organization of Social Service departments is based.

What then is 'family therapy'? If the term means anything, it refers to those methods of intervention which are based on analysing the family as a system. The underlying theoretical assumptions are that the behaviour of individuals is reciprocally linked to that of others in the immediate family network. The 'identified patient's' symptoms are understood as a product of this system, rather than solely in terms of his or her intrinsic physical or psychic make-up. There is a basic conceptual shift from focusing on the individual to seeing him or her as part of a whole which is greater than the sum of its parts. This application of systems theory is perhaps the only generic theoretical assumption of family therapy, but it is no less significant for that (Bertalanffy, 1975). Haley points out that not everybody in the field makes this change in their thinking but argues that it is of great significance, as great as removing the earth from the centre of our model of the universe (Haley, 1971, 1977, 1979).

The other treatment methods discussed in this chapter are the antithesis of this definition of the family therapy approach since they, like other forms of psychotherapy, reinforce the idea of the 'identified patient' as being, or having, 'the problem'. However, the field contains a broad spectrum of theory and practice and some workers would see family work as but one strategy for helping individuals to change. The major research reviews in the field accept definitions of family therapy that specify attempts to change the whole family system. This broad definition is also used here.

The volume and quality of outcome research has increased over the last decade. Earlier reviews quoted the sparseness and inadequacy of the validation of family therapy (Wells et al., 1972) but more recently extensive and detailed summaries of this area have been able to draw on over two hundred studies (Gurman and Kniskern, 1978b; De Witt, 1978; Wells and Dezen, 1978). Only part of the research has concentrated on outcome. Others have directed their effort toward unravelling the relationship between family interaction and the presenting behaviour problems or symptoms (Riskin and Faunce, 1972; Jacob, 1975; Watzlawick and Weakland, 1977).

Outcome studies: an overview

At the beginning of this chapter it was pointed out that 'group psychotherapy has been used to describe a wide variety of procedures' and this is true of family therapy. Goals, means and basic views of behaviour and mankind all vary within the field. Against this background extreme caution must be applied to general conclusions about the efficacy of family therapy *per se*. The extensive reviews which have been published recently acknowledge these difficulties but present us with an overview of the 'outcome' scene to date.

Working from a definition of family therapy which specifies conjoint intervention (i.e. working with a group of family members from at least two generations), De Witt (1978) reviews thirty-one studies. Twenty-three of these are without comparison groups and show similar results to those seen in individual therapy outcome research. Of the eight studies with comparison groups, conjoint family therapy was shown to be superior to no treatment in five, while the remaining three showed it to be superior to non-conjoint methods.

Wells and Dezen (1978) look at the outcome research of family therapy defined in systems terms but specifically exclude behavioural approaches. They conclude from the uncontrolled single-group studies reviewed that two programmes can be identified which demonstrate strong treatment effects. These are the McMaster University and Philadelphia Child Guidance Clinic studies. They consider the results of the controlled studies to be disappointing, identifying methodological shortcomings in many of them.

Three of the controlled studies they do consider adequate (Coufal, 1975; Ginsberg, 1971; Vogelsong, 1975) focus on Parent-Adolescent Relationship Training (PARD). This is a structured training programme, designed to improve communication and the relationship in parent-child dyads. Although the research indicates good results, it cannot be considered family therapy in the full sense of focusing on the whole system. The other controlled studies are the same as those included by Gurman and Kniskern (1978b) and are discussed below.

Following their discussion of the research they conclude:

> At a very broad level it is apparent that family therapy has been legitimised. As a means of delivering helping services, family therapy can no longer be viewed as a rank newcomer of uncertain validity and doubtful status. Both the methodologically adequate studies and certain of the studies judged to be methodologically inadequate contribute to this general legitimising effect. (Wells and Dezen, 1978, p. 266)

The modesty of these conclusions is challenged by Gurman and Kniskern (1978a). They point out the dangers of using conventional criteria for research designs when assessing change in family intervention characterized by interactional systems thinking. Specifically they accuse Wells and Dezen of 'technolatry' and 'methodolatry'. By 'technolatry' they refer to focusing on the technology of family therapy at the expense of looking at therapist characteristics, as if they could be divorced. Thus, they say, Wells and Dezen miss the basic common principle of family therapy, that all behaviour including therapy occurs in an interactional context. 'Methodolatry' is defined as: 'the tendency in worshipping traditional methodology, to let the research methods dictate what are proper data'. In short they suggest that family therapy research needs new and specifically designed multi-dimensional outcome measures.

Gurman and Kniskern (1978b) provide the most comprehensive review of the field to date. They identify eleven studies which contain sixteen comparisons of family therapy with no-treatment controls. Of these studies, eight were considered to be of good or very good design. Two (Reiter and Kilmann, 1975; Stover and Guerney, 1967) focused on treating parents although they used measures of other family change. Although these studies demonstrate that their treatment is superior to control they must be considered marginal to family therapy as defined here. Garrigan and Bambrick (1975, 1977) in two studies use a variety of outcome measures to study the impact of conjoint family therapy with emotionally disturbed adolescents. In the first study they report significant improvement of the interpersonal functioning of the family as perceived by the identified client, but no difference between treatment and control groups on measures of behaviour symptoms. However in the second study, which used ten therapy sessions instead of six, more positive results were recorded. The treatment group showed a reduction in the identified clients' behaviour symptoms in the classroom and at home, and the marital relationship showed an improvement in empathic understanding and congruence.

Katz el al. (1975) found that their treatment group, in which families of moderately disturbed adolescents or children received short-term family therapy, appeared to have improved more than controls on one dimension of family interaction. This was the appropriateness of topic changes within the families' conversations. However, Wells and Dezen (1978) have pointed out that this result is really no better than can be expected by chance.

Stanton and Todd (1976) worked with hard-core heroin addicts. They compared four groups over ten sessions. Two groups received structural family therapy based on Minuchin's approach (see p.136). In one of these groups the family was paid for attending and received a bonus if the addict achieved a drug-free week. One group received an attention placebo (the family met at the clinic and watched anthropological films, which hardly satisfies normal definitions of placebo or blind procedures). The remaining group was designated as a control group. In fact all four groups continued to receive the clinic's normal range of services including group and occupational therapy, detoxification, methadone maintenance and urine analysis. The identified patients' heroin use and work or school adjustment were measured at a six-month follow-up. By both criteria the paid family therapy group produced the best results. The non-paid therapy group was also superior to the placebo and control groups. Although this study provides clear indications of the efficacy of structural family therapy with this notoriously difficult client group, these results are confused by the complex array of variables employed. These workers have continued to develop a family systems approach in combination with other treatment strategies for drug abuse (Stanton, 1979).

Studies by Alexander and Parsons (1973) and Klein (1977) demonstrate better results for a 'behavioural system' family therapy than 'client-centred', 'eclectic-dynamic' family approaches and the control group. These studies are considered in more detail below.

Gurman and Kniskern conclude their review as follows: 'Family therapy appears to be at least as effective and possibly more effective than individual therapy for a wide variety of problems, both apparent "individual" difficulties and more obvious family conflicts' (p.883). They go on to identify certain clinical goals and problems for which specific strategies of family therapy offer the treatment of choice. These are anorexia and other psychosomatic disorders, childhood behaviour problems, decreasing hospitalization rates and juvenile delinquency. However, they caution that current research would not justify new workers being trained exclusively in family therapy techniques. They also warn that like other forms of intervention, family therapy can cause harm and that the deterioration effect seems to be related to therapist and therapist–patient variables.

These reviews demonstrate that within the field of family therapy there are effective treatment approaches. They also suggest that harm can be done in attempting to help in this way, and that many studies failed to identify positive effects of family therapy. Thus it would be folly to assume that their conclusions supported all or even most practices described as family therapy. Truax and Mitchell (1971) have argued that much individual psychotherapy research needs to be redone because the *process* of therapy had been assumed rather than analysed, evaluated and related to outcome. The family therapy research field seems to be in the middle of relearning this point. The following research programmes have identified positive outcomes and described the treatment procedures in fuller detail. They are also

programmes where all the indications are that the treatment procedures were actually followed even though process measures were
not always rigorously applied.

Outcome studies with more specific detail

The families of delinquent teenagers have been the focus of workers
from the University of Utah. These were 'soft' delinquents, that is
adolescents who were running away, described as ungovernable,
truanting, taking soft drugs, etc., although subsequent follow-up
studies investigated *any* contact of child or siblings with the juvenile
court. Their treatment method has been variously described as Short
Term Family Crisis, Family Systems and System–Behavioural Intervention.

The treatment and therapist training programmes described involve clearly defined interventions designed to change family interaction
patterns (Alexander and Parsons, 1973; Parsons and Alexander,
1973; Malouf and Alexander, 1974). The interventions are directed
towards greater clarity and precision of communication and social
reinforcement of changes in behaviour. The rights and responsi-
bilities of all family members are stressed and contracts for change
negotiated on a reciprocal basis.

The overall research design is impressively comprehensive. First,
a study of the interaction in families of delinquent and non-delinquent
children and adolescents was made. Goals for changing the interaction were based on the findings (Parsons and Alexander, 1973). The
treatment was then applied to a randomly selected group. Other
groups were assigned to a client-centred (i.e. Rogerian) family
programme, a psychodynamic-eclectic (i.e. interpretive) family programme and a no-treatment group to control for the effects
of maturation and professional attention. Change in the family
behaviour, as measured on three interaction measures, was significant in the family-systems treatment group. The outcome of the
groups were also tested at six and eighteen months by comparing
recidivism rates for the identified delinquents. The therapy group
demonstrated recidivism rates which were 50–66 per cent lower than
the other groups. This reduction in recidivism was also shown to
be related to changes in family process (Alexander and Parsons,
1973).

One of the arguments for family therapy is that it influences the
whole network and needs to do so because the symptoms are a

product of this system. This line of argument has been used to explain the short-term effect of delinquency prevention programmes which focus on the individual. A further follow-up study was carried out to test the durability of the changes produced in the families, and to check the preventative value of the family-systems approach. Juvenile court records were examined to obtain court referrals for siblings of the initially referred delinquents. Only 20 per cent of families in the treatment group had siblings subsequently appearing at court, whereas 40 per cent of no-treatment contacts and 50 per cent and 63 per cent of the families receiving alternative treatment conditions had siblings in contact with the court (Klein et al., 1977). Gurman and Kniskern (1978b) while acknowledging that these are some of the best outcomes results reported in the field, caution that they do apply to 'soft' delinquency and that 70 per cent of the sample were Mormons, who might be a particularly receptive group because of the stress they lay on family ties.

The programme at McMaster University in Canada has produced outcome figures for 279 families with children or adolescents who were identified as having academic and/or behavioural problems at school. These were treated with a short-term systems-oriented family therapy model which outlines 'assessment', 'contract negotiation', 'treatment' and 'closure' stages of therapy. During this process, goals and expectations are explored and the therapist negotiates tasks which the family are to report back on at the next session. Treatment is ended when all goals and expectations are met. The therapist operates on the McMaster Model of Family Functioning which aims at clarifying problems, negotiating achievable goals and expectations and evaluating and reinforcing task performance (Epstein et al., 1977).

A range of therapist and client variables were researched as well as outcome, using multiple measures. These measures were applied at termination of treatment and at a six-month follow-up. They included therapist and client improvement ratings, goal attainment scaling assessed by independent observers, and recidivism. 70 per cent of families had no further professional contact and 64 per cent attained or exceeded their goals. The more subjective measure produced even stronger results, 74 per cent of therapists and clients rating the family as having improved at termination. The weakness of the programme is the absence of controls or alternative treatment groups (Woodward et al., 1974; Epstein et al., 1977; Woodward et al., 1978).

Structural family therapy has been developed at the Philadelphia Child Guidance Clinic under the directorship of Salvador Minuchin (1974). Their most recently published work on anorexics and asthmatics (Minuchin et al., 1975; Rosman et al., 1976) reports improvements of between 83 per cent to 100 per cent of identified patients. The application of this approach to families of heroin addicts has already been discussed (Stanton and Todd, 1976). No control groups are used (except by Stanton and Todd) but as Gurman and Kniskern (1978b) point out these methodological shortcomings must be seen in the context of the life-threatening conditions being treated. These studies also use the most objective of outcome criteria such as weight gain, blood sugar levels and respiratory functioning, although they do not use family interaction measures.

Structural family therapy places emphasis on intervening in the repetitious patterns of behaviour while the family are encouraged to enact their problems in the treatment session. For instance, families with an anorexic member are typically assessed over a meal. The worker 'joins' the system before attempting to influence the boundaries which delineate, or fail to delineate, the family's various subsystems and coalitions. By being both 'participant' and 'observer' in the family system the therapist attempts to restructure those family patterns of relationships which perpetuate the symptomatic behaviour (Minuchin, 1974). Wells and Dezen (1978), while noting the lack of controls or comparisons in these studies, point out that their data can be seen as a direct replication series of single-case experiments, a type of experimental design which they advocate. Within the research design limitations, the Philadelphia group present the strongest indications to date for the success of family group interventions.

Variables influencing outcome

Gurman and Kniskern (1978b) review the evidence on the various therapist, client and situational variables which influence outcome. Short-term and time-limited therapies provide the clearest significant situational variable. These approaches seem to be as successful as open-ended therapy. This conclusion is supported by findings which indicate that where there is no time limit, most of the positive results are achieved in less than five months. The presence of the father is another factor which is found to play a major role in treatment where a child or adolescent is the identified patient.

Perhaps the most important variables are those related to the therapist and to the patient–therapist relationship. The work of Truax and Carkhuff (1967) and others in individual therapy has highlighted the significance of therapist behaviour. In a treatment method where intervention is specifically designed to change reciprocal behaviour patterns it is hardly surprising that the therapist's own behaviour is highly significant. Gurman and Kniskern's (1978b) review emphasizes this point: 'therapist factors that contribute to both improvement and deterioration in individual psychotherapy are equally powerful in the treatment of relationships' (p.884). They go on to point out that the impact of relationship skills has major importance regardless of the 'school' of therapy applied, and recommend that training should foster these as well as conceptual-technical skills.

The Philadelphia Child Guidance Clinic studies have not researched therapist variables. However, Minuchin stresses the need for therapists to develop their 'joining' and 'tracking' skills, behaviours which seem closely allied to accurate empathy, warmth and genuineness (Minuchin, 1974). The McMaster programme was one of those which identified therapist behaviour skills as being significant (Woodward et al., 1975, 1977). Alexander et al. (1976) have published later research in which they conclude:

> It was expected that the therapist skills of greatest consequence to outcome would be those emphasized in (their own) training manuals ... and formal descriptions of the model. ... These skills have been depicted as the more technical or structural dimensions of a modification technology.
>
> Instead, it was the global quality of relationship skills that made the most significant contribution to outcome variance. (p.662)

The original hope that specific family behaviour patterns would be identified which related to particular symptoms or presenting problems has been largely unfulfilled (Jacob, 1975; Watzlawick and Weakland, 1977). None the less the field has already provided therapists with a variety of concepts and models for analysing family interaction. The Mental Research Institute at Palo Alto has influenced many, if not all family therapists (Bateson et al., 1956;

Watzlawick et al., 1974; Watzlawick and Weakland, 1977). Their research has led to Haley's Problem Solving Therapy (Haley, 1977) and other 'strategic' approaches. Mention should also be made of the Palo Alto group's own therapy outcome study which reported promising results (Weakland et al., 1974). This approach builds on double-bind theory and develops the use of therapeutic paradoxes to shift families into new ways of behaving and problem resolution. Wells and Dezen (1978) criticize the research methods used in this study because other forms of treatment obscure the singular effect of the therapy.

Conclusion

This chapter has been concerned with different ways of utilizing the interrelationships between people to effect therapeutic change in those seen to be clinically disturbed. Groups may simply be construed as a context in which to deal with the problems of individuals in a manner which is more economical than individual therapy, and which allows the possibility of vicarious learning. Generally, though, in group therapy, the relationships between patients or clients are seen to be potentially constructive. By definition, both 'true' therapeutic communities and family therapy focus on effecting change in the relationships *between* individuals, rather than on effecting purely intrapsychic or intrapersonal changes within the context of some contrived or natural social group.

The evaluation of the effects of such treatments is beset by the methodological problems characteristic of any psychotherapy research. If they are to do justice to the treatment, outcome criteria should be tailored to the aims of the particular therapy; however, comparisons between this and other treatments are then hindered. With severely disturbed patients, the use of no-treatment or waiting list control groups becomes increasingly impractical and unethical. There are many other factors which may confound the effects of the therapy such as the concurrent use of drugs or hospitalization. Out-patients or day patients are also likely to have access to numerous sources of help within the community, which may supplement the formal treatment.

It would be fallacious to assume that any of the therapies discussed in this chapter are uniform phenomena. The orientation of therapists, their personal qualities and skills, and the duration and organization of treatment certainly vary widely. In group therapy and therapeutic communities, where patients are seen to be treated, at least in part, by each other, the impact of individual therapists may be lessened. The composition of the group will then be a crucial variable. In family therapy, in which the therapist is the principal agent of change, the qualities of individual therapists are seen to be more significant. Thus a term such as 'group therapy' embraces a multitude of relationships and activities.

Despite these methodological problems, the studies reviewed in this chapter provide considerable evidence for the potential efficacy of groups in clinical contexts. One important conceptual distinction between group therapy, therapeutic communities and family therapy has been suggested: the former identify individuals as being in need of treatment, while family therapy aims to effect change in systems of relationships. While these systems comprise individuals, they are perceived to have some functional identity and dynamics.

Therapeutic communities differ from group and family therapy in that the treatment is continuous and sustained, and may entail participation in a range of therapeutic groups, including in some cases family groups. This has led to therapeutic communities being construed as a multi-faceted metatreatment.

Aside from these conceptual differences between the treatments and their specific practical characteristics, the studies reviewed in this chapter provide some evidence that they may be suitable for different clients or patients.

Neither group therapy nor therapeutic community treatment alone appears to be the optimal method of treatment for severely disturbed schizophrenic patients. The efficacy of psychotropic drugs with such patients is indisputable, and has to some extent reduced the need to develop appropriate psychotherapeutic techniques. Groups seem to have some potential for enhancing social skills and integration, but do not alone constitute an efficient remedy. Such patients seem to have little capacity to benefit from, or even endure, intensive or interpretive therapy, and Fairweather et al. (1960) found that some psychotics deteriorated with such treatment.

The merit of group therapy and therapeutic community treatment with neurotic patients has been reasonably well-demonstrated, although considerable ambiguity remains as to the relative usefulness of behavioural and non-behavioural approaches. Psychoanalytically-oriented approaches appear less promising, on the data available. Of the studies with children it again appears that both behavioural and non-behavioural approaches may be fruitful, except in the case of older children with classroom behaviour problems. Such problems are most typically a function of social deviancy. If deviancy is defined, and perhaps created and sustained, by the individual's social environment, then it need come as no surprise that treatments which approach the problems of the individual out of context are less likely to achieve lasting effects. Some of the most promising results of family therapy are achieved with the families of socially deviant patients, which fits in with this line of thinking.

Research throughout this broad field is impeded by three continuing problems. These are the inadequacy of many change measures, the failure to describe precisely what particular therapists actually do, and the difficulty of obtaining adequate control or comparison groups. Greater progress in linking specific change to specific types of group treatment is most likely to come through studies which achieve more sophistication in each of these areas.

Note

We are grateful to Herbert Pollack for his comments on an early draft of this chapter.

References

Abramowitz, C. V. (1976) The effectiveness of group psychotherapy with children. *Archives of General Psychiatry 33*: 320–6.

Alexander, J. F., Barton, C., Schiavo, R. S. and Parsons, B. V. (1976) Systems–behavioural intervention with families of delinquents: therapist characteristics, family behaviour and outcome. *Journal of Consulting and Clinical Psychology 44* (4): 656–64.

Alexander, J. F. and Parsons, B. V. (1973) Short-term behavioural intervention with delinquent families: impact on family process and recidivism. *Journal of Abnormal Psychology 81* (3): 219–25.

Almond, R., Keniston, K. and Boltax, S. (1968) The value system of a milieu therapy unit. *Archives of General Psychiatry 19*: 545–61.

Almond, R., Keniston, K. and Boltax, S. (1969a) Milieu therapeutic process. *Archives of General Psychiatry 21*: 432–42.

Almond, R., Keniston, K. and Boltax, S. (1969b) Patient value change in milieu therapy. *Archives of General Psychiatry 20*: 339–51.

Anker, J. M. and Walsh, R. P. (1961) Group psychotherapy, a special activity program and group structure in the treatment of chronic schizophrenics. *Journal of Consulting Psychology 25*: 476–81.

Auerbach, R. and Kilmann, P. R. (1977) The effects of group systematic desensitisation on secondary erectile failure. *Behavior Therapy 8*: 330–9.

Baehr, G. O. (1954) The comparative effectiveness of individual psychotherapy, group psychotherapy and a combination of these methods. *Journal of Consulting Psychology 13*: 179–83.

Bailey, K. G. (1970) Audiotape self-confrontation in group psychotherapy. *Psychological Reports 27*: 439–44.

Barcai, A. and Robinson, E. H. (1969) Conventional group therapy with pre-adolescent children. *International Journal of Group Psychotherapy 19*: 334–45.

Barcai, A., Umbarger, C., Pierce, T. W. and Chamberlain, P. (1973) A comparison of three group approaches to underachieving children. *American Journal of Orthopsychiatry 43*: 133–41.

Barron, F. and Leary, T. F. (1955) Changes in psychoneurotic patients with and without psychotherapy. *Journal of Consulting Psychology 19*: 239–45.

Bateson, G., Jackson, D., Haley, J. and Weakland, J. (1956) Towards a theory of schizophrenia. *Behavioral Science 1*: 251–64.

Bertalanffy, L. von (1975) General system theory and psychiatry. In S. Arieti (ed.) *American Handbook of Psychiatry*, vol. 3, 2nd ed. New York: Basic Books.

Boe, E. E., Gocka, E. F. and Kogan, W. S. (1966) The effect of group psychotherapy on the interpersonal perceptions of psychiatric patients. *Multivariate Behavior Research 1*: 177–87.

Bornstein, P. H. and Sipprelle, C. N. (1973) Group treatment of obesity by induced anxiety. *Behavior Research and Therapy 11*: 339–41.

Borowski, T. and Tolwinski, T. (1969) Treatment of paranoid schizophrenics with Chlorpromazine and group therapy. *Diseases of the Nervous System 30:* 201–2.

Bovill, D. (1972) A trial of group psychotherapy for neurotics. *British Journal of Psychiatry 120*: 285–92.

Bovill, D. (1977) An outcome study of group psychotherapy. *British Journal of Psychiatry 131*: 95–8.

Cadman, W. H., Misbach, L. and Brown, D. V. (1954) An assessment of round-table psychotherapy. *Psychological Monographs 68* (384): 1–48.

Caine, T. M. (1965) Changes in symptom, attitude and trait measures among chronic neurotics in a therapeutic community. In G. A. Foulds (ed.) *Personality and Personal Illness*. London:Tavistock.

Caine, T. M. and Smail, D. J. (1969) *The Treatment of Mental Illness*. London: University of London Press.

Claghorn, J. L., Johnstone, E. E., Cook, T. H. and Itschner, L. (1974) Group therapy and maintenance treatment of schizophrenics. *Archives of General Psychiatry 31*: 361–5.

Clark, A. W. (1967a) Conditions influencing patients' response to treatment in a therapeutic community. *Social Science and Medicine 1*: 309–19.

Clark, A. W. (1967b) Patient participation and improvement in a therapeutic community. *Human Relations 20*: 259–71.

Clark, A. W. (1968) The personality and social network adjustment scale: its use in the evaluation of treatment in a therapeutic community. *Human Relations 21*: 85–95.

Clark, A. W. and Yeomans, N. T. (1969) *Fraser House: Theory, Practice and Evaluation of a Therapeutic Community*. New York: Springer.

Clark, D. H (1965) The therapeutic community – concept, practice and future. *British Journal of Psychiatry 111*: 947–54.

Clark, D. H., Hooper, D. F. and Oram, E. G. (1962) Creating a therapeutic community in a psychiatric ward. *Human Relations 15*: 123–47.

Clement, P. W. Fazzone, R. A. and Goldstein, B. (1970) Tangible reinforcers and child group therapy. *American Academy of Child Psychiatry 9*: 409–27.

Clement, P. W. and Milne, D. O. (1967) Group play therapy and tangible reinforcers used to modify the behavior of 8-year-old boys. *Behaviour Research and Therapy 5*: 301–12.

Coons, W. H. (1957) Interaction and insight in group psychotherapy. *Canadian Journal of Psychology 11*: 1–8.

Coufal, J. D. (1975) Preventive-therapeutic programs for mothers and adolescent daughters: skills training versus discussion methods. Unpublished PhD dissertation, Pennsylvania State University.

Cowden, R. C., Zax, M., Hague, J. R. and Finney, R. C. (1956) Chlorpromazine: alone and as an adjunct to group psychotherapy in the treatment of psychiatric patients. *American Journal of Psychiatry 112*: 898–902.

Cowden, R. C., Zax, M. and Sproles, J. A. (1956) Group psychotherapy in conjuction with a physical treatment. *Journal of Clinical Psychology 12*: 53–6.

Daniels, D. N. and Rubin, R. S. (1968) The community meeting – an analytical study and a theoretical statement. *Archives of General Psychiatry 18*: 60–75.

Dawley, H. H. Jr and Wenrich, W. W. (1973) Group implosive therapy in the treatment of test anxiety: a brief report. *Behavior Therapy 4*: 261–3.

De Witt, K. N. (1978) The effectiveness of family therapy. *Archives of General Psychiatry 35*: 549–61.

Donovan, W. B., and Marvit, R. C. (1970) Alienation-reduction in brief group therapy. *American Journal of Psychiatry 127*: 825–7.

Ends, E. J. and Page, C. W. (1957) A study of three types of group psychotherapy with hospitalised male inebriates. *Quarterly Journal of Studies on Alcohol 18*: 263–77.

Ends, E. J. and Page, C. W. (1959) Group psychotherapy and concomitant psychological change. *Psychological Monographs 73* (480): 1–31.

Epstein, N. B., Bishop, D. S. and Levin, S. (1977) McMaster Model of Family Functioning: the McMaster Family Therapy Treatment Model. Unpublished papers from McMaster University, Hamilton, Ontario.

Fairweather, G. W. and Simon, R. (1963) A further follow-up comparison of psychotherapeutic programs. *Journal of Consulting Psychology 27*:186.

Fairweather, G. W., Simon, R., Gebhard, M. E., Weingarten, E., Holland, J. L., Sanders, R., Stone, G. B. and Reahl, J. E. (1960) Relative effectiveness of psychotherapeutic programs: a multi-criteria comparison of four programs for three different patient groups. *Psychological Monographs 74* (492): 1–26.

Falloon, I. R. H., Lindley, P., McDonald, R. and Marks, I. M. (1977)

Social skills training of out-patient groups. *British Journal of Psychiatry 131*: 599–609.

Feder, B. (1962) Limited goals in short-term group psychotherapy with institutionalised delinquent adolescent boys. *International Journal of Group Psychotherapy 12*: 503–7.

Feifel, H. and Schwartz, A. D. (1953) Group psychotherapy with acutely disturbed psychotic patients. *Journal of Consulting Psychology 17*: 113–21.

Felton, G. S. and Biggs, B. E. (1972) Teaching internalisation behavior to collegiate low achievers in group psychotherapy. *Psychotherapy: Theory, Research, Practice 9*: 281–3.

Felton, G. S. and Biggs, B. E. (1973) Psychotherapy and responsibility: teaching internalisation behavior to black low achievers through group psychotherapy. *Small Group Behavior 4*: 147–56.

Ferguson, R. S. and Carney, M. W. P. (1970) Interpersonal considerations and judgments in a day hospital. *British Journal of Psychiatry 117*: 397–403.

Fisher, B. (1953) Group therapy with retarded readers. *Journal of Educational Psychology 6*: 354–60.

Garrigan, J. and Bambrick, A. (1975) Short term family therapy with emotionally disturbed children. *Journal of Marriage and Family Counseling 1*: 379–85.

Garrigan, J. and Bambrick, A. (1977) Family therapy for disturbed children: some experimental results in special education. *Journal of Marriage and Family Counseling 3*: 83–93.

Gelder, M. G., Marks, I. M., Wolff, H. H. and Clarke, M. (1967) Desensitisation and psychotherapy in the treatment of phobic states: a controlled enquiry. *British Journal of Psychiatry 113*: 53–73.

Gillis, L. (1960) Participation – its measurement and relationship to clinical change in psychiatric illness. *International Journal of Social Psychiatry 6*: 288–301.

Ginsberg, B. G. (1971) Parent-adolescent relationship development: A therapeutic and preventative mental health program. Unpublished PhD dissertation, Pennsylvania State University.

Guerin, P. J. (1976) *Family Therapy: Theory and Practice*. New York: Gardner Press.

Gurman, A. S. and Kniskern, D. P. (1978a) Technolatry, methodolatry, and the results of family therapy. *Family Process 17*: 275–81.

Gurman, A. S. and Kniskern, D. P. (1978b) Research on marital and family therapy: progress, perspective and prospect. In S. Garfield and A. E. Bergin (eds) *Handbook of Psychotherapy and Behaviour Change*, 2nd ed. New York: John Wiley.

Hagen, R. I. (1974) Group therapy versus bibliotherapy in weight reduction. *Behaviour Therapy 5*: 222–34.

Haley, J. (ed.) (1971) *Changing Families*. New York: Grune and Stratton.

Haley, J. (1977) *Problem Solving Therapy: New Strategies for Effective Family Therapy*. San Francisco: Jossey-Bass Publishers.

Haley, J. (1979) Ideas that handicap therapy with young people. *Family Therapy 1*: 29–45.

Hansen, J. C., Niland, T. M. and Zani, L. P. (1969) Model reinforcement in group counseling with elementary school children. *Personnel and Guidance Journal 47*: 741–4.

Haven, G. A. and Wood, B. S. (1970) The effectiveness of eclectic group psychotherapy in reducing recidivism in hospitalised patients. *Psychotherapy: Theory, Research, Practice 7*: 153–4.

Herz, M. I., Spitzer, R. L., Gibbon, M., Greenspan, K. and Reibel, S. (1974) Individual versus group aftercare treatment. *American Journal of Psychiatry 131*: 808–12.

Hinds, W. C. and Roehlke, H. J. (1970) A learning theory approach to group counseling with elementary school children. *Journal of Counseling Psychology 17*: 49–55.

Imber, S. D., Frank, J. D., Nash, E. H., Stone, A. R. and Gliedman, L. H. (1957) Improvement and amount of therapeutic contact: an alternative to the use of no-treatment controls in psychotherapy. *Journal of Consulting Psychology 21*: 309–15.

Irwin, E., Levy, P. and Shapiro, M. (1972) Assessment of drama therapy in a child guidance setting. *Group Psychotherapy and Psychodrama 25*: 105–16.

Jacob, T. (1975) Family interaction in disturbed and normal families: A methodological and substantive review. *Psychological Bulletin 82* (1): 33–65.

Jew, C. C., Clanon, T. L. and Mattocks, A. L. (1972) The effectiveness of group psychotherapy in a correctional institution. *American Journal of Psychiatry 129*: 602–5.

Jones, M. (1953) *The Therapeutic Community*. New York: Basic Books.

Jones, M. (1962) *Social Psychiatry*. Springfield, Illinois: Charles C. Thomas.

Katz, A., Krasinski, M., Phillip, E. and Wieser, C. (1975) Change in interactions as a measure of effectiveness in short term family therapy. *Family Process 2*: 31–56.

Kelly, E. W. Jr and Matthews, D. B. (1971) Group counseling with discipline-problem children at the elementary school level. *School Counselor 18*: 273–8.

Kennard, D., Clemmey, R. and Mandelbrote, B. (1977) Aspects of outcome in a therapeutic community setting. *British Journal of Psychiatry 130*: 475–80.

Kilmann, P. R. and Auerbach, S. M. (1974) Effects of marathon group therapy on trait and state anxiety. *Journal of Consulting and Clinical Psychology 42*: 602–12.

King, P. D. (1958) Regressive ECT, chlorpromazine and group therapy in the treatment of hospitalised chronic schizophrenics. *American Journal of Psychiatry 115*: 354–7.

King, P. D. (1963) Controlled study of group psychotherapy in schizophrenics receiving chlorpromazine. *Psychiatry Digest 24*: 21–6.

Kingsley, R. G. and Wilson, G. T. (1977) Behaviour therapy for obesity: a comparative investigation of long-term efficacy. *Journal of Consulting and Clinical Psychology 45*: 288–98.

Klein, N. C., Alexander, J. F. and Parsons, B. V. (1977) Impact of family systems intervention on recidivism and sibling delinquency: a model of primary prevention and program evaluation. *Journal of Consulting and Clinical Psychology 45* (3): 469–74.

Knox, W. J. (1974) Effects of a domiciliary restoration program on state-trait anxiety and self-ideal concepts. *Psychological Reports 34*: 689–90.

Kraus, A. R. (1959) Experimental study of the effect of group psychotherapy with chronic psychotic patients. *International Journal of Group Psychotherapy 9*: 293–302.

Krausova, L. and Hemsley, D. R. (1976) Discharge from a therapeutic community. *British Journal of Medical Psychology 49*: 199–204.

Laing, R. D. and Esterson, A. (1964) *Sanity, Madness and the Family*. London: Tavistock.

Lazarus, A. A. (1961) Group therapy of phobic disorders by systematic desensitisation. *Journal of Abnormal and Social Psychology* *63*: 504–10.

Letemendia, F. J. J., Harris, A. D. and Willems, P. J. A. (1967) The clinical effects on a population of chronic schizophrenic patients of administrative changes in hospital. *British Journal of Psychiatry* *113*: 959–71.

Levene, H. I., Patterson, V., Murphey, B. G., Overbec, A. L. and Veach, T. L. (1970) The aftercare of schizophrenics: an evaluation of group and individual approaches. *Psychiatric Quarterly 44*: 296–304.

Lidz, T., Fleck, S. and Cornelison, A. (1965) *Schizophrenia and the Family*. New York: International Universities Press.

Lipton, S. M., Fields, R. J. and Scott, R. A. (1958) Effects of group psychotherapy upon patient movement. *Diseases of the Nervous System 29*: 603–5.

Luria, Z. (1959) A semantic analysis of a normal and a neurotic therapy group. *Journal of Abnormal and Social Psychology 58*: 216–20.

McBrien, R. J. and Nelson, R. J. (1972) Experimental group strategies with primary grade children. *Elementary School Guidance Counselor 6*: 170–4.

McCollum, P. S. and Anderson, R. S. (1974) Group counseling with reading disabled children. *Journal of Counseling Psychology 21*: 150–5.

McGinnis, C. A. (1963) The effects of group therapy on the ego-strength scale scores of alcoholic patients. *Journal of Clinical Psychology 19*: 346–7.

Main, T. (1946) The hospital as a therapeutic institution. *Bulletin of the Menninger Clinic 10*: 66.

Malouf, R. E. and Alexander, J. F. (1974) Family crisis intervention: a model and technique of training. In R. E. Hardy and J. G. Cull (eds) *Therapeutic Needs of the Family*. Springfield, Illinois: Charles C. Thomas.

Manning, N. (1976) Values and practice in a therapeutic community. *Human Relations 29*: 125–38.

Miles, A. E. (1967) Psychopathy and the therapeutic community. Unpublished PhD thesis, University of London.

Miles, A. E. (1969) The effects of a therapeutic community on the interpersonal relationships of a group of psychopaths. *British Journal of Criminology 9*: 1–22.

Minuchin, S. (1974) *Families and Family Therapy*. London: Tavistock.

Minuchin, S., Baker, L., Rosman, B., Liebman, R., Milman, L. and Todd, T. (1975) A conceptual model of psychosomatic illness in children. *Archives of General Psychiatry 32*: 1031–8.

Minuchin, S., Montalvo, B., Guerney, B. G., Rosman, B. L. and Schumer, F. (1967) *Families of the Slums*. New York: Basic Books.

Minuchin, S., Rosman, B. L. and Baker, L. (1978) *Psychosomatic Families: Anorexia Nervosa in Context*. Cambridge, Mass.: Harvard University Press.

Moulin, E. K. (1970) The effects of client-centred group counseling using play media on the intelligence, achievement and psycholinguistic abilities of underachieving primary school children. *Elementary School Guidance Counselor 4*:85–98.

Murray, D. C., Davidoff, L. and Harrington, L. G. (1975) Treatment of overweight: II – in vivo self-control training. *Psychological Reports 37*: 249–58.

Murray, E. J. and Cohen, M. (1959) Mental illness, milieu therapy and social organisation in ward groups. *Journal of Abnormal and Social Psychology 58*: 48–54.

Myers, K. and Clark, D. H. (1972) Results in a therapeutic community. *British Journal of Psychiatry 120*: 51–8.

Obler, M. (1973) Systematic desensitisation in sexual disorders. *Journal of Behaviour Therapy and Experimental Psychiatry 4*: 93–101.

O'Brien, C. P., Hamm, K. B., Ray, B. A., Pierce, J. F., Luborsky, L. and Mintz, J. (1972) Group versus individual psychotherapy with schizophrenics: a controlled outcome study. *Archives of General Psychiatry 27*: 474–8.

Olson, R. P. and Greenberg, D. J. (1972) Effects of contingency contracting and decision making groups with chronic mental patients. *Journal of Consulting and Clinical Psychology 38*: 376–83.

Parloff, M. B. and Dies, R. R. (1977) Group psychotherapy outcome research 1966–1975. *International Journal of Group Psychotherapy 27*: 281–319.

Parsons, B. V. and Alexander, J. F. (1973) Short-term family intervention: a therapy outcome study. *Journal of Consulting and Clinical Psychology 41*: 195–201.

Pattison, E. M., Brissenden, A. and Wohl, T. (1967) Assessing specific effects of in-patient group psychotherapy. *International Journal of Group Psychotherapy 17*: 283–97.

Paul, G. L. (1967) Strategy of outcome research in psychotherapy. *Journal of Consulting Psychology 31*: 109–18.

Paul, G. L. and Shannon, D. T. (1966) Treatment of anxiety through systematic desensitisation in therapy groups. *Journal of Abnormal Psychology 71*: 124–35.

Persons, R. W. (1966) Psychological and behavioral change in delinquents following psychotherapy. *Journal of Clinical Psychology 22*: 337–40.

Peters, J. J., Pedigo, J. M., Steg, J. and McKenna, J. J. Jr (1968) Group psychotherapy of the sex offender. *Federal Probation 32*: 41–5.

Piper, W. E., Debbane, E. G. and Garant, J. (1977) An outcome study of group therapy. *Archives of General Psychiatry 34*: 1027–32.

Prince, R. M., Ackerman, R. E. and Barksdale, B. S. (1973) Collaborative provision of aftercare services. *American Journal of Psychiatry 130*: 930–2.

Purvis, S. A. and Miskimmins, R. W. (1970) Effects of community follow-up on post-hospital adjustments of psychiatric patients. *Community Mental Health Journal 6*: 374–82.

Randolph, D. L. and Hardage, N. C. (1973) Behavioral consultation and group counseling with potential dropouts. *Elementary School Guidance Counselor 7*: 204–9.

Rapoport, R. N. (1960) *Community as Doctor*. Springfield, Illinois: Charles C. Thomas.

Redfering, D. L. (1973) Durability of effects of group counseling with institutionalised delinquent females. *Journal of Abnormal Psychology 82*: 85–6.

Reiter, G. F. and Kilmann, P. R. (1975) Mothers as family change agents. *Journal of Counseling Psychology 22*: 61–5.

Riskin, J. and Faunce, E. E. (1972) An evaluative review of family interaction research. *Family Process 11 (14)*: 365–455.

Ritter, B. (1968) The group treatment of children's snake phobias using vicarious and contact desensitisation procedures. *Behaviour Research and Therapy 6*: 1–6.

Roback, H. B. (1972) Experimental comparison of outcomes in insight and non-insight oriented therapy groups. *Journal of Consulting and Clinical Psychology 38*: 411–17.

Rosman, B. L., Minuchin, S. L., Liebman, R. and Baker, L. (1976) Impact and outcome of family therapy in anorexia nervosa. Manuscript cited by Gurman and Kniskern (1978).

Sacks, J. M. and Berger, S. (1954) Group therapy techniques with hospitalised chronic schizophrenic patients. *Journal of Consulting Psychology 18*: 297–307.

Santa-Barbara, J., Woodward, C. A., Levin, S., Goodman, J. T., Streiner, D. L. and Epstein, N. B. (1977a) The McMaster family therapy outcome study. I. An overview of methods and results. Unpublished paper, McMaster University, Hamilton, Ontario.

Santa-Barbara, J., Woodward, C. A., Levin, S., Streiner, D. L., Goodman, J. T. and Epstein, N. B. (1977b) The McMaster family therapy outcome study. II. Interrelationships among outcome measures. Unpublished paper, McMaster University, Hamilton, Ontario.

Sarason, I. G. and Ganzer, V. M. (1973) Modeling and group discussion in the rehabilitation of juvenile delinquents. *Journal of Counseling Psychology 20*: 422–49.

Semon, R. G. and Goldstein, W. (1957) The effectiveness of group psychotherapy with chronic schizophrenics and an evaluation of different therapeutic methods. *Journal of Consulting Psychology 21*: 317–22.

Shattan, S. P., Decamp, L., Fujii, E., Fross, G. G. and Wolff, R. J. (1966) Group treatments of conditionally discharged patients in a mental health clinic. *American Journal of Psychiatry 122*: 798–805.

Skynner, A. C. R. (1976) *One Flesh: Separate Persons*. London: Constable.

Slaikeu, K. A. (1973) Evaluation studies on group treatment of juvenile and adult offenders in correctional institutions. *Journal of Research in Crime and Delinquency 10*: 87–100.

Snyder, R. and Sechrest, L. (1959) An experimental study of directive group therapy with defective delinquents. *American Journal of Mental Deficiency 64*: 117–23.

Solyom, L., Shugar, R., Bryntwick, S. and Solyom, C. (1973) Treatment of fear of flying. *American Journal of Psychiatry 130*: 423–7.

Stanton, M. D. and Todd, T. C. (1976) Structural family therapy with heroin addicts: some outcome data. Paper presented at the Society for Psychotherapy Research, San Diego.

Stanton, M. D. (1979) Family treatment approaches to drug abuse problems: a review. *Family Process 18* (3): 251–80.

Steinfeld, G. J. and Mabli, J. (1974) Perceived curative factors in group therapy by residents in a therapeutic community. *Criminal Justice and Behaviour 1*: 279–88.

Stover, L. and Guerney, B. (1967) The efficacy of training procedures for mothers in filial therapy. *Psychotherapy 4*: 110–15.

Swarr, R. R. and Ewing, T. N. (1977) Group psychotherapy outcome with college student neurotics. *Journal of Consulting and Clinical Psychology 45*: 1029–33.

Taylor, A. J. W. (1967) An evaluation of group psychotherapy in a girls' borstal. *International Journal of Group Psychotherapy 17*: 168–77.

Taylor, W. F. and Hoedt, K. (1974) Classroom-related behavior problems: counsel parents, teachers or children? *Journal of Counseling Psychology 21*: 3–8.

Teahan, J. E. (1966) Effect of group psychotherapy on academic low achievers. *International Journal of Group Psychotherapy 16*: 78–85.

Thombs, M. R. and Muro, J. J. (1973) Group counseling and the sociometric status of second grade children. *Elementary School Guidance Counselor 7*: 194–7.

Tolor, A. (1970) The effectiveness of various therapeutic approaches: a study of subprofessional therapists. *International Journal of Group Psychotherapy 20*: 48–62.

Tosi, D. J., Upshaw, K., Lande, A. and Waldron, M. (1971) Group counseling with non-verbalising elementary students: differential effects of Premack and social reinforcement techniques. *Journal of Counseling Psychology 18*: 437–40.

Truax, C. B. and Carkhuff, R. R. (1967) *Toward Effective Counseling and Psychotherapy*. Chicago: Aldine.

Truax, C. B. and Mitchell, K. M. (1971) Research on certain therapist interpersonal skills in relation to process and outcome. In A. E. Bergin and S. Garfield (eds) *Handbook of Psychotherapy and Behavior Change*. 1st ed. New York: John Wiley.

Truax, C. B., Wargo, D. G. and Silber, L. D. (1966) Effects of group psychotherapy with high accurate empathy and non-possessive warmth upon female institutionalised delinquents. *Journal of Abnormal Psychology 71*: 267–74.

Tucker, J. E. (1956) Group psychotherapy with chronic psychotic soiling patients. *Journal of Consulting Psychology 20*: 430.

Vitalo, R. L. (1971) Teaching improved interpersonal functioning as a preferred mode of treatment. *Journal of Clinical Psychology 27*: 166–71.

Vogelsong, E. L. (1975) Preventative-therapeutic programs for mothers and adolescent daughters. A follow-up of relationship enhancement versus discussion and booster versus no-booster methods. Unpublished Ph.D dissertation, Pennysylvania State University.

Waldman, M. and Reiser, M. (1961) Group therapy and personality factors in a work adjustment center. *Journal of Jewish Communal Service 38*: 167–70.

Watzlawick, P. and Weakland, J. H. (1977) *The Interactional View*. New York: Norton.

Watzlawick, P., Weakland, J. H. and Fisch, R. (1974) *Change: Principles of Problem Formation and Problem Resolution*. New York: Norton.

Weakland, J. H., Fisch, R., Watzlawick, P. and Bodin, A. M. (1974) Brief therapy: focused problem resolution. *Family Process 13* (2): 141–68.

Wells, R. A., Dilkes, T. C. and Trivelli, N. (1972) The results of family therapy: a critical review of the literature. *Family Process 11*: 189–207.

Wells, R. A. and Dezen, A. E. (1978) The results of family therapy revisited: the non-behavioural methods. *Family Process 17*: 251–86.

Whiteley, J. S. (1970) The response of psychopaths to a therapeutic community. *British Journal of Psychiatry 116*: 517–29.

Wilcox, G. T. and Guthrie, G. M. (1957) Changes in adjustment of institutionalised female defectives following group psychotherapy. *Journal of Clinical Psychology 13*: 9–13.

Willett, E. A. (1973) Group therapy in a methadone treatment program: an evaluation of changes in interpersonal behavior. *International Journal of Addictions 8*: 33–9.

Williams, M., McGee, T. F., Kittleson, S. and Halperin, L. (1962) An evaluation of intensive group living programs with schizophrenic patients. *Psychological Monographs 76* (543): 1–25.

Wilson, D. L., Wilson, M. E. Jr, Sakata, R. and Frumkin, R. M. (1967) Effects of short-term group interaction on social adjustment in a group of mentally retarded clients. *Psychological Reports 21*: 716.

Winkler, R. C., Teigland, J. J., Munger, P. F. and Kranzler, G. D. (1965) The effects of selected counseling and remedial techniques on under-achieving elementary school children. *Counseling Psychologist 12*: 384–7.

Woodward, C. A., Santa-Barbara, J., Levin, S. and Epstein, N. B. (1978) The role of goal attainment scaling in evaluating family therapy outcome. *American Journal of Orthopsychiatry 48*: 464–76.

Woodward, C. A., Santa-Barbara, J., Levin, S., Epstein, N. B. and Streiner, D. (1977) *The McMaster Family Therapy Outcome Study. III. Client and Treatment Characteristics significantly contributing to Client Outcomes.* Paper presented at the 54th Annual Meeting of the American Orthopsychiatry Association, New York City.

Woodward, C. A., Santa-Barbara, J., Levin, S., Goodman, J. T., Streiner, D. and Epstein, N. B. (1975) *Client and Therapist Characteristics Related to Family Therapy Outcome: Closure and Follow-up Evaluation.* Paper presented at Society for Psychotherapy Research, Boston.

Woodward, C., Santa-Barbara, J., Levin, S., Goodman, J. T., Streiner, D. L., Hussin, L. and Epstein, N. B. (1974) *Outcome Research in Family Therapy: or The Growing Edginess of Family Therapists.* Paper delivered at the Nathan W. Ackerman Memorial Conference, Margarita Island.

Yalom, I. D. (1970) *The Theory and Practice of Group Psychotherapy.* New York: Basic Books.

Zuk, G. (1972) *Family Therapy: A Triadic-Based Approach.* New York: Human Sciences Press.

6 The purposes of group-work in social work

Nano McCaughan

Social work in the UK has now a recognizable, if not very uniform group-work component. The development of this form of intervention has been very slow and uneven. There are a variety of reasons for this which will be discussed later. As we indicate the nature and range of group-work practice, we include in this work with interdisciplinary colleagues as well as work with clients and social work colleagues. The social worker is concerned with a great variety of groups both as leader or member, as an insider or as an outsider.

Social education

Perhaps the most common group-work projects at present used with adults are those groups formed to relieve the feelings of alienation and social difficulties stemming from social isolation. The adults who comprise these groups are generally unsupported parents (mostly women) or elderly people. There are a few examples of work with others who have become isolated, or have isolated themselves because of some labelled 'deviancy' – ex-prisoners, ex-mental hospital patients, alcoholics. The purpose of these groups is to provide a base for lonely, rejected people to form friendships, starting with those in a similar plight; to increase their self-regard and competence in dealing with others by giving information and reinforcing self-assertion. Frequently the group project will offer 'gifts' to the friendless in the shape of communal meals or refreshment, trips and outings, or a social event, with the intention of building cohesion and trust in the group.

Clearly this form of group-work is a substitute for the support and warmth that a natural kin or friendship network most often provides. The group worker would be unlikely to be interested in internal changes in the members, or to use confrontative or insight inducing techniques. The group worker takes a non-directive stance, works at the pace of the members, recognizes and respects defences. This group-work has clearly a *rehabilitative* or *restorative* function. The worker inevitably becomes involved in the practical or material problems of individual members, and although the desired outcome would be that members would learn to tackle their own problems with their environment, the group workers would not be averse to modelling how to do so. There is an increasing use of day centre settings for this type of work. It is easier to combine the two objectives of social education and social skill training in a setting such as a day centre where supports are easily available. These supports include baby-sitting, advice and demonstration to mothers about child development and care, information and advice in tackling organizations in control of income maintenance and housing, leisure activities for those who are reluctant to avail themselves of these elsewhere, and practical care services such as chiropody or physical training for the elderly and disabled.

Examples of this type of group-work are to be found described in such papers as Walker's (1978) account of work with a parents group in a family service unit, and Davies's (1977) report of training volunteers to work with parents in groups.

This form of group-work is difficult to research in any rigorous fashion. The reports are mainly descriptive and outcomes are reported in terms of what changes the workers observed in the members, or the feelings of the members themselves about the group experience. Workers usually have a number of aims in mind in starting the group, none of them very specific. They range from a desire to create a small 'caring' community for friendless people, trusting to luck that in that climate trust and self-confidence will increase, friendships will grow, and members will find the energy to acquire new skills and renovate lost ones. The accounts of some projects indicate that this does indeed happen.

Parfit (1970) made a collection of accounts of group-work of this type with parents. Many of the consumers were unsupported parents living in homeless families' units or in sheltered accommodation. Group-work lasted on average six months. Reports indicate that the members increased in sensitivity to their children's needs and became less possessive of their children. A common problem seemed to be the mixture of hostility and possessiveness experienced towards children. Members were frequently able to take a more positive role in social activities outside their home, particularly where the group experience included social outings. Increase in self-confidence was implied by the members' increasing ability to initiate friendships outside the group, and take up relevant matters with other organizations, schools, local offices of the Department of Health and Social Security, etc. An influential factor in improving relations with children appeared to be the group workers' provision of a play-leader for children, who was able to demonstrate both forms of play and an enjoyment of playing.

The groups were not all plain sailing. The reports frequently mention that the first five or six sessions were uncomfortable for all concerned – perhaps this was a combination of the members' life experience which was currently depressing, and the lack of clear direction for the group. When the purpose is left unnamed or vaguely stated members may remain in a state of ambivalence for a longer time about 'joining'. Certainly there appeared to be a high drop-out rate in the first few sessions, settling down to a steady nucleus later on.

Accounts of unsuccessful group projects rarely find their way into print. This unstructured approach may founder on several accounts.

Composition

The members may be too similar in disposition and have a similar negative life situation. Apathy and despair are contagious and members may feel (in the stage before they can see any potential) that the group is an additional problem in their lives. Workers may be too different from the members who inwardly question their ability to help, particularly if they are hesitant in setting out a view of what might be achieved.

Over-dependency

Unsupported parents, the isolated elderly, and the disabled are frequently vulnerable people, whose needs for affirmation and support are not adequately fulfilled. The 'growth' ethos influencing the worker's actions and response appears to take the form – initially – of establishing the worker as a caring, helpful, giving and permissive person. It is all too easy for lonely people to become attached and dependent on such a person. It is satisfying to the worker to be admired and needed. Group objectives may not be met because the members manoeuvre the worker into doing all the work – leading discussions, suggesting activities, handling difficulties on behalf of the members. Encouragement, withdrawal and confrontation are needed at times to release creative action and risk-taking potential in those accustomed to failure.

Inexperience of group life

Because of the common experience of social isolation among the members of these groups, it is possible that the members lack a suitable internal model of a group to guide their role-taking. Such familiar skills as listening to others, taking a share in the ebb and flow of interaction about a topic, and concentrating on others' actions or words for a time are missing. Learning how to be a group member can cause an undue amount of anxiety and uncertainty for those deprived of the familiar learning opportunities of family life, membership of work and friendship groups. Walker (1978) details the help given by members who had been in other social work groups and this ability to model may be an important factor to consider in composition.

Daily living care

Another type of group intervention (although not primarily seen as that) which is common in social work is the task of caring for the lives of vulnerable individuals in residential institutions – children and elderly people being the main consumers. However, the quarter of a million people in residential care of various types in the United Kingdom include the mentally subnormal, the mentally ill and the physically disabled as well as the needy and disadvantaged. As Payne (1978) states:

> All that the different establishments manifestly have in common is the provision of life's basic – shelter, food, care and protection for a specified group of people who for various reasons cannot maintain themselves or be maintained by members of their families.

People in residential institutions are cared for in group living by groups of staff. Private communication between residents, or between a resident and staff member, are the exceptions rather than the rule. Groups provide the major means of influence, care and context for relationships. Meals, recreation, work or school activities, often sleeping, take place in company with others. The sense of individual identity and uniqueness that Western culture deems so important to personal happiness and fulfilment is difficult to retain without the normal opportunities for privacy and reflection, or for intimate contact with an important other.

Group life can be oppressive, diminishing and punitive to an individual, as well as offering opportunities for participation, influence and leadership. Staff in residential institutions should understand sufficiently the negative pressures that are likely to exist, so as to be able to withstand them themselves and to help and support residents in doing so. These pressures often emerge under the guise of enabling the smooth and efficient running of the institution; they also emerge as a way of handling disagreeable realities on the part of both residents and staff. Examples are provided by the Miller and Gwynne (1972) study of homes for the young chronic sick, in which the authors identify various group defences against facing the realities of severe physical handicap.

There are various aspects of life in residential homes where an understanding of group processes and the pressures of the group on the individual is crucial. Payne (1978) lists these in his paper.

(1) Developing and managing the 'natural resources' of group living.
(2) Managing the tensions of daily living.
(3) Facilitating the integration of the newcomer to the residential setting, and correspondingly, in helping him to prepare for departure from the setting.

(4) In providing opportunities for personal development and life enrichment.

(5) In helping residents find solutions to the interpersonal and other life problems that have often been the cause of their admission into care.

(6) In helping residential staff to exercise constructive and creative leadership in particular through a continuous process of appraisal and review of the events and happenings of residential life.

Clearly it is difficult to generalize in any useful way about the group-work purpose in such a varied field as residential care, which can vary from a large institution for the frail elderly, staffed mainly by ex-hospital trained nurses, to a small family group home. None the less, it is worthwhile exploring one or two research studies in the field of residential care which point to some practical implications for the leadership of these institutions.

Sinclair (1975) studied the quasi-family institutions of probation hostels and in particular the differential effect on the behaviour of the residents of different warden/matron pairs. He found that the warden's performance had a profound effect on the residents, much more influential than that of other staff. Some wardens appeared to provoke a high rate of absconding and committal of further offences. However, even the more successful wardens went through bad patches when their customary performance seemed to have less positive effect. The stress could sometimes be ascribed to the warden's personal or family life, sometimes to other factors in the group of probationers. The interdependence between staff and residents was quite clear. Sinclair was able to isolate qualities of person and attitudes to the residents which made for more or less successful role performance. The study seems to imply that besides selection and training based on these and other findings, residential staff require a consultative, supportive form of supervision including discussion of tension and stress among staff. Strengthened by that process, wardens should gain more insight into and control over their prejudices, realize their own part in provoking behaviour such as absconding, and feel able to use a similar sort of discussion with the residents. The consultant should have at heart the interests of the whole institution, in so far as that is possible.

This kind of research indicates that despite Goffman's (1961) views on total institutions, the specific feature of different settings can have an enormous impact on both the immediate culture and long-term effects of residential institutions. The ideological orientation held by the staff is probably the most important, because on that will depend the organizational structure, staff/resident relations, and resident response. Among the issues studied by researchers into institutions two questions emerge which are of vital interest in developing insight into the nature of staff/resident interdependence. The first is the extent of staff agreement on the values they hold in relation to the people and the regime they work with. Disagreement can be open, covert or sometimes subconscious. Value assumptions may never be openly stated, clarified or challenged. The second question is the effect of staff agreement or disagreement on the culture of the institution and the experience and behaviour of residents.

Social control: group-work with clients in trouble

Social workers are involved with groups of clients where the goal of the intervention is behavioural change of a specific kind – the elimination or decrease of those behaviours that society has classified as deviant through its legislative, judicial and normative processes. The nature and dynamics of deviance as a concept has caused a good deal of soul-searching and conflict among social workers in recent years; in many cases now, especially of minor juvenile delinquency, social workers would wish to state that their primary goal was changing the attitudes of those in authority to the young person, rather than changing the young person's behaviour. None the less, in most instances it is not possible to ignore the consequences of continuing deviant behaviour for the offender, and group-work with this target group might be said to have the goal of re-socialization and behavioural change, but to take place in two modes:

(1) Involuntary clients: young people or adults who are already incarcerated by order of the courts in community homes, borstals, prisons or hostels, as well as those whose non-incarceration was made conditional on attendance at a group run by probation officers or social workers.
(2) Voluntary clients: those whose attendance at a probationers' group, intermediate treatment or other project was more or less a matter of choice for them.

The leader's goals for this type of group-work vary from a specific focus on problematic behaviours with attempts to enlist the co-operation of the deviant individual in changing these, to more open-ended use of activities and discussions designed to demonstrate alternatives to delinquent behaviours. The more control the sponsoring agency has over an individual the less likely is the second alternative mentioned to be used. The worker must then pay great attention to the demonstration and development of group norms, recognizing that resistance will be high and motivation to change will be low.

Recidivist rates show that incarceration in an institution with groups of other offenders or deviants tends on the whole to develop skill and resourcefulness in the behaviours that got the individual locked up in the first place. Special projects however have suggested that if the institution pays attention to and confronts the dynamics of the total staff/residents group interactions, custodial institutions may fulfil the idealistic hopes of providing growth and change. There have been experiments in the field of both mental health and criminology, usually reliant on the commitment and patience of an institutional head (for example, Wills, 1971; Jones, 1952; Burn, 1959). Of special interest is Boyle's (1977) account of the special unit for violent prisoners in Barlinnie Prison, in which he was an inmate.

Diversionary, preventive projects for clients in trouble who are more or less voluntary group members have greatly increased as a result of the development of intermediate treatment, following the Children and Young Person's Act of 1969. Reports of a variety of such projects, some of which indicate the changes occurring in the individuals, have been published by the Department of Health and Social Security (1977).

It is too soon to evaluate what makes for the effectiveness of one project over another or indeed to state that the outcome is equal to the increasing investment of resources in these projects. A pilot study in Manchester (Smith et al., 1970) which contained the unusual feature of an 'untreated' control group, suggested that the 'project' boys were diverted to quite an extent from behaviours which would have led to court attendance, fines and custodial care. However, the basic attitudes towards family and personal relationships did not appear to change so one does not know if the group-work intervention was to prove a temporary rather than permanent hiatus in a criminal career. This kind of speculation indicates the lack of suitable instruments to measure, even crudely, the outcomes of group-work for its consumers, without the financial support needed by a longitudinal study.

Change: group-work to bring about desired individual or community change

This attempt to categorize the various types of group purpose which some social workers and probation officers are engaged in already demonstrates overlap. As we consider a fourth category – voluntary change in behaviour, feelings or role performance – it is evident that consumers in the other categories already discussed might properly belong to this one too. However, there are a number of groups created by social workers to enable the participants to achieve some planned and desired change. One caveat is that while the consumers may feel dissatisfied with their life situation (or an aspect of it) and wish for some change, they do not often have a clear vision of what that change should amount to: or if they do, their experience in a group may alter or modify their vision.

Behaviour and attitudes are frequently transmitted from and kept in being by one's interpersonal relationships. It is, therefore, difficult to change by a deliberate effort on one's own part, unless one expands or changes one's natural group membership. Many of the consumers of social work explicitly wish to change, and in directions in which social work personnel can only offer a limited resource: those in a similar position and with a similar experience can often be in a better position to support, confront or give the necessary information that will help. The group in this instance can offer a safe but hopefully stimulating life space in which the individual can express his dissatisfaction, cast around for alternative solutions, try out new behaviours, receive feedback and discuss transactions that take place with important others outside the group.

In this instance the group should be a temporary experimental and learning resource which does not become more important to the individual than the problem in living he seeks to resolve. The members are helpers as well as helped. Groups like these are set up quite frequently to help individuals deal with situations of chronic or temporary stress: a marriage going wrong, interacting with adolescent children, acquiring friends in a new environment, adjusting to living without an important prop in one's life, retiring and growing old, managing oneself and one's family life in the advent of an illness or a physically or mentally handicapped member. The social worker is somewhat in the position of a referee, ensuring that the individual is not seized on as a victim of the group and exploited as a welcome diversion from the troubles of others; ensuring that the solutions offered are in line with the individuals' basic values and are feasible to their life situation; preventing undue pressure on any individual to conform to group pressures if these are alien to their wishes; and knowing when to suggest termination of the group's efforts or of the participation of individual members.

The characteristics of this form of group-work are that the potential members are aware of the significant problems in their lives and are in some agreement with the group worker about how they can be tackled in the group. The group normally comprises people in a similar situation but not necessarily people of a similar personality. Change groups vary in the explicitness of the contract entered into between the members, and between the members and the leader. One of the difficulties encountered is that there is often a difference in perception between members' views of the cause of their own difficulty and the views of others. Members may enter a group because of an experienced difficulty in making satisfactory social relations; they may attribute this to shyness and insecurity, while the leader and other members may quickly interpret the difficulty as stemming from the member's negative and aggressive attitudes to others. The feedback from others, if its timing is right, can be positively, if painfully, influential in changing the member, but illustrates the dangers of drawing up contracts which are too explicit.

One form of group-work, developing particularly in the USA, where positive and desired change outcomes have been noted, is the use of role-play to train people in social skills or in more appropriate and assertive behaviour. This model has an association with behaviour modification theories, as it is contingent on the members specifying the type and amount of change they desire. An example of this is found in a study by Toselcand and Rose (1978) in which they compared three different approaches used to offer social skills training for older adults. They compared behavioural role-play with two other forms, a problem-solving or cognitive approach and social group-work, using Northen's (1969) psychosocial approach. The psychosocial approach directs attention both toward oneself and toward the social environment within which a problem arises. The behavioural role-play was the most effective immediately, and results lasted over the following three months. The psychosocial approach appeared to have a delayed action as its consumers were deemed to have improved gradually throughout the three months. A further study by Schinke et al. (1975) also indicates that the use of role-play increases the chances of a favourable outcome for people, who can decide in what specific areas of their life they wish to change their interpersonal behaviours. The combination of specificity and practice are clearly the important ingredients in this instance.

Changing behaviour appears to be easier than changing attitudes or beliefs, and it may be that the longer-lasting or more generalized behavioural change is dependent on changing the former. It is more difficult to test or evaluate the amount or type of attitudinal changes. For example, the authors of the Wincroft Youth Project (Smith et al., 1972) were disappointed to find that the young men had not changed their attitudes to family life and interpersonal relations although their behaviour had become more pro-social. It is possible to speculate that those changes may take years to become apparent and in some instances it may be that the experience of the helping adults they encountered will affect, years later, their attitudes to and upbringing of their own children, when they have long since forgotten their group experience.

An evaluation study of considerable interest and potential in brief focused group-work is described by Navarre et al. (1974). The authors designed a series of groups for mothers on AFDC (Aid to Families in Distressed Circumstances), known to case-workers in a Department of Social Welfare in the USA. A rare feature of the study was the comparison with an experimental group with controls – similar subjects randomly selected. The groups were designed to offer a specific problem-solving experience to mothers who had one or more children having learning or behavioural difficulties at school. The mode number of sessions was six for an average member attendance of five. The results of the group-work were very encouraging: mothers in the experimental groups scored significantly higher than controls in total task performance and decision-making at home, in specifically chosen areas of child care tasks and decisions, and in school tasks and decisions, and their children showed significant improvement in a classroom conduct test, although not themselves directly involved in the study.

Another developing model of group-work which relies on the notion of client choice of problem(s) to be tackled and stresses the value of involving group members in actively working towards a chosen goal is the Task Centred Approach. This is described in theory by Garvin (1977) and in practice by Rooney (1977). The characteristics of this model reflect the assumptions of Task Centred Casework (Reid and Epstein, 1972) in that there is agreement about the number of sessions from the outset (eight to twelve is the norm). There is explicit agreement about the method and the difference between the worker's and member's role. At the termination of the group it should be evident whether or not the goals have been achieved. The selection of the problem and the preliminary agreement are reached with each prospective member prior to commencement of the group. There are clear advantages to this form of group-work but possible disadvantages to both the previous models of brief, focused therapy. The group may not succeed for some individuals and so may provide them with a further experience of frustration and failure. They do not take into account the management of the potent forces of group dynamics which may overwhelm rational and explicit agreements about work. They must rely heavily on a capacity to share and give to others which is not necessarily among the current attributes of the members. They ignore the hypothesis that some people are in greater emotional difficulties than others and may learn at a different pace.

Other models of group-work used by workers wishing to help people change are focused more on process than on outcome. The assumption would be that members can only begin to articulate goals which will truly enhance their lives when they have experienced the realities and difficulties of a system whose formal leadership is dedicated to attempting to create a helping, trustful instrument that can offer opportunities both for individuation and mutual help. Schwartz and Zalba (1971) have described this model of group-work (referred to as the *reciprocal* model). The leader's orientation is more crucial than any other aspect at commencement, and the group is viewed as an interactive system open to the influences and initiatives of all group members. Naturally it is more difficult to assess the outcome of less structured forms of group-work such as this, but the editors have included a series of case studies which provide some empirical data.

A good example of the development and maintenance of this type of group is provided by Vickery et al. (1978). Clearly, individuals were helped although they may have joined the group preoccupied by individual concerns. After a time they found themselves forming a club to act as a neighbourhood resource, reaching out to others, perhaps seizing on this community action as an alternative to varying individual feelings of loneliness. The delicate and changing role of the leaders is recorded as they enable the members to move from dependency to autonomy. The importance of recognizing the cultural differences between middle-class group leaders and working-class members is sensitively illustrated. The 'politics' of change in small scale community development is illustrated.

The characteristics of this form of group-work include a lack of stress on the importance of careful composition, the inclusion of the members in working for the resources the environment might give to the group, reinforcement of the effort put in regardless of result, and careful support to emerging leadership of certain members. The disadvantages are that the group may founder and disintegrate because of an initial lack of clear direction, that norms may develop which are inimical to the satisfaction or achievement of certain members, that hidden agendas may devour a disproportionate amount of time and energy, and the difficulty of finding a voice for the group which includes leadership but does not give it undue dominance.

Co-operation and conflict: group-work within organizations and across organizations

Most social workers who are still in touch with clients spend their working day as team members either in a residential, day care or field-work setting. In social services and probation departments which now employ the great majority of social workers in the UK, the team is a vitally important context which shapes the working life of the individual. Work is allocated, caseloads monitored, supervision and professional development provided by the team or by the team leader. The team is very often collectively responsible for all the social work intervention in an area or for a certain number of individuals. Through the senior member the priorities, goals and values of the organization are mediated and interpreted: through his team membership the individual social worker should find his commitment to his work. Working as an integral member of a group is often a new experience for beginning social workers, and one for which all are not well prepared in their basic training. On the whole teaching about leadership and organizational behaviour focuses on management roles: it is difficult for the individual not having achieved such a role to feel and express his own leadership initiative and potential and respond to that in his peers. Many social work teams experience profound problems in working together.

The research carried out by Stevenson and Parsloe (1978) found similar difficulties over a diverse number of teams in integrating non-social workers such as occupational therapists, welfare assistants and home help organizers as team members with a different task. It was found that these individuals were frequently either given too much responsibility in work with clients, or not enough. Decisions about their work were apparently made on the assumption that the team was primarily an interpersonal *sentient* system, rather than a *task* system. Team members expressed a hopelessness about bringing about organization changes which would enhance their work: many legitimate professional grievances were expressed to the researchers as personal complaints, and were not to be shared with colleagues in any formal way. It seems depressingly clear that the social workers interviewed did not have a grasp of organizational issues which affected their work, nor indeed the competence to confront these at an organizational level and attempt to bring about structural change.

Besides their team membership social workers and probation officers find themselves in other work groups, often consisting of other professionals such as magistrates, police, doctors, nurses and school-teachers. Some workers contribute to and manage their membership and work in these groups effectively; for others one suspects the interdisciplinary group becomes an unsatisfactory interpersonal battleground, where individuals are forced to grapple with issues of power, prejudice and needs for self-expression rather than reaching the decisions affecting the lives of others in rational and mutually understood, if not consensual, ways.

The leadership of interdisciplinary groups which are convened in less dramatic ways in the daily activities of hospitals, child guidance clinics and community settings is not of course always the responsi-bility of social workers. However, they find at present little resource in their training opportunities or in current literature to guide their contribution in whatever role they find themselves in. They have to cope with the professional values and ethos of other professions – medicine, the law, education – as transmitted by individuals, as well as with the idiosyncracies of the personal representatives of these systems. Knowledge and skill in utilizing the latter can only be arrived at by experience; however, opportunities for grasping the former could be found and developed, by both cognitive and experiential methods. For example, a number of research/educational institutions both in the UK and USA have followed the lead of the Tavistock Institute in sponsoring experiential conferences in group and inter-group relations which attract members from a variety of professions as well as industrial backgrounds. Professional group associations, beliefs and behaviours can be studied, and the dissonance between stated and operationalized values can be noted and confronted. These conferences are described in various writings, notably Rice (1965), Shaffer and Galinsky (1974), and Palmer (1978).

A grasp of potential underlying dynamics is only a first step. Skill in leadership of inter-disciplinary groups could be developed by research, by supervision and consultancy, and by training. At present this skill is given a low priority in social work judging by the dearth of written materials and courses on the topic.

Some common skill areas in group leadership

There are currently several distinct approaches in use by practitioners of social group-work. These have been usefully summarized by Roberts and Northen (1976). There is not sufficient empirical evidence available to suggest that one approach is better than another, and in the long run the choice of approach will probably be determined by the practitioners' values and basic theoretical or experiential orientation. Some approaches have a distinct continuity with behaviourist psychology (task centred, e.g. University of Michigan, a 'remedial' model); others are derived from systems thinking (e.g. Schwartz, a 'reciprocal' model); a third strand derives from social philosophers such as the educationalist Dewey (e.g. Tropp, 1976, a 'developmental' model). The approach adopted will clearly influence the leader's planning for and behaviour in the group, and it is thus only possible to describe typical skills in broad terms. Some models would suggest that the leader should attempt to transmit these skills to group members at the earliest possible opportunity; others imply that the leader holds firmly to certain tasks leaving the members free to pursue individual change efforts. The identification of skills is an important task for social work teachers. If key areas can be conceptualized and agreed, basic training course curricula and field-work experiences could focus and concentrate on those aspects. A series of typical areas will each be examined.

Group formation

The care with which the group is selected will depend on the purpose and/or the approach adopted. The Task Centred model would indicate a careful selection process for each individual to ensure that the desired changes are compatible and that individuals are not subject by contagion or group pressure to abandon their self-chosen goal. Systems or developmental approaches do not imply such careful selection. The goals are more likely to be developed by members and leaders together once the group-work has commenced.

Composition criteria can be fairly broad: for example, people living in close touch (such as a residential institution) or facing a common situation (such as fostering a child). There is an increasing literature on composition but nothing very conclusive emerges except that it seems wise to steer certain types of people away from group experience at certain times! Whitaker (1978) indicates some useful rules of thumb based on research; Grunebaum (1975) and Parloff and Dies (1977) remind us that 10 per cent of the members of therapy groups suffer some deterioration, presumably as a result of the experience. It is probably not too pessimistic to assume that the same effect may occur in social work groups. However competent leaders are they are not in control of all the experiences offered. Despite the lack of clear guidance it will be useful for the practitioner to develop a policy of composition and test its effectiveness by carefully charting the progress and outcomes for members both during and after the group.

The predilection of the writer is for specified time limits, even if these are to be re-negotiated every three months or so. It is difficult to think of a social work purpose that would demand a very long-term approach. Social group-work should be a means of enabling members to approach and find a niche for themselves in the social resources of their society: if a relevant resource does not exist, the group should perhaps conceive of itself as a self-help system which should function, after a period of social learning, without the interventions of a professional worker.

Role modelling

Thinking of one's behaviour as an influential model for others is a frightening prospect for the more humble and less confident group worker. None the less, this aspect fits with both behaviourist and psycho-dynamic theories. People tend to imitate, identify with and incorporate the attitudes and behaviour of those who are seen as having status and power. There is a substantial body of research in social psychology which backs up this observation. Of course, groups offer a variety of models, and in that lies their richness and diversity. But initially it is likely to be the group worker who is under closest surveillance, depended on and looked to for approbation and security in a new situation. The formation phase is an opportunity for the worker to model behaviours and attitudes that will enhance the work of the group, and to establish the therapeutic norms. Helpful modelling can be given by encouraging clarity, summarizing what has been said, discouraging interruption and irrelevancy, attempting when possible to get closure on a theme, sharing honest feelings, attempting to be in touch with all the members, etc. The skill in this aspect consists in the balance between offering a model (or reinforcing the helpful aspects of members' behaviour) and not taking over the work of the group or attempting to shape it to the worker's liking.

Vitalizing the group

Groups using discussion as the major activity frequently become boring, sterile and repetitive. Another function in which group workers develop skill is in bringing vitality to ailing, dispirited groups. Naturally how one does this depends on an accurate assessment of the trouble. It would clearly be incompetent to attempt to bring enthusiasm into a group which had completed its work and was ready to disband but could not quite face up to the break. The skilful worker can mobilize energy in a number of ways. The members may be despondent about the smallness of the gains, or because of the setback of one member. Praising, evaluating shifts over time, and supporting small steps are possibilities. Another is attempting to bring the reality of problems under discussion into the group room by simulation, role-play, visual aids, etc.

If the assessment of the worker is that the members are silent or withdrawn because of unexpressed anger towards the worker as a member, the role modelling of how to confront this issue openly may release energy.

Managing the group: the executive role

There are usually a number of practical details to be seen to in order to create a continuing atmosphere of work and caring for any group. Some of these are traditionally the province of the secretary of any formal committee: ensuring that an appropriate meeting place is available and prepared; overseeing the provision of refreshments or materials that are to be used; completing written notes or aide memoires; inviting and preparing visiting 'speakers'; facilitating the arrival of new members, and acknowledging the departure of those leaving. These tasks take on different meanings in the pursuit of social work aims through social group-work. It is probably not advisable that workers should feel themselves solely responsible for their execution, but they should ensure that, if these tasks are delegated to members as part of the experience offered by the group, the expected task is clear and the member has the requisite authority and potential competence to carry it out.

The inter-group dimension

No group takes place in a vacuum, however closely involved with each other and with the group experience the members appear to be during the meeting time. The worker should attempt to relate continuously the happenings and movement in the group to other (or potential) groups impinging on the members. This may take the form of putting together a consensus response of the members to policies framed by organizations which affect their lives, including if necessary the worker's own organization. It can take the form of supporting the attempts of members to take part in other group life opportunities: clubs, associations, ad hoc committees, friendship networks. Members may feel disloyal if they speak about desires to move into these activities and the worker should (when appropriate) encourage such developments. The effects of change or attempts by the members to alter situations in their families or in institutions should be carefully explored and reinforced. The success of most social group-work can best be evaluated by changes which occur in the members' lives outside of the actual group experience which is a temporary and transient system. A number of studies have already been discussed which do show that such lasting changes can be achieved.

Interpretation and intervention

The essential skill in group-work regardless of the programme adopted probably lies in the work of grasping and attributing meaning to the minutiae of interaction in the group, and communicating one's grasp in such a way as to further the work. It is rather difficult to discuss this skill in any but broad and general terms. Some approaches in their conceptualizations of worker role tend to assume that workers will always be right, possibly because they have the mandate of a profession or organization to support their efforts. More phenomenological approaches imply that one cannot prepare or plan for intervention in groups, as the passing moment is always the critical one – the worker can only grasp (or fail to grasp) opportunities as they occur.

Ryder (1976) has conceptualized the complexity of judging the type and moment of intervention by group workers in the following useful summary. The elements developed for purposes of examining the components of the skills required are:

(1) Skill in helping the group to diagnose or assess and re-assess itself, including goals, purpose, expectations, structure, programmes, achievements and frustrations or failures.
(2) Skill in helping the group to assess and use each part of each phase in its development for achievement of the group purpose.
(3) Skill in helping the group to assess, use and/or modify various levels of social purpose, including the resources of the sponsoring social service agency.
(4) Skill in helping the group to develop and use a social structure and the relationships within that structure to further its own effectiveness.
(5) Skill in communications of feeling between worker and group, along with skill in facilitating communications of feeling between group members.

Conclusion

The functions of group-work in social work that have been described in this paper mesh well with the current aims and values of the profession: to help steer people through the maze of institutions and rules affecting their private lives which have emerged in a complex society; to ensure that those vulnerable because of age (children and old people) or infirmity are protected from exploitation and given every opportunity to develop and use what potential they have for independent living; to help individuals with material or emotional problems to find within themselves, or in company with others, the resources to resolve those problems; to work with others responsible to ensure that individuals can work and spend their leisure in an environment which affords opportunity for self-expression and for developing a variety of interests and skills, and which demands a care and concern for others. That is the vision – in pursuance of it it is obvious that individuals need to act together, learn to consult and share with one another to achieve collective and individual goals. The field of social group-work contains the potential for addressing both private sorrows and social issues.

References

Boyle, J. (1977) *A Sense of Freedom*. London: Pan Books.

Bradford, L. P., Gibb, J. and Benne, K. B. (1964) (eds) *T-Group Theory and Laboratory Method. Innovation in Re-education*. New York: John Wiley.

Burn, M. (1959) *Mr. Lyward's Answer*. London: Hamilton.

Davies, E. (1977) *Neighbourhood Families*. London: London Council of Social Service.

Garvin, C. (1977) Strategies for group work with adolescents. In Reid, W. J. and Epstein, L. (eds) *Task Centred Practice*. New York: Columbia University Press.

Gershenfeld, M. (1972) Laboratory in-service training. In F. W. Kaslow (ed.) *Issues in Human Services*. San Francisco: Jossey-Bass.

Goffman, E. (1961) *Asylums*. New York: Anchor Books.

Grunebaum, H. (1975) A soft-hearted review of hard nosed research on groups. *International Journal of Group Psychotherapy 25* (2): 185–97.

Jones, Maxwell (1952) *Social Psychiatry: A Study of Therpeutic Commmunities*. London: Tavistock.

McCaughan, N. (1978) *Group Work: Learning and Practice*. London: Allen and Unwin.

Miller, E. and Gwynne, E. (1972) *A Life Apart*. London: Tavistock.

Navarre, E., Glasser, P. H. and Constabile, J. (1974) An evaluation of group work practice with AFDC mothers. In P. Glasser, R. Sarri, and R. Vinter (eds) *Individual Change through Small Groups*. New York: The Free Press.

Northen, H. (1969) *Social Work with Group*. New York: Columbia University Press.

Palmer, B. (1978) Fantasy and reality in group life. In N. McCaughan (ed.) *Group Work: Learning and Practice*. London: Allen and Unwin.

Parfit, J. (1970) *Group Work with Parents in Special Circumstances*. London: National Children's Bureau.

Parloff, M. B. and Dies, R. R. (1977) Group psychotherapy outcome research 1966–1975. *International Journal of Group Psychotherapy 27* (3): 281–319.

Payne, C. (1978) Working with Groups in a residential setting. In N. McCaughan (ed.) *Group Work: Learning and Pactice*. London: Allen and Unwin.

Reid, W. J. and Epstein, L. (1972) *Task Centred Casework*. New York: Columbia University Press.

Rice, A. K. (1965) *Learning for Leadership*. London: Tavistock.

Roberts, R. W. and Northen, H. (1976) *Theories of Social Work with Groups*. New York: Columbia Unversity Press.

Rooney, R. (1977) Adolescent groups in public schools. In W. J. Reid and L. Epstein (eds) *Task Centred Practice*. New York: Columbia University Press.

Ryder, E. L. (1976) A functional approach. In R. W. Roberts and H. Northen (eds) *Theories of Social Work with Groups*. New York: Columbia University Press.

Schinke, S. P. et al. (1975) Behavioural assertion training in groups: a comparative clinical study. Doctoral dissertation, Wisconsin University.

Schwartz, W. and Zalba, S. (eds) (1971) *The Practice of Group Work*. New York: Columbia University Press.

Shaffer, J. B. P. and Galinsky, M. D. (1974) *Models of Group Therapy and Sensitivity Training*. Englewood Cliffs, New Jersey: Prentice-Hall.

Shearer, A. (1979) Tragedies revisited. *Social Work Today 10*: 19, 20 and 21.

Sinclair, I. (1975) Influence of wardens and matrons on probation hostels: a study of a quasi-family institution. In J. Tizard, I. Sinclair and R. V. G. Clarke *Varieties of Residential Experience*. London: Routledge and Kegan Paul.

Smith, C. S., Farrant, M. R. and Marchant, H. J. (1972) *The Wincroft Youth Project*. London: Tavistock.

Stevenson, O. and Parsloe, P. (eds) (1978) Social service teams: the practitioner's view. London: Department of Health and Social security.

Toselcand, R. and Rose, S.(1978) Evaluating social skills training for older adults in groups. *Social Work Research and Abstracts 14* (1): 25–33.

Tropp, E. (1976) A developmental theory. In R. W. Roberts and H. Northen (eds) *Theories of Social Work with Groups*. New York: Columbia University Press.

Vickery, A. Rawcliffe, C. and Ward, V. (1978) Choice of the group as a target of intervention. In N. McCaughan (ed.) *Group Work: Learning and Practice*. London: Allen and Unwin.

Walker, L. (1978) Work with a parents group: individual and social learning through peer group experience. In McCaughan (1978).

Whitaker, D. (1978) The place of theory in the teaching of social group work. In N. McCaughan and K. McDougall (eds) *Group Work: A Guide for Teachers and Practitioners*. London: National Institute for Social Work.

Wills, D. (1971) *Spare the Child*. Harmondsworth: Penguin.

7 Self-help health groups

David Robinson

Over the past quarter of a century there has been a substantial and
rapid growth of self-help groups and organizations which, taken
together, now represent a significant feature of contemporary life.
This is often referred to as the self-help movement, and some have
seen us as moving 'towards a self-help society' (Radford, 1975). Not
surprisingly, a good deal of attention has been given to self-help and
self-help groups by both professionals and governments as well as by
interested laymen and the media. In fact, over the past five years there
has hardly been any wide-circulation newspaper or magazine, or any
journal of social work, sociology, psychology, psychiatry, nursing or
education, which has not carried an article on some aspect of self-help
or on the activities of some particular group. Alcoholics Anonymous,
of course, has been frequently written about, as have Al-Anon groups,
Recovery Inc., Little People groups, Synanon and other drug rehabilitation groups, Gamblers Anonymous, TOPS (Take Off Pounds
Sensibly) Inc., and many hundreds more, including the delightful,
but as yet unconfirmed, Analysands Anonymous, said to be open to
anyone who has been in analysis for twelve years or longer and needs
the help of a power greater than his own – or that of his analyst – to
terminate the analysis.

As well as the main-stream of self-help groups there are other related developments which are often referred to as part of the self-help movement. Among them are the various volunteer schemes; the 'integrity' groups developed by Mowrer (1971) and other small groups; the growing number of self-treatment groups, self-examination and self-care programmes which aim to lessen dependence on the medical professions and, finally, the 'health by the people' and other self-health projects in the developing world which are, at last, being reported (Newell, 1975). In fact, the rhetoric of self-help is all-pervasive. But what are self-help groups, and how do they work?

Until very recently 'self-help' has received surprisingly little systematic analysis either at a broad general level or at the level of particular groups and activities. In fact, the great bulk of self-help literature, apart from that produced by the groups themselves, has tended to be either rather romantic newspaper reporting or the opinions of conventional helpers, which range from the patronizing and condescending to the snide and openly hostile.

Hurwitz (1970), for example, acknowledged that he may have lost his 'professional objectivity' and be displaying 'non-professional enthusiasm' when, at the end of his much-referred-to article on Peer Self-Help Psychotherapy Groups, he sums up as follows:

> It is important to recognise the PSHPG (peer self-help psycho-therapy groups) achieve their goals (of changing people) without the application of specific behaviour modification techniques, without an existential search for identity, without the exploration of human potential, without awareness training to actualize one's potential, without the analysis of the transference neurosis, without psychodrama, without clearing engrams, without creative fighting, without mind expanding drugs, without sensory awakening, without feeling each other up, without taking off one's clothes, and without sexual intercourse between therapists and clients.

Self-help groups achieve their goal, he says, by being:

> fellowships whose members have a common problem. ... Within such relationships, and in the presence of members who acknowledge the help they receive through fellowship, the peers make it possible and desirable to accept each other's efforts to modify their own and others' behaviour.

In this fellowship lies the essence of *mutual* self-care, which Mowrer

(1971) succinctly identified as 'you can't do it alone, but you alone can do it'.

Fortunately, over the past few years there *have* been a number of attempts to analyse the nature of self-help. Writers such as Alfred Katz and Eugene Bender (1976), in particular, and Gerald Caplan and Marie Killilea (1976), have been gathering together the scattered literature in order to discover what self-help is taken to be and to begin to describe what in practice self-help groups do. Killilea (1976), for example, picks out seven characteristics of self-help groups which tend to be stressed. These are:

(1) *Common experience of the members*: the belief that among the primary characteristics of self-help groups is that the care-giver has the same disability as the care-receiver.

(2) *Mutual help and support*: the fact that the individual is a member of a group which meets regularly in order to provide mutual aid.

(3) *The helper principle*: which draws attention to the fact that in a situation in which people help others with a common problem it may be the helper who benefits most from the exchange.

(4) *Differential association*: which emphasizes members' mutual reinforcement of self-concepts of normality and hastens their separation from their previous conception of themselves as deviant.

(5) *Collective willpower and belief*: the tendency of each person to look to others in the group for validation of his feelings and attitudes.

(6) *Importance of information*: the promotion of greater factual understanding of the problem as opposed to intrapsychic understanding.

(7) *Constructive action toward shared goals*: the notion that groups are action-oriented, their philosophy being that members learn by doing and are changed by doing.

On the basis of the massive literature produced by the groups, they most typically see themselves as 'fellowships'. Great stress is put on the *common* problem, position or circumstances, which are collo-quially expressed as 'being in the same boat'. 'Being in the same boat' means, first of all, understanding the problems of others, i.e. 'knowing what it's like'. It is said that only those experiencing the problem can *really* understand. As CARE, the Cancer Aftercare and Rehabilitation Society, put it:

> The organisation consists in the main of cancer patients – people who know what it is like to have cancer, who know the problems, mental and social, associated with the disease. These people we feel are best fitted to give moral assistance and help to patients and families before and after treatment.

It is this understanding based on common experience, say the groups, which produces the necessary common bond of mutual interest and common desire to do something about the problem. And the basic ingredient of this 'doing something' is collectively helping oneself. As SHARE, a self-help group for the disabled, say – to help others is to help yourself. 'SHARE differs from practically all other organizations in the disablement field', they say, 'in that it aims not so much to do things *for* the disabled, as to help them to help themselves.'

In addition to collectively helping oneself, and helping oneself through helping someone else, there is the repeated stress on the importance of 'example' in the sharing of experiences and coping. A point succinctly expressed again by CARE: 'What better therapy than seeing someone who has had exactly what you have got, and who is ... participating in all the normal activities of work and social life.' What better therapy indeed! But being in the same boat, sharing experiences and helping yourself by helping others, while excellent statements of what self-help is, give little indication of how self-help groups actually do their work.

What's the problem?

Before looking at how the groups actually do what they do alone, together, altruistically for themselves, it may be useful to consider why there is any need to do anything at all. In short, what is the problem? Clearly the range of problems, any one of which may be shared in a particular self-help group, is immense. They may be physical, practical, mental, emotional, spiritual or social.

In any aspect of physical condition, mental well-being or social position or activity, there will be those who are technically 'abnormal'. There are those with illnesses such as cancer, or disablements such as amputations, colostomy, stammering, skin blemishes or blindness. There are those with abnormal mental attributes such as feelings of chronic depression, guilt or fear. There are those whose interpersonal behaviour is abnormal, such as those who batter children, make love to them, or choose not to have them; and there are those with some social-situational abnormality such as being a single parent, or homeless, or a mental patient, or divorced. Such technical 'abnormalities', however, are not necessarily a major problem. While there may be practical difficulties they may not be insurmountable. As an article in the popular magazine *Honey* (Brown, 1976) explained, under the heading 'Big Problems for Little People':

> The physical limitations of restricted growth are relatively easy to overcome – or at least learn to live with. Clothes can be made to measure and household appliances, and even cars, can be specially adapted to suit the little person's need. Telephone kiosks, door handles and shaver points can, of course, present problems, but Mr Pocock carries a neat briefcase which opens into two steps for just such eventualities.

Clearly, what turns technical abnormalities into major problems is the way they are interpreted by the people themselves, or by others. To return to the *Honey* article: 'What is distressing for people of restricted growth is the way in which people don't respect the fact that little people have an opinion, a view of life and that they want to contribute.' Despite efforts to discount the attitudes of others, for example by saying 'society doesn't understand', it is easy to see how, for many people, the combination of technical abnormality and social stigma assumes central and overwhelming importance. Listen to how a member of Weight Watchers described it to us (Robinson and Henry, 1977).

> Well, I grew very, very fat over the years and inside me was the slim person that I had always been. But when I was slim I wasn't aware that I was slim ... The only thing I wanted was to be slim again. It mattered, it was the only thing that mattered to me. The only thing. It mattered to me passionately. It meant that when I was fat, wherever I went, I was conscious not of being a woman, not of being a nothing, or of being a something, or of being a friend, or of being a stranger. I was conscious only of being a fatty ... Day and night for years it got me that bad.

Not surprisingly the end result is to lose all sense of personal value. People describe themselves as feeling guilty and ashamed, feeling inadequate, having no identity, no place in life, distressed, angry, and finally alone, since there may be a gradual slide into secrecy, seclusion and isolation. How, then, does self-help work for people like these with problems of technical abnormality and social stigma?

How do self-help groups work?

At first glance, self-help groups appear to do so many different activities for so many different purposes that any attempt to generalize seems futile. Nevertheless, it is possible to draw out a number of dominant themes and practices which, for the sake of convenience, can be summarized under 'sharing' and 'project work'.

Sharing

Sharing is the sharing of information and common experience. The mechanics of sharing range from formal group meetings where, as in Alcoholics Anonymous, a crucial part is taken up with the telling of life stories, to no less important informal meetings between group members; telephone contact networks, correspondence and newsletters, or tape exchanges and radio contacts when the members are geographically dispersed or prevented by their shared problem from meeting face-to-face. In Touch, for example, a self-help group of parents of mentally handicapped children, has a network of correspondence magazines. In these, parents of children with a similar condition take part in a 'magazine' which consists of letters from each of them. When each mother receives the magazine she reads all the other letters and replaces her own last letter with a new one commenting on the points raised. The magazines circulate continuously and so each member gets up to a dozen letters every few weeks whilst writing only one. Some of them have been in operation for several years.

The degree to which 'sharing' is explicitly recognized as a major feature of self-help activity varies from group to group. But irrespective of this, the crucial question is what does sharing mean? How does it actually feature in the day-to-day working of self-help groups? Needless to say, Alcoholics Anonymous, an archetypal self-help group, has recognized the importance of these questions. *Box 514*, the AA newsletter, put it this way:

> Sharing is truly more than a word ... Perhaps we should, from time to time, re-examine what we really mean by sharing – and what it is we are offering to share. What, in other words, is the reality behind the symbolic concept of sharing? What do we really mean, for example, when we say that we share our 'experience, strength and hope'? The problem is not that it is inaccurate to say that we are offering experience, strength and hope – but that the words alone fail to convey the total sense of what we are offering.

The 'symbolic concept' of sharing is *translated into action* in terms of *de*-construction and *re*-construction. De-construction emphasizes the group's attention to specific aspects of their common problems and how these are settled on and then defused, dispersed, and generally coped with. Re-construction emphasizes those activities geared to the production of a new way of everyday life.

Paradoxically, perhaps, the de-construction of the problem initially involves concentrating on it. For a familiar part of the self-help group-work is to help people to settle, from among a whole complex of everyday problems of living, upon one clearly defined problem and agree that it is the 'real' one: admitting that one is 'an alcoholic', for example, or 'a child abuser'. Once 'the' problem is settled on, admitted, acknowledged or brought out into the open, a second stage of de-construction can begin: the sharing of information about practical solutions to technical difficulties. This may be at the level of physical aids, dietary advice, information about official agencies and rights – in short anything which makes it more possible to handle the technicalities of the shared problem. Clearly, the range of specific practical aids being used in self-help programmes is immense.

The third level of de-construction, the most difficult, aims at destigmatization: dispersing the perceived social discreditability of the members and their shared problems. This position is nicely sumarized by the Association of the Childless and Childfree: 'The childless are under the same pressure as the childfree and *their common interest lies in trying to make it quite an unremarkable thing not to have children*.' One way of destigmatizing the problem is by changing members' self-perception, a feat partly achieved by meeting others in the same situation and, therefore, feeling less odd. 'Our self-help groups', said the Director of the National Council for One Parent Families, 'have a double value to lone parents and their children in providing the mutual support that is so helpful to them and also helping the children to have a real social identity by realizing that there are many lone parents and the children are, therefore, not in any way unusual'.

It is common for nearly all groups to direct their destigmatizing efforts towards changing those who are seen as the *cause* of the stigma: 'the general public', or 'society', or just all those who 'do not understand'. The Society of Skin Camouflage says that it 'aims to develop a greater understanding and awareness of our needs and problems in both the public and the medical and allied professions'. In short, then, self-help groups aim to destigmatize the problem by changing both their members *and* outsiders. CHE sums it up this way:

> The Campaign for Homosexual Equality provides a framework within which all women and men – whatever their sexual preference – can work together to end all forms of discrimination against gay people ... And while emphasizing the special needs of gay people that must be catered for, we wish to encourage people of different sexualities to integrate freely and to end the gay ghetto situation.

As well as the de-construction and relief of stigmatized problems, self-help groups can also provide recipes for an altered or re-constructed life. At the same time they provide a forum for putting these recipes into action. The 're-structuring of life' may be more or less explicit and more or less detailed; but at whatever level, the enabling and encouraging of a new way of living and a new way of seeing one's self and one's place in the world is a core aspect of self-help activity. In most cases this re-structuring is accomplished through project work.

Projects

It is difficult to generalize about projects, but basically they can be defined as co-operative activities, planned and organized by the members to achieve certain predetermined goals, and more or less explicit depending upon the particular group. But no matter how elaborate or involving a project is, it is essential that it is important to the members. And, clearly, the most important thing to most members is their shared problem and so, naturally, most self-help project work is based on the core task of helping fellow members with their problem.

Indeed, the whole Alcoholics Anonymous programme can be seen as a collection of 'projects' designed to help fellow alcoholics. From merely telling his own drinking story at a group meeting to 'twelfth-stepping' (i.e. sponsoring newcomers), the AA member is actively helping fellow alcoholics. In learning to tell his story appropriately, for example, the newcomer in AA is transforming his past experience into experience of value which can be put to constructive use. His story provides yet another story for the group to draw on and identify with. It is a means of distancing himself from the drinking experience and it is also his personal example to use in the individual work of 'twelfth-stepping' and 'sponsorship'. As time goes on, the problem experience becomes only a part of the member's story. It is added to by reportable stages in the AA group life, and by aspects of life outside the group which are an ever-growing contrast with the 'problem' time before AA (Robinson, 1979).

Time, and in particular the concentration on particular units or periods of time, is a recurrent theme in much self-help activity. Explicit distinctions are often made between time now and time past, while references to origins and 'the first time' are frequently made. Time is often formally structured in 'steps' and tightly maintained by group members and related to time targets which may be formally celebrated as in Gamblers Anonymous's 'Pin Night' or Weight Watchers' measuring of 'Goal Weight'. Time in the future is devalued while learning to live in the present, 'one day at a time', is stressed. Particular problems may be there for *all time* and since relapses can happen at *any time*, self-help commitment must be *full-time*. To ensure that self-help commitment is full-time, it is not enough for project work to be restricted to formal group meetings; it has to carry over into everyday life, and life outside the group. This is a major feature of self-help activity.

Successful self-help groups are much more than huddle-together sessions for people who feel discriminated against or overwhelmed by a common problem or by some aspect of late twentieth-century life. The groups which offer most to their members are those which manage to combine mutual support for those who share a common problem with projects which enable people to build up a new set of relationships. Some women's self-help groups provide a good example of the way in which self-help can be an opportunity for growth rather than just a refuge from an unacceptable world. An important feature of self-health groups is for women to get to know, understand, monitor, respond to, control and appreciate the nature of the functioning of their own bodies. But in the good groups this is only the beginning. The speculum is the instrument for opening up the passage not merely to one's cervix but to a new way of life. Linda Dove (1977), in a familiar declaration, succinctly makes the point: 'Sometimes it seems that doctors and lovers have had more access to our bodies than we have. We must have power over our own bodies to control our lives.' That is the core of the self-help project method; to settle from among all the problems that one faces on a clear, understandable and manageable one, to 'find' that one can manage it and then build a new life as a person who can control one's everyday problems and, thus, one's destiny. The project method, based on a shared appreciation of the need to structure time and transmitted through 'group talk', is then not just a matter of doing but is a matter of being. It is a matter of being in the group but also of being outside the group. Self-help is a way of life. As the founder of the Association for the Childless and Childfree put it:

> just being together improved morale and made us realize that being childless is not just a case for endless feelings of misery and hidden inadequacy but a chance for another kind of future based on finding the best in ourselves and offering it to others in whatever way appropriate.

Self-help and professionals

Recent years have seen profound changes in the world's political climate. Among other things there has been a concerted effort on the part of many nations to ensure a fairer return for their natural resources and a growing demand for more equitable distribution of the world's wealth, including health services. No one should be misled into thinking, of course, that because the developed countries have highly sophisticated medical services they also have high levels of health. As Dr Mahler (1977), Director-General of the World Health Organization, pointed out, 'medical affluence should not be confused with health abundance'. He went on to remind his European audience of the 'limits of medicine', to warn of the dangers of making people dependent on a medical 'aristotechnocracy' and then, quite rightly, to place issues of health and illness, caring and curing in their political context:

> In many countries the so-called 'health' industry is already consuming a high proportion of the national manpower pool and is approaching the upper limit, beyond which it could be seriously questioned whether medical care, as currently practised, is not becoming detrimental to further economic development.

Medicine, as practised by the medical establishment of developed countries, is certainly seen as a major threat to health; not only in the technical sense of malpractice and inappropriate treatment, and in its insatiable demand for manpower and resources, but in the wider political sense of diverting attention from the social-structural and environmental causes of ill-health.

Self-help groups are often seen as one way of undermining or, at least, counterbalancing the power of the established health professions. Some people, in fact, are confident that a health revolution has started. They have seen the rapid increase in the number of self-help groups as 'a social movement' or even as one manifestation of 'a new era of self-determination'. Some have waxed quite lyrical and seen self-help as a sign of the new Jerusalem. Vattano (1972), for example, considers self-help groups to be 'signs of an evolving more democratic society', while Dumont (1974) feels they represent 'a reification of the aspirations of the Founding Fathers, with their concern for individual rights, balance of power, and de-centralization of power within pluralistic structures'. But what real evidence is there for believing that such revolution is at hand? Claims that it is certainly underplay the variety of self-help groups, with their differing origins, aims, activities, structures, philosophies and political stances. To suggest, for example, as Vattano (1972) does, that self-help groups represent a form of counter-cultural protest with a 'power to the people' political stance is just too gross a simplification to be helpful. For Alfred Katz (1975), such a claim does not withstand a moment's analysis of, for example, the philosophy, values or internal operations of groups like Alcoholics Anonymous or Recovery Inc., two of the largest, most influential and, in many respects, most useful of the self-help groups. 'The aim of groups like AA', he says, 'is exactly that of assisting their members to conform to the values of the dominant middle-class society.'

So, *are* self-help groups the vanguard of the health revolutionaries or the rearguard of the medical establishment? Is self-help, as it is now operating in relation to health, the great alternative which some people hoped for? These are the broad questions which anyone who is interested in self-help will keep coming back to and will answer in accordance with their own confidence and interpretation of the evidence to hand.

The limits of self-help

Although some people believe that self-help groups are paving the way for a radical change in the way everyday problems are handled, and even providing a blueprint for the construction of a new socio-political order, it does not take long to realize that, for a variety of reasons, most self-help health groups seem neither inclined, nor likely to be able, to accomplish any grand political changes.

One of the major limits to self-help is that most groups tend to operate with the same view of health and illness as conventional helpers. Problems, however they arise, are seen to be the responsibility of the individual. The core aim of both conventional help and most self-help is to do something to, or with, people who 'have' problems, in order that they might be better able to find their way around the world as it is. Those self-help groups which look beyond the immediate concerns of their members do little more than press for some adaptation of the current professional or administrative system. They push for recognition of their problem, or for more humane, accessible or competent professional treatment for it.

Concentration on individuals and their problems is, of course, an essential feature of the self-help process. It is the basis upon which sharing and project work can begin to disperse the problem and construct a more bearable life. But it means, as well, that self-help groups rarely focus their attention on any broader structural features of the shared situation in which they find themselves. The fact that modern industrial production concentrates the workforce, and thus the majority of the population, in dense urban centres where 'home-lessness, overcrowding, noise, stress, and loneliness are at their most acute and where the emotional and psychological if not physical health of the population is at its most fragile' (Versluysen, 1977) is never high on the agenda of self-help group meetings. Their attention is much more likely to be given over to making sure that one is serviced properly, rather than to raising the question of whether one needs the service, or of what changes need to be made in order to make it less likely that the 'problem' which needs servicing will arise at all.

Not only do most groups not look at the broad causes of their problems but they may, by their self-help activities, exacerbate them. The Sidels (1976) use the example of neighbourhood associations to make this point:

> neighbourhood-based mutual aid groups provide an excuse for responsible government authorities to avoid fulfilling their obligations. Suggesting that people attempt, with inadequate resources, to build up their own communities or to provide their own services may divert them from seeking their full share of the resources of the entire society.

Another way in which the activities of self-help groups may exacerbate the very health problem they are trying to alleviate relates to the split between the technical and the caring aspects of professional medicine. Many groups develop in response to the low level of human care in many parts of the medical services. For example, CARE say that medically the patient is checked regularly but, since 'the shock, worry and anxiety' goes unheeded this is where the work of CARE starts. In this way, self-help groups are, in many instances, encouraging professionals to avoid the caring aspects of their professional activities and to focus increasingly on its less personally difficult or threatening technological aspects. The activities of articulate middle-class self-help groups may, by taking some of the responsibility for human care away from the professionals, make the medical services even more inhuman and 'technical' for those who are least likely either to cope or complain. On the other hand, reducing professional spheres of activity to the narrow confines of technical expertise could be seen as a step in the right direction by those who want the medical profession's power reduced, by getting them withdrawn from 'community', 'social' and 'caring' commitment to being just one of the many groups of technicians which the lay person calls upon when the need arises.

Clearly everyone involved in self-help groups, however successful they feel they are in alleviating or handling the 'problems' of their members, should ask themselves the following question: 'Is what I am doing likely to increase or decrease the number of people with this problem?' In other words, they must consider the extent to which they collude with the kind of conditions which may have caused, maintained, or accentuated the 'problem' in the first place. That is the core dilemma for everyone who gives 'help', whether they are self-helpers or professionals.

Rather than just tinkering with the existing services, some groups *do* try to wrest control from the professional by disseminating 'technical knowledge' and encouraging the lay person to become their own expert. The separation of the group's experiential knowledge and expertise from the professional's technical knowledge and expertise is an explicit and important political act. Gaining, or regaining, control over aspects of one's own body and life is a clear statement about oneself and one's place in the world. Nevertheless, many self-help groups pre-empt any possibility of building on that base by becoming professionalized clients. Although the self-helpers may gain some control over handling their shared 'problem', the nature of the helping is, often, no different from that given by the professional from whom control has been taken. Rather than offering an alternative to professional services, members seek to 'service' themselves and their fellows as they were once 'serviced' by professional helpers. As Dewar (1976) puts it: 'Rather than changing the content of the help, they merely alter *who* does it. Rather than learning about and dealing with the *cause* of the condition in question, they seize control of currently accepted "cures".'

One of the consequences of this concentration on who gives expert help, rather than on what is the cause of the problem, is that self-help groups tend to remain separated and isolated from each other. The emphasis on the shared particular problem and how it can best be handled for those in that particular group means that there is little sense of common identity across problems. Not only that, but a familiar feature of the self-help world is the bickering and antagonism between self-help groups which are concerned with similar problems. However, one of the severest limitations of the political impact of self-help comes not from the fact that the self-help world is fragmented, but from the groups' willingness to co-operate with professionals for immediate practical purposes.

Professionals are, and always have been, intimately involved with even those self-help groups which are considered to be most independent and self-sufficient. In their wide-ranging review of self-help organizations, Traunstein and Steinman (1973) found that approximately one in three groups were started in close co-operation with professionals. Nevertheless, the nature of the relationship between self-help groups and professionals varies from group to group. Some groups are clearly proud of having close connections with, and the approval of, the medical and other professions and stress these links in their literature. The U and I Club, while claiming that for many women their self-help procedures have eradicated years of cystitis and thrush, also stress that they 'work within the confines of conventional medicine'. Many other groups see themselves as independent from, but closely related to, the activities of professional services. They 'pick up the pieces' or handle aspects of their members' problems which the professions cannot or choose not to deal with.

This 'separate-but-compatible' view of self-help and the professionals is not shared by all groups. For some, it is precisely because the medical profession could not, or would not, deal appropriately with them or their problems that helping themselves is so important. Most women's self-help groups are not just 'picking up the pieces' or providing peripheral support to the professional services, they are trying to change the nature of the medical enterprise. The core issue is 'control', from learning enough about one's own body and so demystifying the processes of health and illness to working for a radical change in the conventional helping services so that when a particular expertise is needed, it will be geared to the conditions, priorities and expectations of those who receive it.

Not surprisingly, there are many professionals who feel threatened by the growing number of self-help groups. Others, recognizing the value of particular self-help enterprises, have proposed that professionals should become directly involved. Mowrer (1971), for example, suggested that professionals could set up self-help groups and that universities should train and supply persons competent to perform this type of function. Others, not surprisingly, think such enthusiasm should be tempered, since it presents a number of problems which the 'facilitators' ought to be aware of. Will professional involvement, asks Jertson (1975), 'contribute to a loss of that one value uniquely cherished by the self-help group; the perceived ability to help itself?'

The day-to-day relationships between self-help groups, their members and professionals are, however, not laid down in the columns of professional journals. They are worked out in particular situations in accordance with the beliefs, inclinations and priorities of the people involved. It is in these situations that control begins to bite. The most obvious way of preventing a successful group from developing a sufficiently firm power base is, quite simply, to take it over. There is no need to 'facilitate', 'regulate', or 'co-operate', when you can 'incorporate'. As Jack Geiger has crisply described it, 'when the counter-culture develops something of value, the establishment rips it off and sells it back' (Jencks, 1976). The dilemma here is that while it may improve patient care, in the sense of providing a wider service of the kind which the group has shown to be of value, it pre-empts the self-help dimension which underpinned the activity in the first place.

Clearly, as self-help groups continue to thrive and prosper there will be many efforts by both professionals and government departments to control them. Only the most crude professional will say that he wants to control self-help groups because they are taking away his prestige, power or fees. Control will be exercised in relation to the issue of 'quality'; the idea that while many self-help groups are useful, or at least not harmful, there are some whose members are hurt by their participation. It follows from this, runs the argument, that self-help groups must be registered or 'evaluated' in order to protect the general public. Those groups which were thought to be harmful or 'inappropriate' would then be 'disbanded'.

To disagree with this argument is not to say, of course, that every self-help group improves the health and happiness of all its members. No doubt there are people who are dead now who would still be alive if they had never gone to a self-help group – just as there are people who are dead now who would still be alive if they had never gone into hospital. But the registration of self-help groups is not the answer to the 'quality control' question. The only thing to do as long as groups are operating within the law is to publicize the fact that some groups seem to be harmful in particular ways for certain people.

The most significant developments in relation to self-help health are likely to result not from governmental or professional concessions in the face of current 'economic reality', but from the day-to-day activities of a – hopefully – ever-increasing number of people who are quietly coming together to share and solve their common health problems, rather than put up with the frustrations and humiliations of professional services and large-scale administrative and State structures. That they do not seek dramatic political changes does not necessarily make their actions politically insignificant. In fact, many of them are operating a self-help 'project approach' to political issues. They are making manageable changes together. If such an approach works for 'insoluble problems' like alcoholism, they argue, why not for any other problem as well? Why not indeed, since undermining the foundations is just as effective a way of toppling a fortress as storming the ramparts!

References

Brown, A. (1976) Big problems for little people. *Honey 10*: 21.

Caplan, G. and Killilea, M. (eds) (1976) *Support Systems and Mutual Help: Multidisciplinary Explorations*. New York: Grune and Stratton.

Dewar, T. (1976) Professionalised clients as self-helpers. In *Self-Help and Health: A Report*. New York: New Human Services Institute, pp. 77–83.

Dove, L. (1977) Self-help centres in Los Angeles. *Spare Rib 55*: 26.

Dumont, M. P. (1974) Self-help treatment programs. *American Journal of Psychiatry 131* (6): 631–5.

Hurwitz, N. T. (1970) Peer self-help psychotherapy groups and their implications for psychotherapy. *Psychotherapy:Theory, Research and Practice 7* (1): 41–9.

Jencks, S. F. (1976) Problems in participatory health care. In *Self-Help and Health: A Report*. New York: New Human Services Institute, pp. 85–98.

Jertson, J. (1975) Self-help groups. *Social Work 20* (2): 144–5.

Katz, A. H. (1975) Some thoughts on self-help groups and the professional community. Paper to the National Conference on Social Welfare, San Francisco.

Katz, A. H. and Bender, E. I. (eds) (1976) *The Strength in Us: Self-Help Groups in the Modern World*. New York: Franklin Watts.

Killilea, M (1976) Mutual help organisations: interpretations in the literature. In G. Caplan and M. Killilea (eds) *Support Systems and Mutual Help: Multidisciplinary Explorations*. New York: Grune and Stratton.

Mahler, H. (1977) Problems of medical affluence. *WHO Chronicle 31*: 8–31.

Mowrer, O. H. (1971) Peer groups and medication: the best 'therapy' for professionals and laymen alike. *Psychotherapy: Theory, Research and Practice* 8 (1): 44–54.

Newell, K. W. (ed) (1975) *Health by the People*. Geneva: World Health Organization.

Radford, J. (1975) Towards a self-help community. *Talking Point* No. 23. Newcastle-upon-Tyne: Association of Community Workers.

Robinson, D. (1979) *Talking Out of Alcoholism: The Self-Help Process of Alcoholics Anonymous*. London: Croom Helm.

Robinson, D. and Henry, S. (1977) *Self-Help and Health: Mutual Aid for Modern Problems*. London: Martin Robertson.

Sidel, V. W. and Sidel, R. (1976) Beyond coping. *Social Policy 7*: 67–9.

Traunstein, D. M. and Steinman, R. (1973) Voluntary self-help organisation: an exploratory study. *Journal of Voluntary Action Research 2* (4): 230–93.

Vattano, A. J. (1972) Power to the people: self-help groups. *Social Work 17* (4): 7–15.

Versluysen, M. (1977) The politics of self-help. *Undercurrents 19*: 25–7.

8 Organization development in industry: perspectives on progress and stuckness

Robert T. Golembiewski

The common wisdom acknowledges that this is a momentous time for organization development, now widely known as OD. On the one hand, numerous signs imply progress – an increasing competence to influence the quality and direction of collective enterprises, burgeoning numbers of practitioners, a growing range of interventions, and so on. At the same time, clear signs of concern force themselves on even the casual observer.

This paper fixates on both progress and concern, and proposes to transcend both via a three-fold argument. In turn, this paper seeks to illustrate both the progress and the concern, to establish their simultaneous legitimacy as descriptions of contemporary OD, and to suggest ways to move tomorrow's OD beyond contemporary progress and concern. The title above says 'industry' but, while that will constitute the prime area for enquiry, the analysis will essentially apply to other areas of OD application as well.

OD as a growing area of action and research

How can we sample the signs of progress in today's OD? Each

approach has its limitations, of course. But each also has approximately the same bottom line, so we need not be timid. A first analysis offers two views of OD's recent favourable ferment. The first view emphasizes several specific indicators, while the second has a broader focus.

Some unmistakable signs of specific progress

Looking back over the brief time-frame of a quarter-century, some very nice things have happened within OD. Seven signs of specific progress serve to illustrate the broader family, and these signs will be presented in no particular order of significance.

First, and perhaps most significantly, OD practice has enlarged its focus to include a frequent emphasis on structural as well as on policy-oriented interventions. Structural OD interventions include the redesign of networks of authority and responsibility in large organizations (Carew et al., 1977), and of jobs or tasks (Frank and Hackman, 1975). Policy-oriented interventions can encompass a broad range, such as permitting increased employee freedom and discretion in the management of time (Golembiewski and Proehl, 1979), and seeking to reduce 'surplus repression' via the elimination of invidious and anachronistic status distinctions between classes of employees (Hulme and Bevan, 1975).

In contrast, over OD's early history the focus had been more or less unrelievedly on interaction-oriented designs. The primary approach involved the use of the T-groups, otherwise known as laboratory training or sensitivity training. The goal was to induce values, attitudes, and behavioural skills thought to facilitate change in organizations, as well as in small and temporary learning groups. Typically, organization members would be sent to 'stranger experiences' in T-groups, with the notion being that participants would return to their worksite with new or enhanced attitudes, behaviours and skills which would get transferred directly into work when the 'seeding' was sufficiently advanced that some 'critical mass' had been attained (Winn, 1971).

This common approach has three major liabilities. This transfer of change often did not occur at all; and even when it did, the home rather than work commonly became the locus of transfer. Moreover, the emphasis on interaction-centred designs severely limited the flexibility of OD practitioners and programmes, since many organizational problems were inherent in structure and policies. In many cases, the emphasis on interaction became seriously counter-productive as organization members sought to introduce relationship qualities experienced in small, temporary, and intimate groups into a collective enterprise whose structure and policies remained unyieldingly work-centred. Finally, interaction-centred designs often had an indiscriminate impact on some worksite problems. In Harrison's terminology (1972, p.57), they often intervened at 'too deep' a level.

Early OD practice did not approximate a monolith, of course. Occasionally, for instance, intact work teams would have a 'family' experience in a T-Group (Kuriloff and Atkins, 1966; Golembiewski and Carrigan, 1970a, 1970b), and positive outcomes were reported. Clearly, this eased the problems of transfer, but the approach did not somehow finesse the other two liabilities sketched above.

Second, the last decade has seen the proliferation of designs with quite specific objectives for learning or change – for role negotiation (Harrison, 1972), for conflict resolution (Walton, 1969; Filley, 1975), for diverse team-building situations (Dyer, 1977), and so on. Concerning team-building, for example, even the journeyman diagnostician should now realize that the selection of a design variant ought to depend on the specific conditions encountered. At least five such types of conditions have been isolated, and appropriate design variants for them have been described (Dyer, 1977). Thus the diagnostician must ask:

(1) Does the need for intervention derive from a 'crisis of agreement' or a 'crisis of disagreement' (Harvey, 1977) in an existing team (see p.213)?
(2) Does the more specific target involve negotiating of appropriate roles?
(3) Is the goal to get a new team off to a good start?
(4) Does a once-successful but now complacent team require revivification?
(5) Does the 'team problem' actually derive from inter-team conflict?

This growing specificity is not pure gain, but it does contrast markedly with earlier general practice. Many observers express concern that some OD practitioners view such target-specific designs as a 'tool-kit', whose components get applied without sufficient diagnosis of the specific locus of application.

In substantial contrast, the earlier OD emphasis had a more generic character, as shown by general prescriptions about 'being open' and 'being in touch with one's self' which needed to be grounded in diagnosis of specific worksites for which interventions could be developed. In many cases, these prescriptions could encourage exotic if not extreme interventions several orders of magnitude more powerful than required. The title of one article in the popular literature graphically projects the character of these common early injunctions: 'It's OK to Cry in the Office' (Poppy, 1968). In some cases, this prescription could be right on-target. In other cases, the injunction could induce puzzlement among those who sought (and required) only some lesser amelioration of their worksite; and it might generate guilt when individuals did not or could not provide the relevant behaviours, or were proscribed from providing them.

Third – as an in-depth complement of the extension in breadth sketched above – substantial research and experience has increased in major ways our knowledge about the costs and benefits of the several specific approaches to OD. Perhaps paramountly, research has enlightened the common wisdom concerning the incidence of trauma associated with various forms of group experience – sensitivity training, NTL T-groups, encounter, and so on (Yalom and Lieberman, 1971). Many were surprised by the incidence and severity of trauma reported by this study, although serious methodological criticisms can be made of it (Cooper, 1975) and although other available estimates of trauma are much lower (Golembiewski, 1972, pp.235–40). Similarly, accumulating experience and research with other types of interaction-centred designs, such as the many varieties of team-building, as well as with structural designs (Frank and Hackman, 1975) and policy-oriented designs (Golembiewski and Proehl, 1979), now permit a degree of choice for interveners not available even a few years ago.

This heightened specificity relates to both diagnosis and prognosis. Consider my own practice with a standard team-building design (Golembiewski, 1979, esp. pp.336–9), the total training time for which approximates 4–5 days from initial diagnosis to reinforcement experience. Given a normal conflict situation, such as a 'crisis of disagreement' (Harvey, 1977), frequent use of the design permits me to tell clients with at least 90 per cent confidence, in the context of Table 8.1:

> If you agree that the dimensions measured by the Group Behavior Inventory are important ones for your team, and if you want the changes sketched below in Table 8.1 to occur in your team, I can suggest a design that almost always works. The design tends to induce changes like those described, changes that tend to be maintained over at least a 3–6 month interval. I do recommend a booster experience during the 3–6 month period, incidentally. I get surprised every once in a while, but not very often.

Table 8.1   Dimensions of group behaviour inventory, and effects predicted to follow from a standard team-building design

Group behaviour inventory dimensions*	Predicted effects of team-building experience
I *Group effectiveness.* This dimension describes group effectiveness in solving problems and in formulating policy through a creative, realistic team effort.	Most members will report higher scores.
II *Approach to versus withdrawal from leader.* At the positive pole of this dimension are groups in which members can establish an unconstrained and comfortable relationship with their leader – the leader is approachable.	Many members will report higher scores, but the manager is a probable exception as are those few cases who try to 'approach' but see it as not working or as inducing punishment.
III *Mutual influence.* This dimension describes groups in which members see themselves and others as having influence with other group members and the leader.	Will increase for most members, with the probable exceptions of those noted under II.
IV *Personal involvement and participation.* Individuals who want, expect, and achieve participation in group meetings are described by this dimension.	Will increase for most or all members, with the possible exception of the manager.

Table 8.1 continued

V	*Intragroup trust* v. *intragroup competitiveness.* At the positive pole, this dimension depicts a group in which the members have trust and confidence in each other.	Will increase for most or all members, with the possible exception of the manager.
VI	*General evaluation of meetings.* This dimension is a measure of a generalized feeling about the meetings of one's group as good, valuable, strong, pleasant, as contrasted with bad, worthless, weak, unpleasant.	Will increase for most or all members.

*Friedlander (1970) isolated these dimensions and developed an appropriate measuring instrument.

Fourth, growing numbers of OD interventions have been extended to very large systems and to employees at all levels of organization (e.g. Kimberly and Nielsen, 1975). Typically, these systemic efforts take one or both of two approaches: survey feedback designs (Nadler, 1977; Golembiewski and Hilles, 1979), which solicit opinions from a broad range of organization members as a basis for ameliorative action, based on feedback of the opinions and subsequent planning sessions; or socio-technical designs (e.g. Thorsrud, 1976), which rest on principles for developing networks of tasks that are more satisfying than the previous structuring of tasks and which often yield higher levels of productivity. The first major round of such efforts, often called quality of working-life (or QWL), has been completed and extensive evaluations are now under way. Initial reactions are complex and mixed (Macy, 1978; Golembiewski, 1979, Part 2, esp. pp.300–30), but there seems no doubt that the evolving QWL technology can be potent even if we seem some distance from routinely predicting effects. In one case, for example, a QWL effort was sold as contributing to the 'democratization' of the worksite and to a more pleasing emotional tone among employees. Productivity might increase, the interveners realized, but this effect would be dealt with if and when it occurred. The results obtained imply a potency that obviously requires fine-tuning. Cost figures improved substantially while worker attitudes and feelings deteriorated (Macy, 1978), due to technical improvements in the structuring of work without an appropriate normative or social context. These technical changes permitted greater efficiency, but with unanticipated side-effects that stressed individuals and their relationships with each other and with management.

Survey feedback and socio-technical designs have dramatically extended both the reach and grasp of OD and provide a significant complement to earlier efforts which often seemed impactful but, with only a few exceptions (most notably that documented by Marrow, Bowers and Seashore, 1967), were restricted to narrow ranges of indicators of success.

Fifth, confidence in interpreting OD effects has increased substantially because of the growing attention to tracking OD effects over extended periods of time. So-called longitudinal studies have never been superabundant (Morrison, 1978), but they can be very helpful in eliminating alternative explanations of the effects of OD interventions.

The point should not be overstated because the OD literature contains some examples of longitudinal studies, both early (Blake, Mouton, Barnes and Greiner, 1964) as well as later (Golembiewski and Carrigan, 1970a, 1970b). Indeed, the granddaddy of all longitudinal OD studies covered eight years (Seashore and Bowers, 1970), and that research began about fifteen years ago.

Sixth, the present OD literature reflects a growing emphasis on objective measures – output, efficiency, scrap, absenteeism, and so on. This is particularly true of the recent flurry of QWL studies (e.g. Macy, 1978), but that concern also characterizes a broad range of work in the private sector as well as in public organizations (Boss, 1979). Such objective measurement has usually been considered to be especially difficult in the public sector, but it has been considered vital in all organizations.

No sharp contrast between the old and new research in OD is appropriate, but one can easily distinguish some central tendencies. 'Old' OD research sometimes gave major attention to objective or 'bottom-line' measures (Blake, Mouton, Barnes and Greiner, 1964). Far more often, however, that research had one of two qualities: either the OD intervention could be related to such measures only by distant chains of effect (e.g. Beckhard, 1966); or the research focused on the measurement of changes in managerial behaviour or organization climate which descriptive studies have often found to be associated with high satisfaction but less often with high productivity (e.g. Golembiewski and Carrigan, 1970a, 1970b). Research with these two qualities does suggest some linkage, but that does not constitute the most powerful proof of OD effects.

Seventh, and in every sense the *summum bonum* of OD experience and research, far more attention has been given of late to *the* essential question in both theory and practice. That question is: Of the several alternative designs for intervening, which will generate the best results under various sets of conditions?

There can never be too much attention to this magnum-question, and in any case today's OD literature certainly does not come close to 'too much'. But one can fairly conclude that the last few years reflect much more of this critical type of research than the entire previous history of OD (Bowers, 1973; Dunn and Swierczek, 1977; Pasmore and King, 1978; Porras, 1979).

Moreover, such research has affected practice to a considerable degree, although we cannot yet report with confidence whether this has been for good or ill. The sharp recent increase in the use of survey feedback designs, for example, has clearly been encouraged by Bowers's (1973) seminal work. Using a very large number of cases, Bowers studied the relative efficacy of five alternative interventions:

(1) Survey feedback, i.e. feedback of survey data plus meetings to plan subsequent change.
(2) Hand-back of survey data, but with no meetings to plan subsequent change.
(3) Process consultation focused on interpersonal relations.
(4) Process consultation focused on task problems.
(5) Laboratory training in 'family' groups (i.e. T-groups for intact work teams).

Although major methodological criticisms can be made of Bowers's work (Golembiewski, 1979, esp. pp.396–7), his results surprised many and seem to have encouraged a major shift in OD practice. Generally, Bowers found that survey feedback designs seemed the most effective in the organizations he studied. What he called 'laboratory training' had a more chequered record, even though it had been the most favoured design at the time. Indeed, not only did laboratory training designs lack a favourable impact, their applications seemed to make matters worse in all the firms studied. 'Favourable' and 'worse' are used here to refer to common-sense evaluations of the direction of change. For example, a design that created greater communication difficulties for parties in an organization would be considered to worsen things.

Pointing to the recent appearance of such comparative research does not disparage OD. This kind of research must build on a substantial cumulative base. Thus alternative designs have to be developed, some consistent evidence of their common effects must be generated, and some substantial sense of important effects to compare must exist. All of these major developments, and many more beside, were required to permit the kind of comparative research referred to here. No wonder, then, that this last feature does not have exemplars in OD's early years.

Some unmistakable signs of progress, broader variety

Four perspectives suffice to illustrate from broader perspectives that OD has made major strides since it first emerged twenty-five years ago. Basically, these perspectives propose that OD is a 'something' that has left definite signs of its coming – a force that is with us, in the cinematic vernacular. In sum, the effects of that force are unmistakable: the terrain of organizational research and action has been affected in major, obvious and permanent ways.

Professional impact. Bustling professional activity constitutes one major sign of OD's arrival as an approach – perhaps even *the* approach – for grappling with the critical issues of our organizational society. Consider membership associations. In the last decade or so, the United States' OD Network has emerged as the major shaper and sharer of attitudes and skills. It now has some three thousand members, mostly practitioners; and it yearly hosts two week-long conferences that often amount to memorable 'happenings' whose kaleidoscopic qualities testify to the energy of OD aficionados and the turf they represent. On the academic side, the same force also has clear effects. The OD Division of the more staid Academy of Management has attracted approximately a thousand members, and that in the first five or six years of the Division's life. More recently, OD has also 'gone international' – east and west, capitalist and socialist, and so on.

Even more noteworthy, major progress toward certification of OD professionals has been made within the last decade. The International Association of Applied Social Scientists (IAASS) is now in its second cycle of five-year reviews of OD practitioners, and that implies a major change. And 'change' here encompasses both meanings that (I am told) comprise the Chinese pictogram for that concept. That pictogram is a composite of the symbols for two other words – one being 'opportunity' and the other 'danger'. In short, certification could develop in traditional ways: as protectionism of those already in the club, and as mindless baffles and socialization hurdles to keep other rascals out. Or new-style certification might become the order of the day: a periodic assessment by caring peers of the performance and development of colleagues, as part of a broader and continuing process of professional association, the most important component of which involves face-to-face meetings that focus on technical and ethical issues related to research and practice.

Institutional impact.   OD's professional ferment at once derives from, and provides momentum for, impact on major institutions. For example, about one-sixth of the total membership of the academically-oriented Academy of Management selects the OD Division as one of their major reference groups. This awesome fact reflects OD's very swift penetration into academic degree-programmes, curricula and courses. The penetration remains most pervasive in business schools, but increasingly also appears in public administration and affairs (Heimovics, 1978).

Not only educational institutions reflect the fact that OD has come their way. Many thousands of business and government organizations have come to value OD, often using a creative blend of internal and external resources. Less well-known is the fact that massive bureaucracies, like the military, recently have begun to produce *thousands* of resource-persons with OD skills, although they do not necessarily get identified in exactly those terms (Schaum, 1978). Such widespread use of OD is impressive in the context of the elemental datum that the first help-wanted ad for an OD 'change-agent' apparently did not appear until 7 October 1963 (Bennis, 1966, pp.113–14).

Research impact.   These professional and institutional effects rest not only on folk wisdom about the potency of OD interventions, but also on a rapidly-accumulating research literature. Bibliographies now generate lists that swell beyond six hundred items (Pate, 1976); and research in depth concerning even narrow families of interventions is now available (Dyer, 1977; Golembiewski and Proehl, 1979). This implies a full tide of effort by anyone's standards.

Significantly, the standards for acceptable OD research have also escalated of late. Many available studies meet rigorous criteria for research design (Morrison, 1978; Porras and Berg, 1978). Moreover, recognition is growing that 'research' comes in several major varieties, depending upon the objective (Porras and Roberts, 1978), which is a helpful antidote to the sterile debate about whether or not the natural-science approach constitutes the only legitimate research method. Most significantly, several scholars have also recently begun efforts to use the growing literature for integrative analyses in which they test sets of hypotheses (Dunn and Swierczek, 1977; Porras, 1979). Such research implies a substantial coming-of-age of the OD literature, especially in that no anomalies have yet emerged in the findings.

Diffusion impact. Efforts to diffuse knowledge and attitudes about OD also reflect its potency, as well as contribute to it. Thus the major success of the Addison-Wesley Series on Organizational Development – begun about a decade ago and now encompassing about fifteen small books – represents one effort at large-scale diffusion. Similarly, as late as a decade ago, no comprehensive texts on OD existed. That deficiency has been vigorously remedied of late (French and Bell, 1973; Huse, 1975; Margulies and Raia, 1979; Golembiewski, 1979, among others).

OD as posing challenges for action and research

Some dark clouds have recently begun to swirl over this golden vista. Discussions about OD's development often reflect a kind of serious in-betweenness which is variously expressed. For example, some see OD as having reached the end of a short cul-de-sac. A more moderate view proposes that 'OD has reached adolescence and is now looking for further ways to enhance its growth to maturity' (Burke, 1976, p.33).

As with human adolescence, this in-betweenness of OD gets reflected in various ways, such as indecision, fervent but shifting emotional attachments, truculence, mercurial shifts in fads that may be passionately embraced while they last, desperate we/theyness, and despair about whether there ever will be a better day. There are arguments about *what* is OD and what is not; there is turmoil associated with *who* is in OD, as reflected particularly in solemn debates about what constitutes appropriate training and apprenticeship, about credentialism, and penultimately about certification of OD practitioners; and there is growing evidence of, and resistance to, efforts to assimilate OD into more traditional but equally troubled areas of academic research such as OB (Organization Behaviour).

The expression we will use for OD's contemporary condition is 'stuckness', which subsequent analysis will approach from two perspectives. Initially the focus will be on several major signs of stuckness. Subsequently we will pay some attention to how OD can become unstuck.

Some unmistakable signs of stuckness

By what signs can OD stuckness be recognized? And how did OD come to be stuck? Basically, the view here proposes that overcoming OD's present condition requires a transition that will not come easily. The focus will be on 'research' and 'application', and the argument will have three major components, the last of which will get the most extensive attention.

Which led in the past? Early OD underwent a classic transition. Historically, OD was research-led. The two 'stems' that have rightly been said to constitute OD's vitals – laboratory education and survey feedback (French and Bell, 1973, pp.21–6) – evolved out of longish research traditions. The emphasis on small group analysis, which so significantly nourishes OD, goes back a century and has more proximate roots in the 'group dynamics' literature whose development extends over fifty years, more or less. The survey stem of OD constitutes a relative newcomer, to be sure, but even so the history of 'scientific polling' goes back at least a half-century.

This lengthy accumulation of knowledge and experience supported OD's great leap forward, a leap occurring with such zest and effect that OD quickly and usefully became application-led. The transformation remains incomplete, but it was very substantial. In gross terms, this effect is now reflected in such common dicta as that application is way ahead of research and theory, or that interveners have to make critical decisions without much guidance from research or theory. The associated mind-set appears in diverse guises. In one mini-history of OD, for example, *the* key event revealingly becomes the creation of the OD Network (Weisbord, 1978, p.3). I do not deny the Network's obvious centrality in the diffusion of OD, and in providing critical support for OD interveners. But the view above has currency only because it fits the fact that OD is now practitioner-led. Otherwise, that concept of OD's genesis is comparable to an explanation of the development of the atom bomb that fixates on Einstein's contact with President Roosevelt. Significant, yes; crucial, no; *the* central event, absolutely not.

This transition occurred quickly and implied some costs and opportunities, as do all such transitions. I propose here only that the transition did in fact occur. Not that everyone is either a white hat or a black hat, of course. Some OD interveners also consider themselves researchers, and vice versa, and some cannot divorce these two roles. But more rather than less, I argue, the balance has definitely swung, with application taking the lead. I see it as no accident that the OD Division of the Academy of Management took form substantially after the profound success of the OD Network, and with only a few of the same people being involved in both ventures. The Academy enthusiasts had strong roots in higher education, both in teaching and research; and the Network has a membership definitely tilted toward practitioners.

Your baby sure is ugly. Both contributing to and being reinforced by this professional history, various different tendencies encourage tension between intervention and research. I sample only. Research tends to lust after control of relevant variable, comprehensiveness, and contribution to knowledge; while application in the field is usually messy, partial, and the only measure of effect employed will often be the self-reports of those involved, even casually gathered. This encourages opposed symbolizations: 'big-domed people' versus 'us practical guys'; a 'white-coat mentality' versus the 'unsung heroes in the trenches'; and so on. Similarly, research may seem to clash head-on with skills relevant at the worksite: methodological criticism versus an optimism that things will work out; punctilious planning of events versus seizing the opportunity of the moment; sanctity of the research design versus tactical expedience; and tentativeness versus resolute gut-feelings that certain interventions really do help.

The contrasts above are clearly exaggerated, but even their milder forms can encourage interveners and researchers to describe the love-child of the other in such terms as: 'Your baby sure is ugly.' Considerations of ego and power can easily exacerbate this treacherous situation. To complicate the situation even more, OD research is being increasingly done by those whose values and skills differ substantially from many OD interveners, for instance when some OB people do OD research. Historically, many OB adherents felt themselves at odds with OD (Cummings, 1978) for numerous reasons. Perhaps the basic difference is that OD advocates a new approach to organizational life and has strong prescriptive roots (Benne, 1964); that is, OD always has rested on a definite normative base (Friedlander, 1976), albeit not always a consistent base consistently applied. In contrast, OB has been more value-free and descriptive. To add further spice, most early OD was interaction-centred, which had the effect of constituting a barrier between OD and OB, the latter having been more structure-oriented.

Sometimes, in addition, you can't win for losing. Today sees greater attention in OD to structure-oriented designs, for example. But that tendency not only constitutes a common interest that could facilitate peaceful coexistence between OB and OD; it can also generate threat and the need to protect one's turf. The latter tendencies get exacerbated by a wicked reality: the market for OD specialists remains strong, whereas in OB a buyer's market exists.

So which should lead today?   In my judgement, application has substantially out-run the foundation of research that supported OD's initial great leap forward, and practice stands in serious need of support from the more sophisticated theory that could in the future support another period of flat-out emphasis on application. Hence I see today's OD as definitely needing to be research-led.

Will that transition occur? Only wiser heads than mine can give a definite answer today, for the question relates to very tangled issues which resist resolution in terms of the textbook ideal: applications and research should stimulate one another, with the specific problem determining priority. Reality places very real roadblocks in the way of this pleasing flexibility. The basic issue is how to protect OD from many of its friends. Pure mass no doubt constitutes the major troublemaker. Overenthusiasm and blatant self-interest, among other factors, can also restrict the needed flexibility. For example:

(1) The small initial cadre of OD interveners and researchers having direct and personal contact with one another has given way to legions, increasingly with specialized interests in intervention or research, but not both, who operate on turfs whose area of overlap and interaction has grown smaller in the last decade.

(2) OD interveners far outnumber experienced researchers, a practical reality that could encourage the latter into exuberant criticism as a counterpoint to the latter's zest to get on with it.

(3) Many interveners emphasize currently fashionable interventions in their practice, and close observers worry that too little attention gets paid to that magical combination which originally led to the development of those interventions: in-depth diagnosis of specific worksites, conditioned by the broad normative consensus that underlies OD, as rightly conceived.

OD as completing another progress/stuckness cycle

In its most simple form, the argument above represents several cycles of stuckness/progress/stuckness/progress. For example, the group dynamics literature got social analysis over some very important barriers to understanding (Golembiewski, 1962, esp. pp.8–18). But that progress soon implied stuckness, and the development of change-agent attitudes and skills was required to exploit this beachhead of knowledge. The initial exuberance with OD followed, but it in turn has had to make its peace with this basic reality: experience with 'the' early answers has been better at raising profound problems than in providing comprehensive solutions. Hence the progress represented by the flurry of the earlier OD applications passes into a growing awareness of stuckness. This loss of innocence is hard to take: denial, resistance, depression, loss of confidence, and truculence are likely knee-jerk responses. I recall the reaction of an OD intervener to a panel variously criticizing the methodology of existing OD research and experience. The intervener obviously spoke for many when he said: 'You guys give me a headache and a heartache. Before you started, I felt pretty good about what I do, and why. Now, I'm not even sure what "it" is that I do. You made galloping variables out of all of my constants.'

Toward transcending four major assumptions

Will OD see stuckness give way to another round of progress? That I cannot say, although I keep the faith.

What must be done to resolve that stuckness? On this question I believe I can be helpful. Basically, we need to realize how much we are in the wicked grasp of four assumptions that once facilitated progress but now contribute to stuckness:

(1) An individual is an individual.
(2) A group is a group.
(3) A large organization is a large organization.
(4) Change is change.

Only after these assumptions are replaced by useful taxonomies of differences will it prove possible to be increasingly precise about designing specific OD interventions for individual clients. And that increasing precision constitutes the only way to move beyond stuckness.

Individual A ≠ individual B.   Few things would ever get started if we initially understood how complicated they would be and what difficulties would be encountered. Not uncommonly, then, simplifications or even little white lies are needed to get the ball rolling. And so it was with OD.

That individual A = individual B has been an assumption that underlies much OD effort, both early and late. Consider the two 'stems' of OD identified by French and Bell (1973, pp.21–6): the laboratory stem, and the survey stem. To begin with, much early thought and practice with the laboratory stem, i.e. that involving T-groups and sensitivity training, implicitly or explicitly accepted this simplifying assumption. In the matter of anticipating psychological trauma, for example, many took the position that individuals can or should take responsibility for themselves, that they were (or should be) alike in that crucial particular. Similarly, opinion surveys just as commonly reflected their version of one person, one vote. Aside from distinguishing those polled in terms of the usual demographics such as age, sex, and so on, opinions were simply aggregated and interpreted in terms of this simple decision rule: one respondent = another respondent.

However useful such a simplification may be as a point of departure for early work, even a little knowledge suffices to highlight the assumption's inadequacy. In general, studies will generate discrepant effects, with the discrepancies deriving in part from the inadequacy of the assumption of the homogeneity of subjects. Consider the T-group, for example. At the zenith of the sensitivity training movement, two careful students highlighted several senses in which individuals differ in profound ways that learning designs have to respect. Campbell and Dunnette (1968, p.78) note that:

> People most certainly differ greatly in their ability to accept the guarantee of psychological safety. To the extent that the feeling of safety cannot be achieved – and quickly – the prime basic ingredient for this form of learning is absent. Its importance cannot be over-emphasized, nor can the difficulty of its being established.

Similarly, recent work suggests that survey feedback designs also have to deal with respondent heterogeneity. For example, important differences in the interpretation of survey findings derive from two ways in which individual A ≠ individual B: a general personality attribute called 'social desirability' (Golembiewski and Munzenrider, 1975); and the diverse performance evaluations that individuals and their work gain in organizations (Golembiewski and Hilles, 1979, pp.243–67). Social desirability (Edwards, 1957) refers to the tendency of individuals to report socially acceptable observations in order to gain approval. Differences between survey respondents in that critical particular can influence the interpretation of findings, but surveys almost never acknowledge that individuals differ in such significant regards. Similarly, recent research indicates that responses vary directly with performance evaluations – the higher one's appraisal, the more positive the terms in which one views the organization and worksite (Golembiewski and Hilles, 1979).

Appropriate learning in OD has been uneven. In sensitivity training some major adaptations have recognized differences between individuals. Thus care is often taken to design a range of activities, to build a supportive social system, to see that each member progresses at a rate comfortable to himself, and so on. Many of these notions always were central to orthodox sensitivity training, but the extensions of theory and practice characterizing the mid-1960s had moved away from them. For example, there was much controversy surrounding the use of designs including non-verbal exercises (Mill and Ritvo, 1969). In survey feedback designs, adjustments have also been attempted (Duckles, 1976), but consciousness remains dim about the need to account systematically for individual differences in interpreting survey findings. What needs to be done is clear, in general, but we still lack tools for distinguishing individuals in relevant ways.

Group A ≠ group B.   The convenience of assuming a homogeneity of groups has a long and distinguished tradition including Aristotle, Le Bon, Freud, and much of contemporary small group analysis (Golembiewski, 1962, pp.9–33). To me, the evidence implies that this tradition is a long-standing and distinguished error, which constitutes a major obstacle to a more-than-superficial analysis.

The OD literature has recognized the awkwardness of this common assumption in two major ways, but incompletely so in both cases. Consider the position that we could more closely tailor OD designs to specific clients if we possessed a taxonomy of group properties or features, and if we had a better understanding of major phases of group development.

A notable study (Bowers and Hauser, 1977) supports with elaborate statistical detail the neglected common-sense idea that differences between group features might determine the OD design of choice. We only sketch Bowers's seminal work. In essence, Bowers had five major categories of data from members of over five hundred work groups:

(1) *Organization climate*, which relates to decision-making practices, communication flow, and so on.
(2) *Supervisory leadership*, which deals with supervisor-to-member relations via factors such as support, facilitation of work, and so on.
(3) *Peer leadership*, which refers to member-to-member relationships.
(4) *Group process*, which deals with group-level phenomena such as co-ordination.
(5) *Satisfaction*, which involves six facets, such as satisfaction with pay.

Using various statistical procedures, seventeen profiles of scores sufficed to classify about 93 per cent of the groups in Bowers's research population, which came from both military and civilian settings. To provide an example of these profiles, four of them represented cases in which the supervisor's behaviour differed from the organizational climate and other behaviours and processes. These were called 'supervisory-behaviour-divergent' profiles.

This typology was put to several uses, including the answering of one question critical at this point in OD's development: did differences in profiles permit one to choose the type of OD intervention likely to work in specific groups? To illustrate, consider 'supervisory-behaviour-divergent' profiles. Would they respond well to team-building via laboratory training, which constitutes a relatively 'deep' and broad-ranging intervention? Or would work groups with such a profile respond better to 'shallower' interventions such as survey feedback, whose targets tend to be quite discrete and 'less personal'? In addition, two other basic interventions were investigated by Bowers for relative goodness-of-fit with the seventeen profiles: interpersonal process consultation, and task process consultation.

Bowers's work clearly relates to central theoretical and practical concerns, but now one can conclude with certainty only that his approach illustrates what OD needs. It is too early to judge whether he provides what OD needs. Existing results (Bowers and Hausser, 1977, esp. pp.92–3) imply that different work group profiles do seem to be more compatible with some OD interventions than with others. And the authors conclude (p.94) that: 'Even in its present crude form, the approach provides a guide for intervention choice.' But the existing data-set has numerous empty cells; and the grouping of specific interventions under such broad labels as 'laboratory training' also requires that one be cautious about making too much of the present findings.

Knowledge about phases of group development would also help in choosing specific OD designs for particular groups. Bennis and Shepard's (1956) classic article amply demonstrates how the most relevant leader intervention at one stage of group development could be absolutely the worst at another. Interveners do without doubt tailor interventions and designs in multiple ways to the specific warp and woof of the organizations within which they work. But the general point often gets neglected by those who have a tool-kit view of OD designs and who leap to prognosis by short-circuiting diagnosis of specific clients. Moreover, too little explicit concern is devoted to this subtle fitting of intervention to client.

Most OD work remains innocent of how one can usefully specify group phases and then tailor designs to them. Consider designs intended to enhance the effectiveness of work teams, which generally and implicitly assume that a team is a team. Dyer (1977) provides a valuable service when he focuses on the very different kinds of designs appropriate to various team conditions. For example, much team-building relies on interaction-centred designs, while problems often inhere in the structuring of work or in policies. Similarly, most team-building has been designed to surface and resolve conflict or disagreement, while recent work implies that many teams experience a 'crisis of agreement' for which very different designs are appropriate. Other sources provide details (Golembiewski, 1979, Part 2, pp.152–64), but the design implications for team-building can be suggested by this brief contrast of two types of crises (Harvey, 1977):

Crisis of agreement	*Crisis of disagreement*
(1) Members have the same or similar concept of the problem-situation.	(1) Members have variously-different concepts of some problem-situation.
(2) Members have the same or similar preference re problem-solution.	(2) Members have different preferences re problem-solution.
(3) Members do not publicly share their views, largely because they fear doing so will mean their separation from a valued association because they are alone in their views, and hence their agreement remains unexpressed in public.	(3) Members may risk open conflict about such differences, but probably will suppress them in the interests of superficial placidity and yet will resist being unsatisfactorily incorporated with some 'them' based on an underlying uncertainty about the rules-of-the-game for resolving differences.

Crisis contrast continued

(4) Members fear taking action on what each knows individually, but which does not get publicly expressed.	(4) Members fear beginning analysis because it will open a Pandora's box of differences.

What design implications inhere in the contrast above? Put simply, designs for surfacing or confronting issues work well in crises of disagreement, while the same designs could be seriously counterproductive in crises of agreement. For surfacing an issue in the latter case could create more problems than it resolved, by posing such broader questions as: 'What is there about us that represses the truth on which we all agreed, but unknowingly? Fear? Stupidity? Cowardice?' Since 'crisis of agreement' seems to be seldom diagnosed, and since common prescription counsels confrontation, much team-building could be ineffective or even counterproductive.

Organization A ≠ organization B.　Now this is something which everybody knows, but there seems no convenient way to act on the knowledge in most of today's OD. Again, a taxonomy is what we need – this time for organizations. Having such a taxonomy to hand, differences in the appropriateness of OD designs under specified organizational conditions could be determined.

Bowers (1973) suggests what is possible in his massive study of 14,000 subjects from twenty-three organizations. His study was described earlier, and suggests (among many other conclusions) that laboratory training was far less effective an intervention than survey feedback in the organizations studied. Bowers does not shrink from emphasizing the point. But how can one square his finding with the reported successes of laboratory training in other organizations, in some of which he participated (e.g. Marrow et al. 1967; Golembiewski and Carrigan, 1970a, 1970b)? A reasonable speculation suggests that the client organizations differed in some essential ways. Thus Bowers allows (1973, p.40) that 'it may be that laboratory-like experiential learning is successful in organisations whose climate is, or is becoming, positive ... but unsuccessful in organisations ...

which are or are becoming, more autocratic and punitive.' The organizations which employed laboratory training in Bowers's study fell in the latter category.

Bowers may be correct and, if he is, that merely strengthens the present point about differentiating client organizations. Alternatively, other explanations might also do the job. Some (Torbert, 1973; Pasmore, 1976) have criticized Bowers's study, emphasizing that several of the treatments were contaminated and insufficiently distinct between types, that assignment to the treatments was not random, that the individual level of analysis was inappropriate, and so on.

Change A ≠ change B.   Moving beyond these first three assumptions requires emphasis on research as contrasted with application. That research will be complicated by a fourth inadequate assumption underlying most OD 'as well as most social science research more generally' which particularly needs setting right. This assumption is that change is simply change.

Several types of change have been recently isolated, and failure to distinguish between them can severely complicate the interpretation of findings. Consider only two kinds of change (Golembiewski, 1979, Part 2, esp. pp.408–17):

(1) *Alpha change*, a change in condition or degree, a variation in the level of some existential state, given a constantly-calibrated measuring instrument related to a known conceptual domain.

(2) *Gamma change*, a change in state, a redefinition of some domain, as in a basic change in the perspective or frame-of-reference within which phenomena are perceived and classified.

Where's the basic rub? Most research acknowledges only alpha change – e.g. does quality X vary between observations 1 and 2? – for which we are relatively well-prepared. The issue is not as simple in behavioural science as it is in determining whether baby's foot has grown between visits to the shoe store. In behavioural science one seldom has the type of measuring instrument whose intervals remain virtually constant between administrations, which we do have for measuring baby's foot. But ways and means do exist in the behavioural sciences for testing the reliability and validity of measuring instruments, given alpha change.

Acknowledging the possibility of gamma change plays havoc with this incomplete but comparatively comfortable knowledge. And OD is definitely in the gamma change business, since most practitioners seek to create new cultures at work, or a new social order. This involves giving new meaning to worksites, e.g. by examining what defines 'co-operation' and how much of that quality is 'enough'. In brief, the goals of OD exacerbate the already-formidable problems of estimating whether or not 'change' has occurred. Analysts must determine, in effect, how much of which kind of change has occurred. Consider reports about a baby's foot-length on two visits to the shoe store, given the complication that the measuring instrument has been modified in some basic and unknown ways. A 'decrease' in foot-length might actually be an increase, or no change at all.

Can such devilish complexities be taken into account in OD research, so as to permit appropriate interpretations of the effects of interventions? The matter is still far from certain but a procedure based on repeated factor analysis has been suggested (Golembiewski et al., 1976) which seems to work tolerably well (Randolph and Edwards, 1978).

If we fail to account for different types of change in OD research, that failure will permit only great tentativeness about interpreting research results. This, in turn, would imply serious problems for OD applications.

OD and a bet on the future

How will things work out? Will standard procedures be developed via research such that the present stuckness will give way to another spurt of progress, to be led by application rather than research? Can OD move beyond general reliance on the four assumptions described above?

I do not know.

Let me briefly state what I do know. Without tolerable working resolutions of such questions, an awkward set of outcomes seems certain. Individual studies will continue to generate diverse effects, perhaps with a more or less definite central tendency, but with many exceptions and anomalies. (How could it be otherwise when studies are limited by the four assumptions described?) In turn, these divergent findings will create problems for many interveners. They will either seek approaches other than OD, which will let some of the air out of the balloon; or interveners will become sceptical about OD research, which will ensure that the air stays out of the balloon; Or perhaps worse still, interveners will become less confident about what their instincts indicate to them and hence less effective as interveners, if indeed they do not despair about intervening at all.

References

Beckhard, R. (1966) An organizational improvement in a decentralized organization. *Journal of Applied Behavioral Science 2* (1): 3–26.

Benne, K. D. (1964) From polarization to paradox. In L. P. Bradford, J. R. Gibb and K.D. Benne (eds) *T-Group Theory and Laboratory Method*. New York: John Wiley.

Bennis, W. G. (1966) *Changing Organizations*. New York: McGraw-Hill.

Bennis, W. G. and Shepherd, H. (1956) A Theory of Group Development. *Human Relations 9* (3): 415–37.

Blake, R., Mouton, J. S., Barnes, L. B. and Greiner, L. E. (1964) Breakthrough in organization development. *Harvard Business Review 42* (6): 133–55.

Boss, R. W. (1979) It doesn't matter if you win or lose, unless you're losing. *Journal of Applied Behavioral Science 15* (2): 198–220.

Bowers, D. G. (1973) OD techniques and their results in 23 organisations. *Journal of Applied Behavioral Science 9* (1): 21–43.

Bowers, D. G. and Hausser, D. L. (1977) Work group types and intervention effects in organizational development. *Administrative Science Quarterly 22* (1): 76–94.

Burke, W. W. (1976) Organization Development in Transition. *Journal of Applied Behavioral Science 12* (1): 22–43.

Campbell, J. P. and Dunnette, M. D. (1968) Effectiveness of T-group experiences in managerial training and development. *Psychological Bulletin 70* (1): 73–104.

Carew, D. K., Carter, S. I., Gamache, J. M., Hardiman, R., Jackson, B. and Parisi, E. (1977) New York State Division of Youth. *Journal of Applied Behavioral Science 13* (3): 327–39.

218 Small Groups and Personal Change

Cooper, C. L. (1975) How psychologically dangerous are T-groups and encounter groups? *Human Relations 28* (3): 249–60.

Cummings, L. L. (1978) Towards organizational behavior. *Academy of Management Review 3* (1): 90–8.

Duckles, R. L. (1976) Work, workers, and democratic change. Unpublished doctoral dissertation, Wright Institute.

Dunn, W. N. and Swierczek, F. W. (1977) Planned organizational change. *Journal of Applied Behavioral Science 13* (2): 135–58.

Dyer, W. G. (1977) *Team Building*. Reading, Mass.: Addison-Wesley.

Edwards, A. L. (1957) *The Social Desirability Variable in Personality Assessment and Research*. New York: Dryden.

Filley, A. C. (1975) *Interpersonal Conflict Resolution*. Glenview, Ill.: Scott, Foresman.

Frank, L. L. and Hackman, J. R. (1975) A failure of job enrichment. *Journal of Applied Behavioral Science 11* (4): 413–36.

French, W. and Bell, C. H. Jr (1973) *Organization Development*. Englewood Cliffs, New Jersey: Prentice-Hall.

Friedlander, F. (1970) The impact of organizational training laboratories on the effectiveness and interaction of ongoing work groups. *Personnel Psychology 20* (3): 289–307.

Friedlander, F. (1976) OD reaches adolescence. *Journal of Applied Behavioral Science 12* (1): 7–21.

Golembiewski, R. T. (1962) *The Small Group*. Chicago: University of Chicago Press.

Golembiewski, R. T. (1972) *Renewing Organizations*. Itasca, Ill.: F. E. Peacock.

Golembiewski, R. T. (1979) *Approaches to Planned Change*. New York: Marcel Dekker, Parts 1 and 2.

Golembiewski, R. T., Billingsley, K. and Yeager, S. (1976) Measuring change and persistence in human affairs. *Journal of Applied Behavioral Science 12* (2): 133–57.

Golembiewski, R. T. and Carrigan, S. B. (1970a) Planned change in organization style based on the laboratory approach. *Administrative Science Quarterly 15* (1): 79–93.

Golembiewski, R. T. and Carrigan, S. B. (1970b) The persistence of laboratory-induced changes in organization style. *Administrative Science Quarterly 15* (3): 330–40.

Golembiewski, R. T. and Hilles, R. (1979) *Toward the Responsive Organization*. Salt Lake City, Utah: Brighton Publishing.

Golembiewski, R. T. and Munzenrider, R. (1975) Social desirability as an intervening variable in interpreting OD effects. *Journal of Applied Behavioral Science 11* (3): 317–32.

Golembiewski, R. T. and Proehl, C. W. Jr (1979) A survey of the empirical literature on flexible workhours: an update. Paper presented at Annual Meeting, American Psychological Association, New York.

Harrison, R. (1972) Role negotiation. In W. W. Burke and H. Hornstein (eds) *The Social Technology of Organization Development*. Washington, D. C.: NTL Learning Resources.

Harvey, J. (1977) Consulting during crises of agreement. In W. W. Burke, (ed.) *Current Issues and Strategies in Organization Development*. New York: Human Science.

Heimovics, R. D. (1978) Organization Development in SPAA Curricula. *Southern Review of Public Administration 1* (4): 477–85.

Hulme, R. D. and Bevan, R. V. (1975) The blue-collar worker goes on salary. *Harvard Business Review 57* (1): 104–12.

Huse, E. F. (1975) *Organization Development and Change*. St Paul, Minn.: West Publishing.

Kimberly, J. R. and Nielsen, W. R. (1975) Organization development and change in organizational performance. *Administrative Science Quarterly 20* (2): 191–206.

Kuriloff, A. H. and Atkins, S. (1966) T-group for a work team. *Journal of Applied Behavioral Science 2* (1): 3–26.

Macy, B. A. (1978) A theoretical basis for and an assessment of the Bolivar quality of working life experiment: 1972–1977. Paper presented at Annual Meeting, Academy of Management, San Francisco, Cal.

Margulies, N. and Raia, A. (1979) *Conceptual Foundations of Organization Development*. New York: McGraw-Hill.

Marrow, A. J., Bowers, D. G. and Seashore, S. E. (1967) *Management by Participation*. New York: Harper and Row.

Mill, C. and Ritvo, M. (1969) Potentialities and pitfalls of nonverbal techniques. *Human Relations 13* (1): 1–3.

Morrison, P. (1978) Evaluation in OD. *Group and Organization Studies 3* (1): 42–70.

Nadler, D. A. (1977) *Feedback and Organization Development.* Reading, Mass.: Addison-Wesley.

Pasmore, W. A. (1976) The Michigan ICL study revisited. *Journal of Applied Behavioral Science 12* (2): 245–51.

Pasmore, W. A. and King, D. C. (1978) Understanding organizational change. *Journal of Applied Behavioral Science 14* (4): 455–68.

Pate, L. E. (1976) A reference list for change agents. In J. W. Pfeiffer and J. E. Jones (eds) *The 1976 Annual Handbook for Group Facilitators.* La Jolla, Cal.: University Associates.

Poppy, J. (1968) New era in industry: it's ok to cry in the office. *Look* 9 July: 65.

Porras, J. I. (1979) The comparative impact of different OD techniques and intervention intensities. *Journal of Applied Behavioral Science 15* (2): 156–78.

Porras, J. I. and Berg, P. O. (1978) Evaluation methodology in organization development. *Journal of Applied Behavioral Science 14* (2): 151–74.

Porras, J. I. and Roberts, N. (1978) Toward a typology of organization research. Research Paper No. 470, Stanford University, Graduate School of Business.

Randolph, W. A. and Edwards, R. G. (1978) Assessment of alpha, beta, and gamma changes in a university-setting OD intervention. Paper presented at Annual Meeting, Academy of Management, San Francisco, Cal.

Schaum, F. W. (1978) The strategy and practical realities of OD in the U. S. Army. *Southern Review of Public Administration 1* (4): 449–62.

Seashore, S. E. and Bowers, D. G. (1970) Durability of organizational change. *American Psychologist 25* (1): 233–6.

Thorsrud, E. (1976) *Model for Socio-Technical Systems.* Oslo, Norway: Work Research Institutes.

Torbert, W. R. (1973) Some questions on Bowers' study of different OD techniques. *Journal of Applied Behavioral Science 9* (5): 668–71.

Walton, R. E. (1969) *Interpersonal Peacemaking.* Reading, Mass.: Addison-Wesley.

Weisbord, M. (1978) The Wizard of OD. *OD Practitioner 10* (2): 1–7.

Winn, A. (1971) Reflections on the T-group strategy and the role of change agent in organization development. Unpublished MS.

Yalom, I. D. and Lieberman, M. A. (1971) A study of encounter group casualties. *Archives of General Psychiatry 25* (1): 16–30.

9 Organization development in schools[1]

Matthew B. Miles
and Michael Fullan

Introduction

One of the perennial dilemmas in the study of change in people concerns whether or not the primary emphasis is on the individual or the group (see especially Hartman, 1979). This dilemma appears in even more complex form when we remember the fact that the groups in which most people work and learn are embedded in an organizational setting. Thus, when considering any effort to change or improve the way individuals are functioning, we must attend not only to their interaction with their work group(s) and to the group's functioning, as would be the case in 'stranger' groups, but to the role expectations for individuals drawn from the surrounding organizational contexts, the relations between their groups and other groups, and so on. It is no longer the case that the group exists only to support individual change, but that both individual and group change occur in the context of efforts to improve the overall functioning of the organization.

Organization development (OD) is a system-oriented change strategy adapting familiar methods of group-work (notably its emphasis on here-and-now relationships) to the 'semi-permanent' setting, where a consultant works with 'intact' groups, role relationships and persons who have a more or less enduring connection with each other.

This article focuses on OD in educational settings, particularly schools. The first part reviews the current state of knowledge in the research literature, while the second part presents the findings from our own study of seventy-six school districts in Canada and the United States where sustained OD programmes were in operation. In the conclusion we formulate a revised and more comprehensive definition of OD, as well as considering the implications of our study for the future of OD in schools.

Review of OD in schools[2]

OD programmes characteristically involve a consultant, based either externally or internally to the organization (either in a line or staff position), who aids system members in collecting data about organizational problems and functioning, analysing them, and taking corrective problem-solving action. It is a form of action research applied to organizational life. Successful OD programmes usually extend for several years, and desirably become institutionalized to enable continuing 'self-renewal'.

There have been both pessimistic (Blumberg, 1976; Derr, 1976) and optimistic (Miles, 1976) views on the prospects for diffusion of OD in schools, along with some sceptical discussions (Fullan, 1976). Lack of thoroughgoing data on OD in schools was the primary driving force for our study.

Values and goals of OD

A good sense of OD can be obtained by considering common definitions of OD in the literature.

Miles and Schmuck (1971, p.2) suggested that: 'OD can be defined as a planned and sustained effort to apply behavioural science for system improvement using reflexive, self-analytical methods.'

In one of the most recent reviews six years later Alderfer (1977, p.272) refers to the practice of OD as: 'Aimed toward improving the quality of life for members of human systems and increasing the institutional effectiveness of those systems.'

French and Bell (1973) include the following elements in their definition:

Organisation development is a long-range effort to improve an organisation's problem solving and renewal processes, particularly through a more effective and collaborative management of organisation culture – with special emphasis on the culture of formal work teams – with the assistance of a change agent or catalyst, and the use of the theory and technology of applied behavioural science, including action research.

Friedlander and Brown (1974, pp.315–316) differentiate two basic approaches to OD: *people-oriented* approaches, which attempt to change organizational processes primarily in order to increase human fulfilment; and *technology-oriented* approaches aimed at changing organizational structures primarily in order to increase task accomplishment.

Several writers have struggled with the lack of balance and the absence of a simultaneous focus on *both* organizational productivity and human fulfilment (or quality of life) in organizations. For example, Friedlander and Brown (1974) observe:

Though most OD practitioners and researchers in some degree value both organisational task accomplishment *and* human fulfillment, there is an organisational press in favour of the former. ... Within the hierarchical fabric of everyday organisational power struggles, OD researcher/consultants typically represent the control needs of management. The needs of those lower in the organisation for a higher quality of life, for an expanded range of occupational life choices may seldom be known or acted upon by the consultant.

In addition to the question of balance between organizational and individual accomplishment, a more practical set of problems concerns the use of the term OD which has been applied to all activities directed at individual or group change within the organization. Bowers (1977, pp.53–7) describes some of these in terms of superficiality and commercialism. Superficiality refers to short-term preprogrammed one-shot workshops, not linked to the needs and activities of the organization, and involving only a few members of the organization. Commercialism includes such things as over-advocacy (making exaggerated claims about appropriateness and payoff) and consequent aversion to rigorous evaluation.

If we take the definitions and critiques of OD together, a number of conclusions are warranted *vis-à-vis* the meaning of OD. First, a definition of OD would include at least the following key words: *planned change, long-range;* a focus on *group processes* and *techno-structural* factors in order to improve both *task accomplishment* and the *quality of life of individuals;* often using the assistance of a *change agent;* always using *behavioural science techniques* to gather valid data and use it in a *reflexive, self-analytic* fashion.

Second, using these key words as guidelines, we can immediately rule out all those activities which address only parts of the organization or the problem, or which are in Bowers's terms superficial. It appears that many activities which go under the label of OD are not really OD at all, though they might be called 'OT' for 'organizational training'. This has contributed both to a confusion about what OD is, and to a reputation that OD is irrelevant or inconsequential. The presence of 'OD'-labelled activities which do not meet the general definition can also be seen as a kind of vulgarization stemming from users' eagerness to appear up-to-date, innovative, etc., along with unwillingness to expend the time and resources needed for serious effort.

Third, the *values-in-practice* of OD programmes may not in fact address the human side of development with as much integrity as they address the organizational side, despite the intentions of OD consultants.

Fourth, since OD not only has to *address*, but also to *balance* a number of complex factors – individual and organization, process, task and structure, etc. – over a long period of time, it is understandable that OD has had uneven success, especially since most definitions of OD do not stress the problem of balance.

Having identified the purpose and meaning of OD and some of its underlying problems, we are now in a position to investigate more precisely how OD actually works or operates in school districts as described in recent studies.

Operating characteristics in school districts

There are a number of recent studies of the operation of OD programmes in schools which provide substantial data on the use of OD. Runkel and Schmuck's (1974, 1976) review of their own OD projects, Bassin and Gross (1978), Coad et al. (1976), Cohen and Gadon (1978), and Mohrman et al. (1977) are the main sources on which we draw.

Without doubt, the most intensive and substantiated work on OD in schools has been carried out by Richard Schmuck, Philip Runkel and their colleagues at the University of Oregon, who have been working with school districts since 1967 (see Schmuck et al., 1972; Schmuck et al., 1975; Schmuck et al., 1977; Runkel and Schmuck, 1974, 1976). Fortunately, they have carried out their own review of research findings from twenty studies based on their work in a number of elementary and junior high schools as well as working on a district-wide basis to establish and train internal cadres of OD specialists to serve all the schools in the district (for the latest overview of their work see Runkel and Schmuck, 1976).

They identify an initial list of the conditions found to be important for the operation of OD, classifying these in four categories – start-up, transition, maintenance and effects.

Entry or start-up is one of the main themes in the OD literature. It includes both the conditions and state of readiness for OD as well as the way in which OD is introduced. In summarizing several factors related to readiness Runkel and Schmuck state:

> Our evidence indicates that success in OD consultation in facili-
> tating structural change is strongly influenced by the social-psy-
> chological readiness of the client organisation to change. Readi-
> ness is greatest where openness of communication is valued and
> communication skill is high, where there is a widespread desire for
> collaborative work, where the administration is supportive or at
> least not negative toward the intervention, where there is a good
> agreement at the outset about the educational goals to be reached
> by restructuring, and where the staff does not have a history of one
> 'innovation' after another that has failed to produce rewarding
> outcomes. (Runkel and Schmuck, 1976, p.13)

According to Runkel and Schmuck, a certain amount of organizational readiness is important as a precondition for OD getting
started and/or being productive – a desire or value for *open communication* and *collaboration*, sufficient *administrative support, goal
clarity* and the *absence* of *previous failures* in innovation. In other
places in their writings they emphasize that strong direct support
from central administrators is necessary, as well as the principal's
commitment, support and involvement at the district level (see also
Schmuck et al., 1975).

Two other factors which they list as essential are the need to focus on subsystems, and participation in the decision by all subsystem members: 'The successes of OD consultation, we believe, are due in large measure to our insistence upon bringing entire subsystems into the consultation' (Runkel and Schmuck, 1976). Also: 'OD is more likely to help a school achieve a significant structural change when the staff's decision to move into innovation is public and almost consensual' (p.17).

In their comparison of successful and unsuccessful experience in six elementary schools (Schmuck et al., 1975, p. 356), they make the same point more specifically:

> A crucial aspect of these early days, we are convinced, was the way group and individual decisions were made to participate in the project. We believe strongly that the total staff should hold at least three or four meetings over a period of about two months to discuss OD.

Under the category of *transition*, Runkel and Schmuck include events during the initial use (e.g. the first year) of an OD programme – the amount of consultation time, the use of consultants, the continuity of leaders and the sequence and pacing of the programme.

In working in relatively small or medium-sized organizations (mostly elementary schools) Runkel and Schmuck have found that a total of approximately 160 hours of each staff member's time in direct OD training and work over the period of a year is necessary for major results to occur. In fact, at the other end of the scale they found that 'staffs receiving fewer than 24 hours of OD help actually declined in their communicative adequacy' (p.19). They cite some schools which evidenced positive changes after only forty-six hours or even fewer, but caution that a total of twenty-four hours or so is dangerously low because it opens problems which cannot be resolved in such a short time. Thus, a single workshop or two or three workshops which total four days or less fit the latter time frame.

On the use of consultants – an issue we pursue throughout our study of OD – they claim: 'Consultation in OD is more likely to help a school modify its organisational structure when the staff makes frequent, knowledgeable, and proactive (not passive) use of outside consultants' (Runkel and Schmuck, 1976, p.19). They also conclude that continuity of the principal is important, in particular that he or she stay with the organization until at least a year after the outside consultants leave.

The last aspect of the transitional period concerns sequence and pacing. For example, according to Runkel and Schmuck, constant communication, especially rapid feedback of diagnostic information, is necessary as a basic condition for further development (pp.20–1); and the sequence of change works best if it proceeds *from* communication and problem-solving skills *to* structural and curricular changes (Runkel and Schmuck, 1976, p.21; Schmuck et al., 1976, p.362).

Concerning *maintenance*, Runkel and Schmuck make only one major observation – that maintenance of the OD programme requires a team of inside organizational specialists who will operate as a built-in subsystem of OD consultants. In their own work in some school districts they have built the programme on the training of OD specialists within the district who operate in a staff relationship to the needs of the organization (see Runkel and Schmuck, 1976; and especially Schmuck et al., 1977, chapter 12).

Other case studies of OD programmes in schools that were mentioned at the beginning of this subsection provide mostly supportive evidence but also suggest some additional factors. The common findings can be summarized as follows.

Entry is critical, it depends on strong specific support from top management; either a certain level of organizational readiness must exist, or the OD programme must be designed in a way which convinces school people that it is task relevant, practical in the short run, and will not be unduly costly in time or money. On the other hand, Runkel and Schmuck provide strong and convincing evidence that a minimum time expenditure of not less than four person days per staff member is essential. There must be some willingness to invest a certain amount of time and energy. Moreover, OD does cost some money, and programmes which are totally dependent on outside money will most likely not receive commitment from the beginning. Some financial investment from the district and the schools would seem to be an accurate indicator of the potential success of the programme. Decision-making about whether to become involved in an OD programme is somewhat complicated. It appears that different routes are possible depending on the conditions. Ideally all administrators and teachers could be involved in some pre-start OD activities as a precondition to decisions to participate which would be made at a later time during the early transition phase. Also, the development of political skills and an orientation toward working with power relations in the organizational setting are explicitly advocated by some authors (Beer, 1976).

During the transition phase, active involvement, support and understanding of the programme by top management and by principals are essential. When this is present (see Runkel and Schmuck, several aspects of Bassin and Gross, Cohen and Gadon), the programmes seem to get off to a good start. When it is absent (see Milstein (1978); Mohrman et al.; Coad et al.) the programme experiences problems or goes nowhere. Sustained training and work over the period of two years also seem to be necessary for implementing OD programmes during the transition phase. The establishment and use of OD consultants internal to the school system combined with proactive use of *external* consultants is also important. Programmes which do not build this internal capacity, and/or which build up a dependency on one or more external consultants, are probably heading for trouble. Harvey (1975) and Weisbord (1977) also stress the point that the external OD consultant should not be viewed as or operate as a *change agent*. His or her job is to enhance the capabilities of internal managers and other personnel to make effective change decisions within their own organization – a claim which makes a great deal of sense and which is clearly supported in our case studies of successful OD programmes (Fullan et al., 1978, vol. IV).

Prospects for longer term institutionalization (e.g. after the first two years of activity) can be traced to the previous two phases. If active involvement of administrators, use of district funds (as opposed to total reliance on external funds), and development of internal consultant capabilities at the co-ordination and school levels have not been foci of the entry and transition phases, it is unlikely that the programme will survive beyond the first two years.

Outcomes of OD efforts in school districts

Most people consider questions about the real impact of OD on organizations and its members to be the most fundamental to its long-term worth for social systems. Depending on one's values and interests these questions include effects on human processes in organizations, member attitudes and satisfaction, organizational performance and productivity. The case studies reviewed contain varying degrees of evidence about the impact of their program- mes.

Runkel and Schmuck (1976) cite a wide range of effects of OD from the various projects (some twenty case studies in all) in which they have been involved:

> Our research and the analyses of others indicate that OD methods (properly chosen, sequenced, and applied) can increase a school's spontaneous production of innovative social structures to meet internal and external challenges, improve the relationship between teachers and students, improve the responsiveness and creativity of staff, heighten the influence of the principal without reducing the influence of the staff (and vice-versa), expand the participation of teachers and students in the management of the school, and alter attitudes and other morale factors toward more harmonious and supportive expectations. (Runkel and Schmuck, 1976, p.23)

Among other examples they refer to one of their main projects which involved OD training for six elementary schools changing from a traditional structure of self-contained classrooms to differentiated staffing with a multiunit structure (see Schmuck et al., 1975). The results showed that three of the six schools were highly successful in developing and maintaining the organizational relationships and member satisfaction in the new multiunit structure.

Other findings summarized by Runkel and Schmuck are similar in that they report both some successes and some failures concerning more effective collaboration among teachers, increased participation in curriculum planning, and in some cases 'spill-over' effects on the relations between teachers and students. But the latter effects were not measured in very many cases, and their measurement sometimes depended only on the perceptions of teachers.

All in all Runkel and Schmuck claim that the rate of success (which might be something around 50 per cent in their opinion) is note- worthy 'considering the large number of failures currently being reported in the literature' (p.25).

An independent assessment was conducted of Bassin and Gross's (1978) High School Renewal Project. Data were collected in a sample of twelve of the initial twenty-four schools active in the programme in 1976. The evaluator measured both processes occurring during the programme and subsequent effects. Bassin and Gross (1978) acknowledge major limitations in the evaluation, notably no pre – post evaluations or other quantitative data on student achievement, and the fact that data collection was limited to the minority of those in each school who were directly involved in the project.

When commenting on the significance of the changes the authors say:

> Over the thirty schools, the significance of change varies from very substantial to nothing at all. However, both very great and nothing are extremes. In most schools there are changes that do affect hundreds of students. For the most part, the schools remain basically the same, with improvements interspersed throughout. (p.87)

Cohen and Gadon (1978) in a study of OD in a small school system report that after two years of OD work, new management changes were 'firmly entrenched' (p.68). Evidence for this statement seems to come from the observation that new committees were operating regularly and dealing with key issues with which they had not previously dealt. Quantitative data are presented on the accomplishment of twelve goals as perceived by administrators comparing two points in time – September of the second year of the contract with April of the second year. These results show gains (of one-half a point or more on a seven-point scale) for three of the twelve goals, losses on one item and virtually identical scores on the other eight goals (Cohen and Gadon, 1978). So the accomplishments were not great, based on the data presented.

The evidence in Mohrman et al. (1977) in a study of a survey feedback programme indicates that there was limited success. Seven of the nine schools proceeded to the second year of the programme. Of the seven we find that the OD model was in full use in three of the seven schools, and feedback sessions were conducted in four of the seven schools. What these data tell us is that the programme was *implemented* in only three or four schools. Moreover, they do not indicate the *effects* of this implementation either on member satisfaction or on any kind of organizational performance criteria (save for a few comments on one of the elementary schools and one of the subgroups within a high school). At best we can say that some behavioural changes might have occurred in three or four of the schools of the nine which participated.

In conclusion, two points stand out. First, the quality of the evidence on impact of OD programmes on school districts is uneven. Second, to the extent that we do have evidence, success or failure of OD does seem associated with the presence or absence of the operating characteristics which we identified in the previous section.

OD programmes in school districts

In our review of the literature we were able to obtain a relatively comprehensive picture of OD and its use in a small number of school districts. We did not, however, know anything about the extent of use of OD or about the nature of its operation and impact on a large scale. We set out to identify all possible examples of sustained or serious use of OD in school districts in Canada and the United States. We did locate and gather extensive data on seventy-six school districts. Our findings are presented in the following four subsections.

Characteristics of the sampling and the sample

We mailed a twelve-page questionnaire to a sample of 390 US and Canadian school districts which had been nominated by one or more OD consultants.[3] We provided a definition of OD, and asked specifically whether such a programme had been operating for at least an eighteen-month period since 1964. If the answer was yes, we requested that the remainder of the questionnaire be filled out: it asked for details on the characteristics of the programme and its activities, how it got started, how it was supported financially, the impact of the programme, and its future in the district.

Our definition of OD on the questionnaire read as follows: 'A sustained attempt at system self study and improvement over a period of at least eighteen months, focusing on change in organizational procedures, norms, or structures using behavioural science concepts.' In one sense the definition was rigorous in that we were interested in serious attempts at OD – a minimum of eighteen months in duration. In another sense the definition was deliberately general because we wanted to identify a variety of types of OD and to find out what people in school districts considered to be OD.

The final refined sample of eligible cases consisted of seventy-six school districts in Canada and the United States in which sustained OD programmes had been carried out.[4] Phone calls were made to districts in order to verify ambiguous data. The majority of respondents were local district administrators. Seventy-six per cent of the districts were in the United States, with the remainder in Canada. The regional spread was wide: only in the Midwest were there as many as 20 per cent in a single region. The settings were also diverse: 38 per cent were suburban districts, long considered more likely to innovate – but 41 per cent were urban or metropolitan, and 21 per cent towns or villages.

The median district had 15 per cent upper-middle-class parents, 35 per cent white collar, 30 per cent blue collar, and 15 per cent semi-skilled or unskilled parents. When we characterized districts as to their overall socio-economic balance, we found that 34 per cent had a predominantly middle-class composition, and 61 per cent were predominantly working class; 5 per cent had no single class level predominating.

Operating issues in OD programmes

The questionnaire asked for information on many different aspects of the programme. First, we were interested in the initial problems for which OD was seen as a potential solution. The most frequently mentioned 'start' issues were 'communication' (25 per cent), reorganization/redesign (11 per cent), goals and goal-setting (10 per cent) and decision-making (8 per cent). Only 5 per cent mentioned student issues as such. When start issues were aggregated into more general areas, we found that 32 per cent mentioned task-oriented organizational issues (such as problem-solving, co-ordination), 21 per cent were concerned with educational output (goal-setting, effectiveness), and another 25 per cent with internal education issues (such as curriculum, classroom climate, programmes, finance).

A total of 41 per cent mentioned socio-emotional issues (communication, trust). Other areas included structural issues (18 per cent mentioned items such as reorganization or consolidation), external education issues such as school–community relations (13 per cent), personnel issues (10 per cent), and the functioning of subsystems such as teams (4 per cent). Perhaps the most interesting finding here is the emphasis on task-oriented, goal-oriented items, and the educational-programmatic context. Though socio-emotional starting problems were frequently mentioned, it seems as though the really painful issue is 'getting the job done'. Educational goals may be diffuse, but that does not hinder the districts in our sample from being concerned about them.

We also asked about the conditions which made it possible for OD to begin. Here, the responses focused heavily on the behaviour of top management: 41 per cent mentioned the commitment or support of existing top management and 21 per cent mentioned an initiative taken by a *new* top manager. Twenty-one per cent also acknowledged the presence of a grant or other extra funds, 21 per cent cited a problematic or changing situation, and 18 per cent mentioned the initiative of an internal change agent. Seven per cent mentioned an external consultant and 7 per cent said a study or survey had provided start conditions.[5] We see here a good deal of support for the idea that OD diffusion in education really depends on top management as gatekeeper.

The questionnaire asked respondents to divide the OD work in their district into phases, and to characterize the work in each phase. First phases varied in length from one to eighty-four months, with a median of eight months. The most frequently mentioned problems dealt with during the first phase were 'communication' (22 per cent), along with 'planning' (19 per cent), 'goal-setting' (27 per cent), and 'problem-solving' (16 per cent). Table 9.1 shows the aggregated results for the problems mentioned according to Phase I and Phase II: the figures are percentages of districts mentioning one or more issues in that category. Though it is getting ahead of our story, Table 9.1 also shows the percentages of districts mentioning one or more desirable outcomes in each general category as well – both expected and unexpected outcomes.

We note that, if anything, task and output orientation increased or was maintained during the early phases, with decreasing emphasis on socio-emotional issues as such. The increase in 'personnel' issues (which included such items as performance review, staff development and hiring) suggests that many projects included a 'training' component as soon as things were reasonably launched. Similarly, subsystem functioning proved to receive more attention. We should note here that, in relation to *initial problem*, organizational-level outcomes (task and socio-emotional) are well achieved – but that outcomes involving educational issues (programmes, curricula, etc.), either external or internal, are achieved by a somewhat smaller percentage than those initially mentioning them. This lends some – though not strong – weight to the criticism that OD tends to be oriented toward interpersonal relationships rather than focused on the more directly educational issues.

Table 9.1 Initial problems, those worked on during early phases of OD effort, and achieved outcomes

	Initial problem	Phase one	Phase two	Achieved outcomes (expected)	Achieved outcomes (unexpected)
	%	%	%	%	%
Task-oriented	32	41	30	37	5
Output	21	28	22	20	8
Eductional issues (internal)	25	12	20	14	8
Socio-emotional	41	28	15	47	28
Structural	18	5	4	13	1
Educational issues (external)	13	4	3	4	9
Personnel	10	12	21	18	12
Subsystem functioning	4	5	13	4	0

We were also curious about what it took to support the enterprise. We have already identified the presence of many internal change agents. We found that only 26 per cent of the districts said they had an actual group of OD specialists or trainers within the district. However, 55 per cent of districts provided release time for administrators and teachers, 51 per cent mentioned an OD planning or steering group, and 48 per cent a district-level co-ordinator. OD co-ordinators within a particular school were much less frequent (19 per cent).

The question of how much OD really costs any organization is not easy to answer. The financial resources provided for the OD effort as a whole varied wildly in this sample: one district said it got by with $600, while another spent $1,500,000. Even when these figures are adjusted to an annual cost, the range is still very substantial (from $200 to over $750,000). Over the whole sample, the *median* annual amount spent was only $5 – $10,000, less than half of one teacher's salary. We anticipate the reader's curiosity by saying that annual costs do seem to make a difference in overall impact, as we will see in the next subsection, but do not necessarily cause people to favour OD efforts – and are *negatively* related to how institutionalized the programme becomes.

We asked the respondents whether the OD programme had been formally evaluated – 29 per cent left the item blank, 21 per cent said no, 4 per cent said not yet, 3 per cent said no, but we plan to, and 43 per cent gave various responses indicating yes (e.g. yes, but unavailable; yes, in preparation; yes, a district evaluation; and yes, an external evaluation). Thus, about 50 per cent of the programmes had not been formally evaluated and there was no indication that they would be.

To summarize this section: once beyond the stereotypic label of 'communication' as a presenting problem, we found that instrumental issues – task functioning among the adults in the school, outputs, and the educational programme – take centre stage; socio-emotional issues are also initially important. However, instrumental issues are important not only for the 'start' situation but also for the first two phases of the typical effort.

OD begins, typically through top management initiative, with the support of added resources. Entry conditions involving data collection or the support of internal or external consultants are quite rare. However, once the enterprise is under way, about half of the districts support the effort with structures or roles such as steering groups, district co-ordinators and release time. Building-level co-ordinators are found in a quarter or less of the districts.

Finally, dollar expenditures vary extremely – probably more than their relation to efficacy justifies. Regarding the question of efficacy, formal evaluation of the OD programme is carried out in about half of the cases, although thorough evaluation studies are in the minority.

Outcomes

We were naturally concerned to develop a general measure of the success of OD programmes, both to see what these programmes appear to have accomplished for their users and to provide a dependent measure against which we could test explanatory variables. The initial criteria of OD 'success' that we generated were:

(1) *Impact* on the school district as a system (including impact on students).
(2) Positive *attitudes* toward OD, especially those which bear on whether it should be used in schools more generally.
(3) *Institutionalization* or durability of the OD effort.

That is, a 'successful' OD effort is one that makes a difference locally, has become 'built in', and has partisans who have positive, even 'evangelistic' attitudes that will encourage wider diffusion of the effort to other districts. Although these are self-reported indicators of success, we did find variations. We also used open-ended questions to develop measures of impact based on *specific* descriptions of changes.

It does not seem wise to combine the above three criteria into a single measure: they are only moderately correlated with each other, and the factors that 'explain' their occurrence also vary a good deal. The discussion which follows first gives a *descriptive* account of how the districts fared in their outcomes, then reviews the more systematic outcome measures we developed, and their relationship. Finally, we examine *explanations* – why these outcomes seem to have occurred (or not) in our districts.

Impact (expected).   When we asked respondents to describe what good consequences had occurred of an *expected* sort, the most frequent mentions went to 'improved communication' (20 per cent). Other specific expected positive outcomes were 'planning' (8 per cent), 'decision-making' (10 per cent), 'improved relationships' (8 per cent), 'productivity' (8 per cent), 'new educational programmes' (8 per cent), and 'commitment to change' (6 per cent). If we use aggregated categories for the diverse outcomes described, we end up with an interesting finding: 47 per cent mention socio-emotional improvements in organizational functioning, and 37 per cent task-oriented ones (see Table 9.1). This suggests support for the view that successful OD tends to induce a cultural shift (in social processes) along with task-oriented results.

Other frequent categories included organizational output improvement (20 per cent), internal educational issues (14 per cent), personnel issues (18 per cent), and structural changes (13 per cent). Direct changes in students are rarely mentioned here (4 per cent), but see p.239.

We were also interested in *why* these changes were seen to have occurred. Coding and aggregating the reasons given is quite striking. Although many districts (30 per cent) gave credit to background conditions such as capable staff, dollar investment, administrative support, etc., the dominant explanation (50 per cent) is given in terms of socio-emotional aspects of the OD process itself, such as 'partici-pation', 'more open communication', 'commitment', 'humane atmos-phere', and the like. Another 14 per cent mentioned more general properties of OD, such as feedback, capable consultants, etc. The other major cluster, quite naturally, stresses results (21 per cent) – 'we planned it that way', 'the change effort caused it', 'good vehicle for problem solving'. Task-focused aspects of OD, such as 'clearer role expectations', 'better management system', etc., were invoked by only 7 per cent of districts in explaining good outcomes, even though the OD process often seemed to have been launched with task-centred hopes and rhetoric.

Impact (unexpected/desirable). To a researcher, *un*anticipated good consequences are always of interest – 59 per cent of our sample mentioned such changes when asked. The most frequent unexpected gains were 'spinoff' or extension to new participants (16 per cent), 'improved communication' (14 per cent), and 'increased acceptance of change' (11 per cent). For our aggregated categories, we note with interest that 28 per cent mentioned unexpected socio-emotional outcomes in organizational functioning, as contrasted with 5 per cent mentioning task-related ones.

Impact (unexpected/undesirable). Our next question focused on whether there had been undesirable or negative consequences of the effort. Though we seemed to be dealing with a population of satisfied users, it turned out that 68 per cent could point to at least one negative outcome, a finding which increases the plausibility of the remainder of our data.[6] The results were scattered: 13 per cent mentioned 'resistance', 11 per cent 'refusal to participate', 12 per cent 'feelings of fear or job insecurity', 11 per cent mentioned 'general negativism toward OD activities', 12 per cent mentioned 'overload or too-heavy time commitments required'. Only 4 per cent mentioned 'programme failure' as a negative outcome and 5 per cent saw the presence of 'programme ineptness'. When these are classified more generally, it appears that 24 per cent mentioned direct negative consequences of the *programme activities* (such as feelings of threat or work overload) and 35 per cent mentioned more general *attitudes* toward the programme (such as personal defensiveness, lack of interest, criticism of 'games' or outside helpers); 9 per cent saw programme weaknesses as such.

The explanations for these bad outcomes were scattered but centred mostly on 'poor communication' (12 per cent), along with 'resistance, fears' (18 per cent), worry about being 'too personal' (6 per cent), 'lack of commitment' (8 per cent), and 'resistance to new ideas' (8 per cent). Only 6 per cent mentioned poor planning or implementation issues; it appears that explanations centre mostly on behaviour of negativists rather than on that of the advocates of OD.

Impact on students. Since schools are supposed to exist for students, we thought we should ask explicitly whether the OD programme had direct (or even indirect) effects on students, in or out of the classroom. Interestingly enough, 70 per cent said that such effects had occurred; 18 per cent were unsure or said it was too early to tell, and 12 per cent left the item blank. Of the fifty-three districts who mentioned student effects, over half (53 per cent) mentioned various 'soft' effects, notably 'improved learning atmosphere', 'improved relationships' and 'attitudes', while only 13 per cent mentioned gains in achievement scores. If we take a sceptical stance, note that for only 37 per cent of all districts were *specified* 'soft' student effects mentioned, and achievement gains were noted in only 9 per cent.

The specific explanations for student effects were extremely scattered, and only half the respondents offered them. For example, 49 per cent mentioned various pedagogical reasons, such as the fact that the programme focused directly on improvement in the classroom curricula: 28 per cent credited socio-emotional aspects of the OD programme, and 10 per cent the task side; 23 per cent felt that the good results of the programme generally had induced classroom changes, and another 15 per cent commented on good programme activities. Only 13 per cent mentioned background conditions. The moral seems to be that OD is reported to change student experience at least on soft variables – *if* it is well executed and has a clear linkage to the classroom.

Impact on other change efforts. The OD programmes in our study were not occurring in a vacuum – 39 per cent of the districts said that multiple instructional innovations were taking place, another 49 per cent mentioned one or two such changes, and only 12 per cent failed to mention any other instructional innovations. Thirty-five per cent of districts were attempting to cope with some form of legally-required change during the time of the OD programme (e.g. desegregation, bilingual programmes), and 46 per cent mentioned concurrent changes in key personnel, including replacement of top management, expansion, cutbacks, and reorganization.

When asked about the pace of educational change efforts occurring concurrently with the OD programme, 61 per cent said it was faster than usual, 30 per cent about the same, and only 9 per cent said it was slower. We asked if the OD effort contributed to this. The findings were quite clear: 63 per cent said the OD programme had directly caused a 'few' (30 per cent) or 'many' (33 per cent) other change efforts, and *no* respondent said OD had slowed down or blocked other change efforts. Extensive cross-tabular analysis provided clear evidence that OD programmes did stimulate (and support) the adoption of new instructional practices, lending weight to the idea that increased 'organization health' might be expected to add to innovativeness (Miles, 1965). So at least as seen from the school district viewpoint, OD tends to stimulate other educational change efforts in addition to the direct effects we have already noted.

Positive attitudes.   The second criterion of success concerned whether districts currently held a positive attitude toward the OD programme and the dissemination of OD to other school districts. On the whole, they seemed relatively satisfied with the way their programmes had been executed. When asked if they would have done anything different, 51 per cent said yes. The most frequent after-the-fact wish was that the programme should have gone more slowly (21 per cent), then came better planning and preparation (21 per cent) and the need for better commitment from the top (16 per cent). Others included more use of outside consultants (10 per cent), better involvement of parents (10 per cent), and the need for better evaluation (10 per cent). The implication of the first three items is that OD may well have been launched a bit precipitously.

When we asked our respondents whether they thought that OD should be used more widely in this country's schools, 64 per cent said they definitely thought so, 26 per cent said 'Yes, probably', 7 per cent were not sure and 3 per cent passed. No one expressed doubt or definite disapproval.

Districts where attitudes toward OD seem so positive, on balance, might be expected to do some proselytizing, a behaviour which bears on whether OD will diffuse more widely. We found that of our districts, 60 per cent had explained their OD programmes at conferences or workshops, 40 per cent had sent consultants to other districts, 37 per cent had visited other districts to explain their work, 37 per cent had sent out reports or materials, and 29 per cent had written articles on their OD experiences. We also found that 74 per cent had had informal contacts with people from other districts, and 51 per cent reported that others visited them. So while dissemination efforts are not widespread across our districts, a moderate amount of diffusion effort seems to be occuring. Our sample, by and large, thinks OD is a good idea for schools.

Institutionalization.   The final measure of success referred to whether OD was going to continue in the district. As of the spring of 1977, 88 per cent said it was in fact still going on. The primary explanations for continuance were the good results obtained (23 per cent), the commitment and hard work of participants (15 per cent), and the support of top management (14 per cent).

When respondents were asked to predict the future of OD in their districts, 8 per cent said it would not continue and 14 per cent were uncertain. Another 24 per cent said that OD would continue, but with some qualifications (go more slowly, or on a contingent basis, or unevenly), 38 per cent said it would continue (but gave no qualifications), and 16 per cent said it would continue, expand and get further institutionalized. The gross figure is that 78 per cent of districts predicted continuation.

Factors correlated with outcome measures.   In order to analyse factors that account for different degrees of success, we developed indices using the questions just described to measure the three criteria. We then ran three step-wise multiple regressions on a total of forty-seven predictor variables, one regression for each outcome variable.

Factors related to impact.   The best predictors of impact were scale of effort and technical support. Length of programme ($r = 0.36$), use of federal funds ($r = 0.24$), number of outside consultants ($r = 0.37$), and expenditures for materials ($r = 0.22$) were correlated positively with impact. 'Task' orientation ($r = 0.29$), efforts with a 'structure' (r = 0.17), and 'system' focus (r = 0.31) were also correlated with impact, but 'personnel-development' approaches (r = −0.16), i.e. approaches that focus more on individual staff and leadership development as distinct from more system-oriented programmes, were negatively correlated with impact. OD support mechanisms internal to the district were also important, particularly the presence of an OD steering group (r = 0.22) and the number of inside OD consultants (r = 0.28).

Attitudes toward dissemination of OD. As with impact, scale of effort and technical support for the OD programme are associated with positive attitudes: length of programme (r = 0.34), expenditures for materials (r = 0.37), presence of a district OD co-ordinator (r = 0.31), and number of outside consultants (r = 0.16) are correlated with attitudes toward diffusion. Structural emphasis (r = 0.12) and especially task orientation (r = 0.25) continue to be important.

The major new variable is focus on educational issues. Positive attitudes about the usefulness of OD and the tendency to proselytize are more likely when the initial emphasis of the programme (the problem for which OD was to be the solution) is on educational matters internal to the school district (r = 0.23). Users of OD are more likely to want to disseminate it to other districts when it is clear that the OD programme has been of strong educational use.

Factors related to institutionalization   The most important finding in terms of whether or not the programme has continued or will continue in the district is that large-scale programmes are *less* likely to become institutionalized. Those with larger annual costs (r = −0.12), more contact with outside consultants (r = −0.28), and expenditures for new positions (r = −0.14) have negative relationships to institutionalization. Further, the amount of federal funds involved is correlated slightly negatively to institutionalization (r = −0.12). Further analysis revealed that districts receiving *some* federal money did as well as districts receiving no federal money, but districts in which the *majority* of funds came from federal sources were less likely to continue the programme – a finding that is familiar from other studies of educational-change implementation.

Second, there is a clear indication that structural (r = 0.18) and system-oriented approaches (r = 0.21) are associated with institutionalization, but personnel development ($r = -0.13$) is again a counter-indicator.

Summary of factors related to outcome.   Impact, positive attitudes, and continuance of OD programmes are more likely to occur when the OD approach is task-oriented and has a structural, system-oriented focus (not a personnel-development one); impact and attitudes are more positive when the scale of effort and technical support are large, although larger size interferes with the likelihood of institutionalization. Overall, it seems that OD programmes are more successful if they are of moderate size, focused on educational issues, and characterized by a task-oriented, structural, system-changing approach with technical support through the use of internal OD consultants and OD materials.

General OD approach and outcome.   One other comparison is necessary in order to understand more fully what types of OD programmes have the greatest effect on outcomes. We carefully examined the descriptions of the OD programmes and their characteristics as described by the district, and were able to classify the approaches to OD into eight different categories. These categories and their relationship to the three outcome measures are contained in Table 9.2, which is arranged in a rough order from indeterminate, person-centred approaches to system-oriented, 'classical' approaches.

Table 9.2 shows that the weakest approaches as far as *impact* was concerned were 'personnel development' (those focusing primarily on individual learning as such), 'accountability', 'indeterminate' and 'curriculum change' (though N's are small in the latter two). Most clearly, the 'personnel development' approach is under-performing (we might note that 50 per cent of the fourteen cases fall in the lowest impact category). On the other end, 'classical OD' is achieving the best results (if we discount the two desegregation cases); 'MBO/PPBS' and 'overall school improvement' are near the mean for the sample as a whole.

Looking at *attitude*, the results are broadly similar: 'personnel development', 'indeterminate' and 'accountability' are less frequently achieving dissemination-prone attitudes; 'classical OD' does well. The main differences are that more 'MBO/PPBS' districts show a much stronger positive attitude outcome, as do 'curriculum change' districts.

Table 9.2   Percentages of districts showing high to moderately high outcome

General approach	N	Impact	Attitude	Institution-alization
		%	%	%
Indeterminate (workshops, meetings, etc., but approach not clearly defined)	5	40	20	20
Personnel Development (emphasis on skills, personal growth, etc.)	14	29	43	79
Desegregation (racial attitudes, behaviour)	2	100	100	50
Curriculum Change (specific projects, or comprehensive)	5	40	60	80
Accountability (systematic assessment and planning, often state-specified)	8	37	37	62
MBO or PPBS (as central feature)*	9	55	78	78
Overall school improvement model**	6	50	50	100
'Classical' OD***	27	66	63	89
	76	51	55	78

*MBO stands for 'Management by Objectives', and PPBS for 'Program Planning and Budgeting System'. Each is a systematically developed programme for goal-setting, planning and performance review.
**Includes IGE (Individually Guided Education) and programmes sponsored by National Academy of School Executives.
***Districts classified as having 'classical' OD programmes ordinarily reported much attention to issues such as system-level communication, problem-solving, norms, group functioning, and, generally, the human side of the organization; the consultants they used were often those mentioned in Schmuck and Miles's (1971) book on OD in schools; the materials were usually drawn from the general OD literature. A few mentioned the Schmuck et al. *Handbook of OD in Schools* (1972).

When we turn to *institutionalization*, 'classical OD', along with 'overall school improvement', and 'curriculum change' are again outperforming the rest of the sample. The weakest institutionalizers are 'accountability' and 'indeterminate'. 'Personnel development', though it performed poorly in both impact and attitude, tends to be institutionalized about as frequently as the average district in our sample, raising the interesting possibility that 'personnel development' may be easy to diffuse and institutionalize because it does not represent a very fundamental change.

It seems fair to conclude that the 'classical OD' approach is most likely to show positive outcomes of all three types, followed by 'MBO/PPBS' and 'overall school improvement' schemes. All these approaches share a coherent, structured, system-oriented approach.

The 'indeterminate' approach is clearly most inferior, followed by 'personnel development' – we infer because of its emphasis on persons and their skills as targets rather than on system functioning. We should also note that 'accountability' schemes fare poorly; it is possible that standardized and often legally-required schemes lack acceptance by districts and/or the flexibility to have real impact or attitudinal effects and do not get institutionalized once the stipulated period of use is over.

On balance, then, conceptually coherent, system-oriented approaches to OD work best, while focusing on the learning of individuals as such, or having no clearly defined approach, tend not to work well.

Case studies

We wished to verify our survey findings via intensive data collection in a few OD sites. Space permits only the conclusions.[7] Three case studies were carried out: one was a combined survey feedback and professional-development approach in a large urban Canadian district, the second was an MBO-linked approach in a moderate-sized suburban US district, and the third was a curriculum-based approach in a small US district. Many themes from the district study were reconfirmed in the cases, particularly the roles of top-management support needed for programme initiation, the need for structural and educational task emphasis, the importance of strong and sustained inside change agent presence, the low dollar cost and high time costs, and the existence of reasonably clear (but poorly evaluated) obtained benefits. These benefits were limited, however, in extent of staff coverage and student impact. But some new themes appeared: (a) the importance of a clear, coherent programme vision, accompanied by careful prior planning; (b) the possibility that OD programmes are easier to launch when the external environment is not turbulent; (c) the importance of a close working partnership between a sophisticated inside change agent and the top manager of the district; (d) the idea that the OD programme is not an 'extra' but a 'way of life' in the district; (e) the importance of 'multiplier' effects achieved by steady attention to the training of internal trainers; and (f) the likelihood that real institutionalization may take five years or more to achieve.

Conclusion

The question of what OD 'is' is not simple, and is subject to a good deal of debate in the general OD literature. Our present inclination is toward a revised definition of this sort:

> Organization development in school districts is a coherent, sys-tematically planned, sustained effort at system self-study and improvement, focusing explicitly on change in formal and informal procedures, processes, norms or structures, using behavioural science concepts. The goals of OD include *both* the quality of life of individuals as well as improving organizational functioning and performance.

The revisions should be noted. The requirement of *coherence and systematic planning* may be too normative, but does serve to distinguish OD from haphazard efforts casually labelled 'OD', as increasingly seems to be the case in our experience. The emphasis on *explicitness* indicates that OD deals directly with organizational phenomena and their alteration, rather than inducing changes indirectly through some other vehicle. The inclusion of both *formal and informal* organizational issues makes for more thoroughness, and excludes simply-'official' rearrangements. The emphasis on *quality of life of individuals* and on *organizational performance* highlights the dual goal of OD and the potential problems in pursuing these goals in a balanced way. The inclusion of *educational content* acknowledges that such work is a primary task of school districts, but indicates that curriculum-focused work is not necessarily OD in the absence of the preceding qualifiers. The label 'sustained' is perhaps best left unspecified, though the eighteen-month figure is probably useful as a guide, given the year-by-year planning often characteristic of school districts.

Our findings show that OD can be beneficial to districts regardless of their size, wealth, location, or socio-economic character. Districts which define their needs in task-oriented, educationally focused terms and consider structural changes a possibility are more likely to be successful, particularly if the superintendent supplies strong initial support.

The most striking finding in regard to personal change in educational OD programmes is that a primary focus on such change is self-defeating. Rather, personnel development programmes must go hand in hand with attention to group and organizational issues. Persons in organizations are as much defined by their roles and group memberships as by their 'personhood', and exclusive focus on the latter proved unproductive in our sample.

In summary, OD programmes have a favourable cost-benefit ratio: they can reasonably be expected to improve organizational climate and functioning, increase instructional innovations, and improve student outcomes. Dollar costs are less than a half of 1 per cent of total budget, easily comparable to in-service education costs; personnel time investment is large (ten days a year per person), and programmes require about five years for firm institutionalization. Programme effects such as resistance, defensiveness and insecurity are natural, but do not seem to jeopardize programme success.

Systematic programmes with a well-developed framework, aimed at structural change rather than just personnel training are more effective. They are steadily supported by top management, must be carefully planned at initiation, and have a district-level co-ordinator probably spending at least a third of his time. Competent outside consultants (perhaps twenty days a year) can aid with early planning and programme development, and with developing a team of well-trained inside consultants – an essential component for OD effectiveness and continued use. The team's usefulness in extending the OD programme to all parts of the system will be facilitated if systematic re-usable programme components or packages are developed and locally adapted. A full-time OD specialist, working closely with the superintendent, is desirable in districts of a thousand or more staff.

Although our data located many more OD-using districts than most knowledgeable people thought had existed, it seems quite unlikely that more than 1 per cent of US and Canadian districts are now engaged in OD. OD appears to be a good way to increase instructional innovation, to increase participation by all levels of personnel, and to improve various aspects of task and socio-emotional functioning, *if it is done right*, i.e. if the programme meets the requirements in the definition of OD, and if it is implemented in a way which includes the key operating characteristics identified in our review of the literature, and in our school district analysis. However, the incentives for adoption are not universally present in school districts. Not all districts (or their communities) want to innovate; not all superintendents and principals wish for more upward influence on teachers' parts; and not all districts feel a clear need for better functioning, even though external observers might claim that any social system has its poorly functioning aspects. In any case, the future of OD in school districts is clouded by the scarcity of well-articulated programmes and practices which are consistent with its underlying principles and goals. This may also be true of OD's use in other types of organization, but it is especially problematic in schools due to the recency of its emergence and to the adverse environmental conditions which are now demanding more of OD and other educational innovations than was the case in the 1960s.

So the prospects for OD in the future of schooling in these two countries are not clear. On balance, we believe that encouraging the further diffusion of OD is worthwhile, and that some deliberate, stimulative efforts can be mounted for a relatively small cost. Without such efforts, OD in schools will probably continue to diffuse slowly, and/or to suffer the fate of vulgarization that has occurred with most other complex and substantial educational innovations, from 'progressive education' onward.

Notes

1 We would like to thank Gib Taylor and Joan May for their considerable help in carrying out this study. An account of the total study is available in Fullan et al. (1978), vols 1–5.
2 For a more complete review of the literature on OD, especially as applied to schools, see Fullan, Miles and Taylor (1980).
3 Data on a total sample of 308 OD consultants engaged in supplying OD training to schools, either as inside or outside change agents,

were also collected, but are not described here. See Fullan et al. (1978), vol. 3.

4 We received a 42 per cent return on the mailing, but about one half of these returns proved not to be OD, not sustained, not based in school districts, or were duplicates from schools within the same district.

5 Percentages add to more than 100 because some respondents mentioned two conditions.

6 Negative results did not vary in frequency according to level of impact. Rather, they simply seem to be routinely reported accompaniments of OD work.

7 See Fullan et al. (1978), vol. 4 for full details.

References

Alderfer, C. P. (1977) Organization development. *Annual Review of Psychology 28*: 197–223.

Bassin, J. and Gross, T. (1978) Organization development: a viable method of change for urban secondary schools. Paper presented at the American Educational Research Association, Toronto.

Beer, M. (1976) Comments on the preceding articles: on gaining influence and power for OD. *Journal of Applied Behavioral Science 12*: 44–51.

Blumberg, A. (1976) OD's future in schools – or is there one? *Education and Urban Society 8*: 213–26.

Bowers, D. (1977) Organizational development: promises, performances, possibilities. *Organizational Dynamics 4* (4): 50–62.

Coad, R., Miskel, C. and van Meter, E. (1976) The effects of an organization development program on satisfaction, group process, climate, leadership, and student achievement. Paper presented at the Annual Meeting of the American Educational Research Association, San Francisco.

Cohen, A. and Gadon H. (1978) Changing the management culture in a public school system. *Journal of Applied Behavioral Science 14*: 61–78.

Derr, B. C. (1976) 'OD' won't work in schools. *Education and Urban Society 8* (2): 227–41.

French, W. and Bell, C. (1973) *Organization Development*. Toronto: Prentice-Hall.

Friedlander, F. and Brown, L. D. (1974) Organization development. *Annual Review of Psychology 75*: 313–41.

Fullan, M. (1976) OD in schools: an overview and critique. In *Organization Development*, Management in Education Course, E.321, Unit 6, Open University Press: 43–51.

Fullan, M., Miles, M. B. and Taylor, G. (1978) *OD in Schools: The State of the Art*. Final report to National Institute of Education, vols 1–5.

Fullan, M., Miles, M. B. and Taylor, G. (1980) Organization Development in schools: the state of the art. *Review of Educational Research 50* (1): 121–83.

Hartman, J. (1979) Small group methods of personal change. In M. Rosenweig and L. Porter (eds) *Annual Review of Psychology 30*: 454–76.

Harvey, J. (1975) Eight myths OD consultants believe in . . . and die by. *OD Practitioner 7* (1): 1–5.

Miles, M. B. (1965) Organizational health: figure and ground. In R. O. Carlson et al. *Change Process in Public School*. Eugene, Oregon: Center for Advanced Study in Educational Administration.

Miles, M. B. (1976) Critique: diffusing OD in schools. *Education and Urban Society 8* (2): 242–54.

Miles, M. B. and Schmuck, R. (1971) Improving schools through organization development: an overview. In R. Schmuck and M. B. Miles (eds) *Organization Development in Schools*. Palo Alto, California: National Press Books.

Milstein, M. M. (1978) Evolution of an internal change teams expectations, design and reality. Paper presented at the American Educational Research Association, Toronto.

Mohrman, S., Mohrman, A., Cook, R. and Duncan, R. (1977) A survey-feedback and problem-solving intervention in a school district. In P. Mirvis and D. Berg (eds) *Failures in Organization Development and Change*. Toronto: John Wiley.

Runkel, P. J. and Schmuck, R. A. (1974) Findings from the research and development program on strategies on organization change at CEPM-CASEA. Eugene: Centre for Educational Policy and Management, University of Oregon.

Runkel, P. J. and Schmuck, R. A. (1976) Organization development in schools: a review of research findings from Oregon. Eugene:

Centre for Educational Policy and Management, University of Oregon.

Schmuck, R., Murray, D., Smith, M., Schwartz, M. and Runkel, P. (1975) *Consultation for Innovative Schools: OD for Multiunit Structure*. Eugene: Centre for Educational Policy and Management, University of Oregon.

Schmuck, R., Runkel, P., Arends, J. and Arends, R. (1977) *The Second Handbook of Organization Development in Schools*. Palo Alto, California: Mayfield Publishing Co.

Weisbord, M. (1977) How do you know it works if you don't know what it is? *OD Practitioner 9* (3): 1–9.

Name index

Subject index